composition STUDIES

Volume 53, Number 2
Fall 2025

Contents

Editors' Introduction

Editing in the Age of Generative AI
Jacob Babb and Zachary Beare

Articles

Access Denied: Black Women's Experiences with Mentorship and Professional Development in Rhetoric and Composition Graduate Programs   15
Talisha Haltiwanger Morrison and Malina Anderson

Addressing and Overcoming Barriers in the First-Year Writing Classroom: The Story of an International Graduate Teaching Assistant of Color   36
Jainab Tabassum Banu

Where Chance and Invention Collide: Scrap Writing in the Composition Classroom   54
Danielle Koupf

Generative Artificial Memories: Teaching AI Text Generators as Rhetorical Memory Devices   70
John J. Silvestro

Fumbling Toward Co-Territorialized Spaces: Composition Pedagogy and Dual Enrollment   89
Joe Courchesne, Jennifer DiGrazia, and Wyatt Hermansen

Pandemic-Era Workload in the Online Writing Classroom: Lessons in Sustainability for the Future   104
Jennifer Sheppard

Course Designs

AI & Writing: An Experimental First-Year Composition Course   124
Laura J. Panning Davies and Kate Navickas

Composing from Desire: Third Places in the First-Year Writing Curriculum   137
Charissa Che

Where We Are: Teaching Writing in the Second Trump Administration

Composition in the Shadow of Campus Protests 150
Jonathan Alexander

"As Long as There's Fire," with Apologies to David Bowie 155
Ryan Skinnell

Composition Among the Ruins 163
Lydia Wilkes

Until I Hit Ocean 171
Patti Poblete

Book Reviews

Navigating AI's Writing Revolution: A Review Essay and Call for Deliberation 174
Jason Tham

Feminist Technical Communication: Apparent Feminisms, Slow Crisis, and the Deepwater Horizon Disaster by Erin Clark 184
Reviewed by Brigida R. Blasi

Masking Inequality with Good Intentions: Systemic Bias, Counterspaces, and Discourse Acquisition in STEM Education by Heather M. Falconer 188
Reviewed by Shuvro Das

Cultivating Critical Language Awareness in the Writing Classroom by Shawna Shapiro 193
Reviewed by Ananta Khanal

"K for the Way:" DJ Rhetoric & Literacy for 21st Century Writing Studies by Todd Craig 198
Reviewed by Megan Palmer

Multimodal Composing and Writing Transfer edited by Kara Poe Alexander, Matthew Davis, Lilian W. Mina, and Ryan P. Shepherd 202
Reviewed by Abigail Robinson

composition STUDIES

Volume 53, Number 2
Fall 2025

Editors
Jacob Babb
Zachary Beare

Book Review Editor
Wenqi Cui

Managing Editor
Bethany Ober Mannon

Content Editors
Abby Buckner
Jaclyn Fiscus-Cannaday
Roberto Sebastian Leon
Marie Pruitt
Rhiannon Scharnhorst
Madeline Scott
Carina Jiaxing Shi
Othniel Williams

Blog Editors
Emily Brier
Daniel Libertz

Social Media Editors
Skyler Meeks
Othniel Williams

Editorial Consultant
Jaclyn Fiscus-Cannaday

Former Editors
Gary Tate
Bob Mayberry
Christina Murphy
Peter Vandenberg
Ann George
Carrie Leverenz
Brad E. Lucas
Jennifer Clary-Lemon
Laura R. Micciche
Matt Davis
Kara Taczak

Advisory Board
Chen Chen
 Utah State University

Kristi Murray Costello
 Old Dominion University

Scott Gage
 Texas A&M – San Antonio

Kristi Girdharry
 Babson College

David Green
 Howard University

Talisha Haltiwanger Morrison
 University of Oklahoma

Christina LaVecchia
 University of Cincinnati

Erin Lehman
 Ivy Tech Community College

Cruz Medina
 Santa Clara University

Kris Messer
 Community College of Baltimore County

Nathalie Singh-Corcoran
 West Virginia University

Alexis Teagarden
 University of Massachusetts, Dartmouth

SUBSCRIPTIONS

Composition Studies is published twice each year (Spring and Fall). Annual subscription rates: Individuals $50 (Domestic), $80 (International), and $25 (Students). To subscribe online, please visit https://compstudiesjournal.com/subscriptions/.

BACK ISSUES

Back issues, five years prior to the present, are freely accessible on our website: https://compstudiesjournal.com/archive/. If you don't see what you're looking for, contact us. Also, recent back issues are now available through Amazon.com. To find issues, use the advanced search feature and search on "Composition Studies" (title) and "Parlor Press" (publisher).

BOOK REVIEWS

Assignments are made from a file of potential book reviewers. If you are interested in writing a review, please contact our Book Review editor at wcui9@jh.edu.

JOURNAL SCOPE

The oldest independent periodical in the field, *Composition Studies* publishes original articles relevant to rhetoric and composition, including those that address teaching college writing; theorizing rhetoric and composing; administering writing programs; and, among other topics, preparing the field's future teacher-scholars. All perspectives and topics of general interest to the profession are welcome. We also publish Course Designs, which contextualize, theorize, and reflect on the content and pedagogy of a course. CFPs, announcements, and letters to the editor are most welcome. *Composition Studies* does not consider previously published manuscripts, unrevised conference papers, or unrevised dissertation chapters.

SUBMISSIONS

For submission information and guidelines, see https://compstudiesjournal.com/submissions/.

Direct all correspondence to:

> Zachary Beare, Co-Editor
> 2211 Hillsborough Street
> Campus Box 8105
> Raleigh, NC 27695-8105
> compstudiesjournal@gmail.com

Composition Studies is grateful for the support of North Carolina State University and Appalachian State University.

©2025 by Jacob Babb and Zachary Beare, Co-Editors

Production and distribution is managed by Parlor Press, www.parlorpress.com.

ISSN 1534–9322.

Cover art by Michael J. Day.

https://compstudiesjournal.com/

Editors' Introduction

Editing in the Age of Generative AI

Jacob Babb and Zachary Beare

One of the great privileges of editing this journal is that we have an insiders' view of what our disciplinary colleagues are thinking about and researching. Jacob often repeats a line—likely garbled by faulty memory at this point, nearly a decade down the road, but the sentiment is still the same—that he heard from Lisa Mastrangelo and Barb L'Eplattenier when he was transitioning into a co-editorial role at *WPA: Writing Program Administration* back in 2016: "You'll never be as familiar with research in your field as when you're a journal editor." As editors, we read submissions from scholar-teachers interested in the wide array of pedagogical and research areas of interest to our readers. It should come as no surprise to our readers that submissions on generative AI vastly outnumber submissions on any other topic of interest to the journal at this time. Readers will discover pieces that address generative AI in every section of this issue. As a new writing technology, generative AI is at the forefront of the minds of many scholar-teachers in our field.

The pace of the development of generative AI since 2022, when ChatGPT first began generating texts that routinely crossed our paths in writing classrooms, has been frankly astonishing. The complexity of texts created by the multiple generative AIs now available has increased to the extent that it can be difficult or simply impossible to determine whether something we are reading was written by a human being or generated by an algorithm that feeds, often illegally, on published texts—including texts published by many scholars in writing studies. The proliferation of such a technology cannot help but disrupt our conceptions of literacy and education, just as other major advances in technology in the past have done, such as the personal computer, the printing press, and ballpoint pens. As writing scholars, we recognize that writing itself is a technology that has had profound impacts on oral cultures.

Positioning the rise of generative AI as another technology that disrupts the status quo and generates a new instantiation of the literacy crisis is a useful framing for our discipline, since we have long thought of these crises as at times overblown and exaggerated for political purposes. Situating generative AI in that lineage encourages us to attempt to take the long view, to understand that new technologies often create ethical and pedagogical concerns among the general populace as well as among those of us who work in education. Yet this AI-powered disruption feels substantively different compared to previous iterations of the literacy crisis. Perhaps this difference is based on the fact that we are still very much in the thick of this paradigm shift, and because we still exist in that moment, we have no sense of what the aftermath of the generative AI literacy crisis will look like. We have no idea what this technology will look like in the next twelve months, let alone over the course of the next decade. Perhaps this emergent technology feels more dire or more exciting, depending on your perspective on generative AI, because the rise of the technology overlaps with rapid climate change, socioeconomic instability, and political uncertainty, along with a dwindling public trust in higher education. So much uncertainty and anxiety extend from multiple points of origin, even when many of those points have significant overlap with one another. Generative AI highlights all of these concerns in different ways.

On the humor website McSweeney's, American studies scholar Brian Michael Murphy recently published "How I Learned to Stop Teaching and Love AI," a satirical article whose title recalls Stanley Kubrick's 1964 classic political satire film *Dr. Strangelove, or How I Learned to Stop Worrying and Love the Bomb*. In this short piece, Murphy asserts that he "used to resist, but no more," instead giving in to the power of AI to conserve human energy and to increase efficiency in previously definitionally human endeavors such as writing, painting, dance, and sports. He remarks that "many publishers are still not interested in work composed by AI, and so this piece was written by me, a human. Hence the wordiness, ineptitude, and inefficiency of the prose." Murphy's satirical article highlights what we stand to lose by turning over the power of creation to machines in the name of efficiency, that economic concept that is so vital to the sustenance of capitalism. According to Murphy's satirical framing, and according to decidedly less satirical framing from Silicon Valley developers and enthusiasts, humanity would certainly fare better if we could just get those pesky humans out of the way of production.

Maybe we show our hand by framing our introduction in terms of disruptive technologies and diminished human creativity. Maybe we indicate our own leanings toward a refusal stance on generative AI by citing a satirical article. You might be on to us, reader.

Look, we could have been much more overt. In previous discussions about this introduction, we contemplated calling it an AI hallucination. We considered referring to the practically endless parade of AI-like constructs that populate science fiction, such as the novel generating machines in George Orwell's prescient 1949 *Nineteen Eighty-Four*, the endlessly printing prayers of the generative devices called Soul Scrolls in Margaret Atwood's equally prescient 1985 *The Handmaid's Tale*, or the haunting sorrow of the smart house that continues to conduct the daily business of a suburban family with great efficiency, even after that family was killed via nuclear annihilation in Ray Bradbury's 1950 short story "There Will Come Soft Rains." Science fiction offers countless examples of AI and AI-like technologies that devalue or destroy humanity, from HAL 3000 in Kubrick's *2001: A Space Odyssey* to the seeming inevitability of robotic rebellion in James Cameron's *The Terminator*, the prequel to the vastly superior *Terminator 2: Judgment Day* (not sorry for holding that opinion), or in Lana and Lilly Wackowski's *The Matrix*. The rush of recent horror films that explore how AI can undermine humanity, or how AI reflects how humanity corrupts itself, such as Drew Hancock's *Companion*, Chris Weisz's *Afraid*, or S. K. Dale's *Subservience*, all build on our interest in using narrative to contemplate when technology goes from helpful tool to a self-aware force with agency. (We could rattle off numerous other science fiction texts that support such ambivalence, but we don't want to wear out our welcome. Corner us at a conference if you want more of that discussion—at your own risk.) All of these texts explore and express cultural anxieties about different kinds of machine intelligences and forms of textual replication—anxieties that we as editors and scholar-teachers in writing studies share as we have observed the rapid growth and proliferation of generative AI and its integration into multiple technologies that we all use on a routine basis. We could have written about all of that in our introduction. Instead, we only wrote about thinking about writing about those observations in a masterful demonstration of editorial restraint.

However, we find that we remain somewhat ambivalent about the future of generative AI, an ambivalence we believe is important to maintain because of the numerous perspectives we have the privilege of engaging with as journal editors. Within writing studies, we can see the emergence of a spectrum of perspectives on how generative AI may be used in composing and in teaching composition, from eager embrace of this new technology on one end to staunch refusal to use the technology on the other end, and we have already signaled our leaning toward one side of this spectrum. We imagine most readers have spent time reflecting on where they find themselves on that spectrum.

Our own ambivalence toward generative AI reflects a conscious choice to avoid reaching a firm conclusion about these emergent technologies at this time. We do not see ourselves as neutral on the issue; as writing teachers and writing program administrators, we have both taken stances on generative AI within our classes and our writing programs. However, as editors, we strive for that neutral position. We like to think of ourselves as reserving judgment, particularly as companies begin to find that AI may not be as profitable as they had hoped, as colleges and universities begin to find that faculty and students may not be as eager to embrace AI as they had assumed, and as the companies creating these generative engines face resistance against their machines that consume human-produced texts and natural resources at a staggering pace.

As editors, we have an ethical imperative to maintain an open mind. We are the first readers of the works submitted to the journal, and we fully admit that we bring our own perspectives, expertise, and biases along with us when we read these submissions. After all, editors are human too—at least until Silicon Valley tells us we aren't. But even though we bring all our human baggage with us when we read submissions, we see it as an obligation to consider with great care any argument authors present to us in their submissions, regardless of our own views on generative AI or, frankly, any other topic that informs the intellectual and pedagogical inquiries that shape our discipline. We also have personal leanings and stances on issues such as alternative grading, writing transfer, contingent labor, disciplinary history, writing program administration, multimodal composing, and many other topics routinely addressed by authors in our discipline. Because *Composition Studies* publishes articles on all aspects of the field—as our website states, "We welcome work that doesn't fit neatly elsewhere"—we must remain intellectually open to any arguments and research that authors submit to the journal.

We also understand that our editorial role makes us stewards of the journal and of our authors' intellectual property, and that responsibility has pushed us, as it has other journals in the field, to compose a policy about generative AI. We have spent a significant chunk of 2025 discussing, drafting, and revising our policy statement on generative AI. Our aim was to create a policy informed by four values:

- Cultivating trust and respect
- Striving for transparency
- Investing in revision and ongoing reflexive inquiry
- Embracing peer review and stakeholder input

This statement establishes how we will respond to authors who use generative AI in their work; we are not opposed to the usage, but we think there should be a rationale for its use as well as a clear indicator of where and how generative AI has been used in a manuscript. More importantly, the statement declares the journal's intent to protect the intellectual property of authors to the best of our ability. For instance, we call on reviewers not to upload manuscripts they are reviewing to any large language model (LLM) for any reason, since these manuscripts are not the intellectual property of the reviewers. We are calling this statement "an evolving document," because we must continue revisiting this policy as the technologies associated with generative AI continue to evolve at a rapid pace. We also call it that because we recognize that, while our editorial positions come with the ethical obligation to protect the work of our authors, we are facing technologies that may undermine our efforts to do so. We persist all the same.

We invite you to read the policy, entitled "A *Composition Studies* Policy on the Use of Generative AI: An Evolving Document," which is housed on our website (compstudiesjournal.com) under the Submissions tab. We want to thank the members of the Advisory Board for providing invaluable feedback for revision of the document; for such a complex and rapidly changing subject as generative AI, a range of perspectives was critical to producing a policy that will help authors, reviewers, and readers. We also want to give a special thanks to content editor Marie Pruitt, with whom we have co-authored a forthcoming chapter on generative AI and scholarly editing. Marie was pivotal in helping to shape our discussions about the ethical implications of generative AI as we wrote and revised this policy statement. Thank you, Marie! Our policy would not be nearly as nuanced without you or without feedback from our Advisory Board.

Before we discuss the exciting contents of this issue, we want to welcome five new members to the journal's Advisory Board:

- Kristi Murray Costello, Old Dominion University
- Talisha Haltiwanger Morrison, University of Oklahoma
- Erin Lehman, Ivy Tech Community College
- Kris Messer, Community College of Baltimore County
- Alexis Teagarden, University of Massachusetts Dartmouth

We are so grateful to Kristi, Talisha, Erin, Kris, and Alexis for their willingness to serve in this role to support *Composition Studies*, and we are looking forward to working with them.

We are also thrilled to welcome Skyler Meeks to the editorial staff, who is joining Othniel Williams as a social media editor. Perhaps we are biased, but we think *Composition Studies* has one of the best social media presences of any of the journals in writing studies, and we are so glad that Skyler and Othniel are doing their best to put a spotlight on the work of our authors.

In This Issue

Issue Cover

Putting aside the parental reminders that "it is what is on the inside that counts" and that one "shouldn't judge a book by its cover," we have to say that we think the cover of this issue is pretty darn cool. As editors, we have committed to continuing the journal's tradition of having interesting and visually engaging covers. In discussing how we might secure such covers, one of our thoughts was to reach out to scholars in the field who also happen to be visual artists, and this issue is one result of that strategy. The cover image, playfully titled "Peekaboo Raccoon," is a digital photo from Michael J. Day. We are confident many of our readers will be familiar with Michael's kindness, energetic presence, and eagerness to mentor and support graduate students and early-career scholars. And if you happen to be a regular attendee of the Computers & Writing Conference, you might know Michael as the guy constructing the elaborate display of official t-shirts documenting the history of the Computers & Writing Conference.

For those of you who may not know Michael, he is professor emeritus of English and former director of First-Year Composition at Northern Illinois University. He has authored and edited countless publications in composition and digital rhetoric. In retirement, he divides his time between walking in the woods with a camera, editing and exhibiting photos digitally and in print, and co-authoring a book on Japanese Chicago with his wife. For the past five years he has published a hyperlocal wildlife calendar to benefit the NIU library.

Michael offers the following statement about his work:

"Peekaboo Raccoon," 2024

Digital Photograph

My daily ritual is to walk along the Kishwaukee river through the Northern Illinois University campus and a local park, watching and listening, trying to capture in light, color, and form in what I see. I have a special affection for wild creatures, especially birds, whose colors, shapes, and poses captivate me, and I have worked hard to identify the birds around me even through their songs. Through my photos, I want to share the many faces of nature, the wildness of spirit, and the interplay of light and shadow woven into the tapestry of the natural world. As I wander through nature, I keep watch for faces peering out of the woods, in bushes, and, as this one, out of a natural hollow in a tree.

Articles

This issue of *Composition Studies* features six articles that utilize a variety of methodological approaches to explore an array of professional and pedagogical issues situated in a range of institutional locations. While articles are queued for publication largely based on when they are accepted, it is always exciting when they serendipitously speak to one another in interesting ways, and we think the pieces in this issue do just that. Though they rely on different methodological approaches and slightly different foci, both the article by Talisha Haltiwanger Morrison and Malina Anderson and the article by Jainab

Tabassum Banu inquire into the experiences of women of color graduate students in the United States. Though on the surface, Danielle Koupf and John J. Silvestro appear to be writing about very different topics (scrap writing and generative AI text generation, respectively), both explore issues connected to memory, materiality, and mental processing. Finally, though Joe Courchesne, Jennifer DiGrazia, and Wyatt Hermansen examine the complexities of co-taught dual enrollment courses and Jennifer Sheppard examines pandemic-era workloads in online writing courses, both highlight complexities of pedagogical labor, point to the myriad roles of relationships in that work, and demonstrate that sometimes lessons can only be learned through retrospective reflection.

Course Designs

This issue features two Course Designs. Charissa Che describes a themed first-year writing course named "Intercultural Communicative Competence," in which students are invited to be sojourners (which Che differentiates from tourists) in a new culture to gain knowledge about that culture as they examine a particular cultural tension and possible avenues for addressing that tension. Next, Laura J. Panning Davies and Kate Navickas offer a collaboratively designed experimental first-year writing course on AI and writing that invites students to study how generative AI affects writing and writers, offering a space for students to build critical literacy about and to experiment with using generative AI.

Where We Are

We have invited four scholars—Ryan Skinnell, Jonathan Alexander, Lydia Wilkes, and Patti Poblete–to share different perspectives on the potential future of composition studies in the second Trump administration. We posed the following questions for our contributors to reflect on as they developed their responses for this issue's Where We Are:

- What does this moment mean for our field and its possible futures?
- How is this moment impacting the wellbeing of faculty and students?
- How is this moment impacting curriculum and pedagogies?
- How is this moment shaping issues of academic labor, contingency, and precarity?
- How might composition studies, literacy sponsorship work, and rhetorical education be essential in responding to, resisting, and/or critiquing this moment?
- How might acts of resistance and persistence in this moment vary depending on institutional and geographic contexts?

- How does this moment resonate with and/or differ from other historical moments the field has faced?

The contributors' responses explore a range of interconnected topics, including the targeting of individual institutions and higher education in general, campus protests, climate change, citizenship, and nationality. Collectively, these responses reflect trepidation, determination, and—occasionally—hopefulness about postsecondary writing instruction, the pedagogical and intellectual endeavor that brings all readers of this journal together.

We won't lie. It is hard to read these contributions—at least we thought it was. But that's part of the point. We are grateful for the clear-eyed perspectives of Skinnell, Alexander, Wilkes, and Poblete. If we are all to continue to be stewards of our discipline and its pedagogical imperative to teach students to use writing as a tool for exploration and for building new knowledge, we must continue to strive to address the concerns of the world around us with as much honesty and intellectual integrity as we can.

Book Reviews

We present a robust range of book reviews in this issue, as always with thanks to book review editor Wenqi Cui for her work with authors to prepare these reviews. The section starts with a review essay by Jason Tham, covering three works on writing and generative AI. Tham's review essay will undoubtedly be helpful to those readers who want to find a way into the scholarly discourse within writing studies on these emergent technologies. Tham concludes by noting that these early works on generative AI establish "frameworks for inquiry that future scholarship can build upon, challenge, and ultimately transcend in service of genuinely humane approaches to technological change." The section also includes five book reviews that collectively demonstrate the breadth of concerns addressed in writing studies, from feminist technical communication (Blasi), systemic bias in STEM education (Das), and critical language awareness (Khanal) to DJ rhetoric (Palmer) and the overlap of multimodal composing and transfer (Robinson).

Work Cited

Murphy, Brian Michael. "How I Learned to Stop Teaching and Love AI." *McSweeney's*, 25 Aug. 2025, www.mcsweeneys.net/articles/how-i-learned-to-stop-teaching-and-love-ai.

Articles

Access Denied: Black Women's Experiences with Mentorship and Professional Development in Rhetoric and Composition Graduate Programs

Talisha Haltiwanger Morrison and Malina Anderson

Our study brings together existing scholarship on mentorship for graduate students and Black female graduate students' experiences. We interviewed five self-identified Black women who completed graduate degrees in rhetoric and composition (rhet-comp) between 2018 and 2022. We found striking similarities across the participants' experiences, despite all having attended different institutions and programs. Findings reveal that Black women often crave mentorship and professional development and seek out programs intentionally based on their scholarly and professional goals. However, the participants in this study discovered that experiences and opportunities available to others were not universal, as programs in the field were unprepared or unwilling to provide holistic and culturally inclusive support for them as emerging Black women scholars. Further, the women often had their requests for mentoring and leadership opportunities denied and were forced to seek out external resources and support. We conclude that many rhet-comp graduate programs remain underprepared to provide appropriate mentorship and professional development to Black women graduate students. The field of rhetoric and composition needs a robust review of its graduate support systems that engages, listens to, and responds to Black women's experiences.

Mentorship as a personal and professional relationship can be a critical guardrail within academia. Graduate student success strategies often include implementing mentorship programs for students, which has been acknowledged as a practice that can contribute richness and success to program experiences and beyond. Our study examines the availability of and access to mentorship and professional development in graduate rhetoric and composition programs. Specifically, we examine how, or if, such opportunities are available to Black women in these programs and how these students perceive their availability. We found that, despite our participants' keen interests in mentoring and professional development, their programs often offered inadequate and unequal access to these experiences. Several of their needs would go unfulfilled, leading them to locate external resources and opportunities. Further, we found that Black women may turn to more culturally appropriate resources outside of their programs and academia entirely as a form of resistance to the hostile environments within it.

Graduate programs in rhetoric and composition, which are still predominantly White, are spaces in which Black women's resistance may simply be continued existence and perseverance. We contend that, although the general need for mentoring in graduate programs is indisputable, Black women graduate students in rhet-comp programs are unique in their challenges, standards, and needs. Our study seeks to home in on these voices. We listen attentively and with respect to those who know these experiences intimately, and we hope that this study will be one of a burgeoning whole of scholarship centered on Black women in rhetoric and composition that supports their scholarship and personhood in tandem.

Literature Review

A review of the literature on rhet-comp graduate programs, graduate mentoring, and Black women graduate experiences in rhetoric and composition or other graduate programs reveals the crucial role of mentorship in graduate school. This review also uncovers a need for restructured and more explicit mentoring opportunities for Black women graduate students, as well as a need to identify and honor the unique perspectives that these students bring to their programs and fields. To better understand these perspectives, we reviewed articles on mentorship definitions, mentoring resources and structures (or lack thereof), the isolation or invalidation as experienced by Black women graduate students, professionalization in rhetoric and composition programs, the whitewashing of Black women's research, peer mentorship, and strategies of resistance. The literature specific to Black women graduate students explicitly utilized Black Feminist Thought (BFT) or related frameworks to analyze findings. Articles that focused on Black women graduate student experiences were notably developed within predominantly and historically White institutions (PHWIs); this is particularly relevant for our study, as four of our five participants also studied at PHWIs, and all five programs were predominantly White.

Mentorship is a critical factor in the success and satisfaction of a graduate program. E. Shelley Reid identifies that, while not everyone makes a great mentor in graduate programs, students generally benefit from formally establishing a mentor as early as possible. One obstacle in establishing such pairings is the nature of a graduate program, which provides a (relatively) short amount of time to achieve a large amount of intellectually, emotionally (and sometimes physically) challenging labor. Reid makes clear that peer mentoring is not sufficient on its own and that programs "do not have the luxury of waiting for mentoring to 'just happen,'" given the pace at which many programs move

(70). The social aspects of graduate programs are another obstacle for students, including Black women students. Rachelle Winkle-Wagner suggests that Black women university students' success can and should be measured beyond individual factors, with emphasis also on relationships and collective support. Yet the "outsider within" role that many Black women scholars take on in their programs impedes their integration and acceptance, therefore impeding their scholarship, efficacy, and satisfaction (Henderson et al.; Wilson et al.; Apugo, "Hidden Culture"). Waiting for this socialization and integration to happen "naturally," without explicit strategies, mentor program development, resources, and goals further impedes students' work within rhetoric and composition programs (Reid).

Scholarship repeatedly identifies mentorship as critical both laterally (peer) and with "superiors;" which could be professionals or academics with experience, particularly those older than the mentee (Reid; Miller et al., Haggard et al.). The meaning of mentorship in academic and professional spaces has evolved over time, and recent definitions emphasize two important factors of mentoring relationships: career-related and psychosocial guidance (Haggard et al.; Minnet et al.; Miller et al.). Although Dana L. Haggard et al. argue against both the possibility and desirability of a single, comprehensive, or streamlined definition of success, they acknowledge "core attributes [that distinguish] mentorship from other kinds of interpersonal relationships" (300). A good mentor(ship) can be defined as one who "provides students with the kinds of apprenticeship that teach[es] them professional habits [and] necessitate[s] the interpersonal relationships [that] students obviously crave" (Miller et al. 404-05). Our study focuses primarily on mentorship experiences with some attention to professional development, which we understand to be more limited and time-bound than true mentorship. We note that professional development often aims to help develop specific skills or knowledge, whereas mentorship is grounded in a sustained, supportive relationship appropriate and responsive to the given context (Miller et al., Haggard et al). We further define mentorship here as a relationship or network that provides explicit and/or personalized support and direction for a graduate student's self-defined professional, academic, and, at times, personal success. Professional development is often included as part of a broader mentorship experience (Walkington; Patterson-Stephens et al.).

This understanding of the relationship between mentoring and professional development acknowledges that graduate student support should be expansive and come from a variety of sources, even when the student is assigned or has found a designated mentor. Mentoring is essential for Black women, who often face devaluation or questioning of their work or very place in academia; they may have their research "whitewashed" by being asked to "broaden the scope" of their work or by being challenged on the relevance or importance of work that focuses closely on racialized and/or gendered experiences (Wilson et al; Minnet et al.; Apugo, "'We All We Got'"; Henderson et al.; Walkington; Apugo, "Black Women"). For Black female students, having mentors who look like and relate to them can positively impact their abilities to withstand these efforts and to locate and express their Blackness in predominantly White institutions and areas of study (Wilson et al.; Minnett et al.; Apugo, "'We All We Got'"; Henderson et al. Patterson-Stephens et al.). This relatability may also help a student "seek comfort and external validation after negative encounters with White faculty and peers" (Wilson et al. 703) as she asserts her identity—and how it influences her research—within a PHWI context and within the field of rhetoric and composition. Both Reid and Betty L. Wilson et al. note, however, that cross-cultural mentoring is not inherently detrimental. Short-term, peer-based, cross-cultural mentoring in rhet-comp programs may not have as significant an impact as long-term cross-cultural pairings, but it can still be beneficial (Reid 61). For these types of relationships, especially between a Black woman mentee and a White mentor, it is essential for White faculty to be mindful of potential whitewashing and cultural insensitivity and to actively, attentively work to eliminate both (Wilson et al. 703). So, it is not impossible to have a strong cross-cultural mentoring relationship, but these pairings should still be chosen with care and intention (Grant and Simmons; Grant).

Black women's epistemologies often face censorship and delegitimization when programs, especially at PHWIs, are not designed to integrate and respect non-White perspectives, and faculty are not prepared to address, let alone mentor, Black scholarship (Walkington 53; Wilson et al. 699). Lori Walkington notes that while Black women's inclination to study their own communities may help them find a sense of purpose as scholars, this focus may inhibit mentorship from senior scholars in their program who do not feel comfortable or are not interested in providing support for this research. As a result, Black women graduates may continue to struggle with confidence and obtaining the unspoken academic know-how even after completing their degrees. This is one factor that leads to attrition rates for Black women faculty, who earn degrees at high rates but face barriers to tenure due to discrimination, both explicit and implicit expectations for increased service, and unclear workload expectations (Kynard; Garrett et. al.). Obstacles to career advancement do not end for those Black women who do obtain tenure, as they may get "stuck" at the associate level without access to privileged positions such as full professorships and executive administrative positions (Alcalde; Grant and Simmons). Stacy D. Garrett et al. found that some Black women scholars choose to stay at the associate level after finding the tenure and promotion process to be unclear, unsupportive, and even traumatic. M. Cristina Alcalde notes that Black women hold just 1.6%

of full professorships in the US. Talisha is one of just 12 tenured or tenure-line Black women faculty at her R1 institution, where there are only 21 full-time Black women faculty in over 850 total. The result on this campus and others is more Black women graduate students seeking mentorship than there are Black women mentors available, which Jari L. Minnett et al. call a "deficit of availability" (214). This disconnect creates both a gap in mentoring resources for Black women graduate students and a cyclical exclusion of Black women's perspectives in academia, which adds a potential hindrance to career success and coping abilities (Grant; Apugo, "'We All We Got'"). We acknowledge all of these as contributing factors to the experiences of Black women graduate students, such as those we discuss below.

Methods

Data Collection

The data from this study were taken from five interviews with former rhetoric and composition graduate students, four of whom were PhD students and one who was a master's student. These interviews make up the first part of a larger study by the first author on mentoring and professional development experiences of Black women graduate students and early career Black women scholars in rhetoric and composition. Each participant in this round self-identified as a Black or African American woman between the ages of 20 and 50. Although bi- and multi-racial Black women were included in the recruitment call, no participants in this study identified as bi- or multi-racial Black women. All participants are also US citizens, born and raised in the United States.

It is no secret that the field of rhetoric and composition is not overflowing with Black women scholars. The dearth of Black women scholars in this field and many others is part of the motivation for this study, but it also makes it more difficult to conduct interview studies and maintain participant confidentiality. To protect participants' confidentiality, we are providing minimal information about each participant. Below, we provide brief introductions to each participant intended to help orient readers to the later discussion and analysis:

- Soraya is in her late 30s and currently works as an assistant professor. She completed her PhD at a large public research university in the Midwest. Soraya selected her doctoral program based on her career goal to obtain a tenure-line position at a similar institution.
- Flora is in her late 40s and currently works as a lecturer and writing center administrator. She completed her PhD at a large public research university in the Northeast. She selected her program based

on advice from a former student and her desire to receive professional development in writing pedagogy.
- Comfort is in her mid-40s and is an assistant professor and writing center administrator. She completed her PhD at a large public research institution in the Midwest. She selected her doctoral program based on her research interests and advice from mentors from her undergraduate and master's institution.
- Lenox is in her late 30s and works as a visiting assistant professor. Lenox earned her PhD from a large public research university in the Southeast. She selected her doctoral program based on advice from her mentor and her interest in both academic and non-academic career paths.
- Candice is in her early 20s and works as a marketing assistant. She completed her MA at a mid-sized private university in the Southeast. She selected her master's program based on advice from undergraduate professors and her research interests. She also felt it would allow her to continue exploring both academic and non-academic career paths.

Each participant in this study attended a rhetoric and composition program at one of five different institutions located in the South, Midwest, and Northeastern US and completed their graduate programs between 2018 and 2022. One participant notably attended most of her courses online due to COVID-19 pandemic protocols.

Examining recent graduates, as opposed to current students, works well for our research questions for several reasons: (1) participants have an opportunity to reflect on their experiences and consider how, if at all, they have applied lessons learned to their current work; (2) we can capture any mentoring and professional development experiences that may be targeted towards degree candidates, such as mentoring around completing the dissertation or applying to jobs; and (3) we believe it reduces possible anxiety or apprehension about responding to interview questions. Current graduate students may have felt less comfortable openly discussing any negative experiences if they felt it might put their degree in jeopardy. Talisha was responsible for the design of the study. She contacted and recruited participants through a selective recruitment process, using listservs, Facebook postings, and direct outreach to potential interviewees. Malina assisted with data analysis and with writing this article manuscript. First-round interviews on which this article is based took place in January 2023 and lasted 60 to 90 minutes each. They were semi-structured with a specific set of questions but allowed space for further or tangential inquiry. In the analysis that follows, participants will be referred to using pseudonyms; each was given the option to provide one or have one assigned for her. Participants were compensated for their participation with a $30 gift card to one of three options of their choice.

Positionality

When conducting any study, particularly an identity-focused study such as this, we feel that researchers generally should attend to their unique positionalities. The primary investigator of this study identifies as a Black woman. I (Talisha) was drawn to this study based on my own experiences as a Black woman in the field, and I intentionally sought out a Black female research assistant. The undergraduate research assistant, Malina, identifies as a tri-racial African American, White, and Filipina woman. As Black women, our positionality made us less inclined to question or counter the experiences of our participants and more likely to validate or relate to parts of their stories.

Analysis

This IRB-approved study (protocol # 14590) used a grounded-theory methodology (Charmaz and Belgrave; Charmaz and Thornberg) that analyzed data while it was being collected. Interviews were audio recorded with the permission and notification of participants, then transcribed. This study asked three questions: (1) What are the mentoring and professional development experiences of Black women in rhetoric and composition programs?; (2) How do Black women in the field define mentoring and professional development?; and (3) What mentoring and professional development opportunities do Black women need or desire from their rhetoric and composition programs?

Transcriptions then went through several rounds of coding. We performed one round of coding on each transcript separately, then came together to compare themes. After the first round, we created a single document that compiled the shared and refined codes and organized data per participant. From the data, we identified three primary themes that guide our analysis below: (1) desire for mentorship and professional development, (2) denial of and subsequent outsourcing for mentorship, and (3) Black women's needs for and ideal forms of mentorship. In the section below, we discuss these three themes and draw conclusions about how to better support Black women graduate students in the field.

Desire for Mentorship and Professional Development

One thing that quickly became apparent when speaking to the women in this study is that they all deeply desired experiences that would help them prepare for their future careers. They spoke clearly about wanting to diversify their experiences in specific ways, build upon skills they felt they would need, and be mentored by established scholars in the field. Research has shown that Black women college students, including graduate students, are often intentional about their educational journeys and seek out and create pathways to success (Winkle-Wagner; Apugno "We All We Got"). Scott L. Miller et al. identified graduate students of all races and genders in rhetoric and composition as relatively "nontraditional," bringing to their programs specific professional needs and sacrifices that they'd made to pursue further education. Even in 1997, the authors noted that programs in the field needed to adjust to the changing climate of higher education and realities of academic job markets. They insisted that programs "*need* to be (more) accountable" to students and their future careers (400, emphasis added). Failure to build accountability and properly support and prepare students might lead to dissatisfaction and frustration (397, 404). Research on Black women graduate students across fields suggests that these frustrations are often heightened for Black female students. The stories of the women in this study also affirm those findings, even though the participants—even prior to beginning their programs—were thinking actively about what they needed as developing scholars and were working to obtain it.

As we noted in the participant overview, our participants each chose a graduate program that they felt was best able to provide the mentoring and professional development they needed. This was one way for them to create pathways to their future career goals. For example, Soraya explained that she selected her program because she felt it was the best place for her to grow and that the faculty at her chosen institution were best equipped to help her meet her goals. As she put it, she wanted to work with faculty whose work "aligned with [her] research interests and where [she] desired [her]self to be placed." Soraya had a clear goal for herself and her future to become faculty at an R1 institution, and she reported that a tenure-track position at an R1 was the program's ultimate goal for its graduates. So, theoretically, Soraya and the faculty in her program began on the same page for what her future should be.

Other participants also shared insight into their decision-making processes. After spending time researching programs, three of the participants—Comfort, Candice, and Flora—decided where they wanted to go. For various reasons, they applied only to those programs, to which they were all accepted. Decision strategies were based on a number of factors and restraints such as geography, affordability, and perceived strengths of the programs. Soraya and Lenox applied to and were accepted into multiple programs, each choosing the one they felt best equipped to help them reach their goals. Lenox attended an HBCU for both her bachelor's and master's degrees. For her doctoral degree, she wanted to attend a PHWI because she knew that her future work environment would likely be a predominantly White space, and she "needed to be able to navigate that professionally." Effective mentoring can assist in preparing Black women graduate students for careers at PHWIs in the ways that it helps mentees find their place, voice, and confidence in their field(Grant and Simmons; Grant). Lenox was hoping her program would provide her with such mentoring in addition to a different racial environment than that of her previous educational institutions. She also selected her program because she felt it would provide her with more options professionally. Unlike Soraya, who was focused on becoming a tenure-track professor, Lenox was open to a career in academia or industry work in professional writing. Her program "allowed for diverse career paths" that would prepare her to transition outside of the academy if she chose, and she wanted specific mentorship around these alternative career options.

Comfort was one of the women who only applied to one program. She had a strong relationship with her existing mentors, who encouraged her to apply for her doctoral program based on her research interests and career goals. Like Soraya, Comfort was seeking a career in academia. Her selected program had a strong reputation for producing influential scholars and supporting the types of research she was interested in. After researching the program for herself, Comfort agreed with her mentors that it seemed to be a good fit. Flora and Candice were similarly encouraged to apply for their programs. Candice was working in the writing center at her undergraduate institution and considering graduate school. Her mentor encouraged her to go to a regional writing center conference and meet with people from a prospective MA institution that the mentor thought would be a good fit based on Candice's research interests in both writing centers and digital media. Flora also selected her program based partly on a conference experience. An acquaintance she spoke with at the conference was currently enrolled in Flora's future doctoral program and encouraged her to apply. Flora was seeking professional development around teaching writing to support her new consulting business, which had started to receive requests for faculty development. She sought out an academic discipline and program that she thought would provide deep pedagogical knowledge about teaching and supporting writing in various forms.

After arriving in their programs, several of the women sought out professional development and mentoring right away. Some, like Candice, looked for support for race/identity-centered research, or for someone to help them maintain their momentum and identify diverse career paths, like Lenox. The women did so among faculty, program- and institution-wide resources, and, sometimes, more advanced students in their programs. They were seeking familiarization and professional exposure to the field. Lenox described PhD programs as "a different beast" from master's programs, stating that the former necessitate genuine mentorship and development through both inter- and intraracial relationships. However, each woman in this study expressed an explicit desire for mentoring that would support her research, which was shaped in some way by her racialized and gendered identities. Moreover, some of the women expressed the desire for guidance and mentorship around how their Blackness would be perceived in professional spaces. Many noted the importance and desire to be seen in their programs. When Candice reflected on her program, she said that if she had had a mentor who was a person of color, it "woulda gave me a little more guidance as far as my research process goes. I'm thankful for the opportunities I had, but I feel like I woulda had a little less hardship and challenges if I had connection to a scholar/professor who's been there, who's been in my shoes." As students, our participants were not oblivious to the fact that they were being specifically perceived based on their racialized identities, nor did they expect that their graduate school experiences would be simple or easy. However, they did expect and want mentorship that would help them shape their research and identity in the academy and workforce.

Access Denied: Outsourcing Mentorship

As the previous section shows, the women in this study were eager for professional development and leadership opportunities as well as sustained mentor relationships. They arrived at their programs hoping to be mentored in a way that would guide them toward their future careers. Most of them had a clear idea of what they wanted that future to be and at least some idea of what they needed to make it happen. While some might question if the women had realistic expectations of what their program could do for them, many of the women had heard positive things about their chosen programs' student opportunities and outcomes. The programs were known for placing graduates in tenure-track positions, equipping graduates with skills to move into industry, or, in Candice's case, preparing graduates to go on for doctoral work. What these particular students discovered, however, was that the experiences and opportunities available to others were not universal. The women in this study often had their requests for mentoring and leadership opportunities denied. Sometimes this was an outright denial; other times, the women were redirected elsewhere or told to figure things out themselves. Despite bringing her concerns to leadership in her program several times, Candice did not receive the support that she needed in her master's program and felt "like [she] was getting gaslit and ignored." Candice was told to broaden her research topic or focus to be more "relevant" and that faculty in the program could not direct her towards specific research on race and teaching. These experiences influenced her decision not to pursue a PhD, as she had originally planned to do.

Faculty and program infrastructure at times made it explicitly clear to several of our participants that their unique experiences and needs for support did not fit and that they should look elsewhere for what they needed.

For example, Flora was frequently told about her research on Black writers that her program "didn't do that." She was encouraged to transfer to the Africana Studies department or to another institution entirely. In a program with no Black faculty or other faculty of color, Flora, like Candice, was faced with White scholars who could not or would not support her research. Other women were similarly encouraged to generalize their teaching and academic pursuits, focusing less on Black women and people of color. They were forced to decide for themselves how, or if, they would find the support to continue their work, as it was clear that their programs could not fully provide such.

Another of Flora's experiences offered a stark example of denied mentorship around teaching. As noted above, Flora decided to apply to rhetoric and composition programs specifically for the professional development in writing pedagogy. And, rhetoric and composition is one of few fields in which graduate students regularly have the opportunity to serve as an instructor of record. However, she discovered that her program offered very little training for its graduate instructors. She stated that her graduate teaching assistant (GTA) training course taught students to build a syllabus but did not provide much support for actual instruction, and overall, the training practicum "wasn't helpful." Further, the course and the program overall offered little that felt culturally inclusive or relevant for her as a Black woman GTA. Soraya's experience with teaching reflects Flora's in the lack of support she felt as a Black female instructor. However, Soraya expressed that she felt simultaneously attacked and invisible as a Black woman composition instructor. Recounting stories of her teaching experience, Soraya shared that students at her predominantly White institution often made comments about her speech or the way she dressed. They complained that she "only wanted to talk about Black stuff." Soraya insisted that her course did not focus on "Black stuff" but did acknowledge how some of the issues discussed in class disproportionately affect Black people. When she went to her faculty for support, she was told, "Oh, it's fine. Your students are just airing out their concerns about other stuff," and "Don't take it personally." Soraya described her interactions with faculty as "acknowledgements without any empathy. Without any strategy" that would prepare her to handle such moments in the future. Similarly, she reported being told by faculty that they did not "see [her] as a Black woman" and that she was "just a GTA" like "everybody else."

The field of rhetoric and composition's use of graduate student labor for writing courses is often discussed and debated in ways beyond the scope of this article. However, given the field's fairly unique use of this labor, we contend that it is another area where programs and the field overall must improve its attention to Black women students like Soraya. Soraya felt that the responses she received from her faculty minimized the reality of her experience, including her students' fixation on her race, and refused her the mentorship and guidance she sought on how to be a Black female composition instructor, including dealing with students' anti-Blackness and disregard for Black female authority figures. It's important to note here that Soraya's doctoral institution was similar to the type of institution she wanted to work in one day. She knew that the culture and racial makeup of her future institution may be very similar to her doctoral institution, and she looked to current faculty for support on how she could navigate biased feedback from students. Instead, her faculty refused to engage with her as a Black woman in a way that she said was a "severe detriment to [her] education and [her] development" as a scholar. Soraya also offers one of the most explicit examples of being denied professional development. Soraya reported that she did not feel supported in her program. As she states, "I didn't have a lotta faculty that I felt were backing me," and as a result, Soraya didn't think she belonged in the program. From Soraya's story, it seems her program gave her several reasons to feel this way. Particularly, after a single negative incident early in her program in which she yelled at a classmate, Soraya's faculty refused her leadership positions and took away those she had been placed into. Some faculty, even years later, refused to write her recommendation letters for fellowship applications. The reaction from her program after the incident impacted her success and opportunities for the rest of her time in the program. Soraya reported feeling isolated and directionless in her program. She expressed regret for the incident and agreed that her behavior had been inappropriate. However, she maintained that the refusal of her faculty to grant her any leadership and professionalization opportunities for the duration of her program was unfair. Because she was denied opportunities within her program, Soraya felt pressure to take on immense amounts of service work to build connections in the field and strengthen her CV. She struggled to balance these obligations while also finishing her dissertation and producing the publications that would help her obtain the tenure-track job she desired.

Soraya's experience highlights both the limited space for Black perspectives along with the need for diverse mentorship and faculty in graduate programs. In her example, the unwillingness of faculty in Soraya's program to actively engage identity-specific experiences or scholarship stemmed from an effort to generalize all graduate student experiences, perhaps for the sake of purported equality. Color-blindness, or resistance to recognizing racially-centered motives and experiences, reaps real-time repercussions, doubly so when the need to have culturally-inclusive and relevant mentorship is ignored for the same mission of generalization. This makes seeking out external support a dire necessity for the survival and success of Black women graduate students who are denied mentorship and support. In Soraya's case, there was a single Black woman in a faculty or leadership position in her program; as it was, the best advice that this faculty member would provide was "That's what happens." Finding support and mentorship among those who share your culture has important benefits: in Lenox's experience, she relied on both an external mentor—an established Black woman scholar in the field—and on informal peer mentoring, through which she and other students "would share information, share documents, present with one another, and just share wisdom back and forth."

These reported experiences are consistent with other scholarship on the discrimination and oppression that Black women experience on college campuses. The participants' environment greatly influences their experiences, persistence, and success; thus, an environment resistant to scholarship focused on Black woman experiences, or hostile to those who hold such identities, often leads to "suboptimal coping mechanisms such as code-switching and hypervigilance" (Apugo, "Hidden Culture" 53). According to Danielle Apugo, such practices can lead to additional stress, feelings of not belonging, and pressure to "mask" one's Blackness, all of which can create psychological distress and burnout for Black female students, leading to attrition from their programs. For other Black women, however, the belief or feeling that their university does not want them and will not support them is a motivating factor that drives Black women graduate students to identify culturally-relevant networks that they can trust (Apugo, "'We All We Got'"; Henderson et al.). Comfort's time in her program reflected this phenomenon. Although she did not face efforts to whitewash or diminish her scholarship, she did not trust her program to support her needs as a Black queer woman, including addressing racism that she faced or witnessed. Instead, she found peer mentorship in community spaces wholly outside of the university. Apugo notes that trust is essential for Black women graduate students in mentoring relationships and that this trust can often be difficult to establish in mentoring relationships across identity categories, leading Black women to foster mentoring relationships outside of their immediate contexts ("'We All We Got'"). We saw this in Candice's experience, as she created her own network of support through an online community she built to connect with other women of color. These types of actions become a necessity for many Black women as a means of simply being able to move forward in their programs, especially when they find themselves in institutions or programs unwilling to validate their experiences and encourage their development as Black feminist scholars.

What Mentorship Could (or Should) Be

Our participants who found external mentor relationships identified the ways in which those relationships became lifelines. All shared what they, upon completing their degrees, felt would have made their journeys easier and the type of mentors they wished their program had provided. According to our participants, good mentors are collaborative, intentional, validating, and engaged in "vision work," or work that helps mentees identify their vision for the future and outline concrete steps to make those goals reality. Good mentors offer perspective, a listening ear, and support when needed. They help their mentees develop or refine a plan for themselves as scholars and teachers. The participants' ideal forms of mentorship would include guidance for teaching philosophies and securing job offers, balancing teaching and publishing responsibilities, and defining a scholarly identity. It would be mutually beneficial and include both lateral and hierarchical relationships that provide a network of support and development.

Institutionalizing mentorship opportunities is vital to support and retain students of color (Minnett et al.; Apugo, "We All We Got"; Henderson et al.). Most of our participants discussed the unique experiences, and therefore unique needs, of Black women students in their mentor relationships. In a mentoring relationship, Black women graduate students need a mentor who will, according to Comfort, "allow [them] to be weak, who allow them to break down, who allow them to not be okay—and [the mentor] can rebuild them so they can be okay." Soraya homed in on this as well. Especially within a PHWI, she emphasized the validating role of mentoring, particularly the importance of telling Black women graduate students to "celebrate your Blackness. . . . [what] makes you unlike everyone else in your goddamn program . . . Blackness is not a monolith [and] you do not have to reach whiteness" to be successful or worthwhile to the program.

Indeed, consistent with our review of the literature, validating students' internal worth is a key factor in effective mentorship that could influence Black women graduate students' experiences and satisfaction with their program (Wilson et al.). Candice, who keenly focused on race studies and dynamics, shared that, had she had the support and understanding that she needed throughout her thesis process, she would have continued on to a PhD program, which was her original plan. It was her negative experiences in her master's program that discouraged her from pursuing academia. The pushback on her research topic and the need to outsource for support whilst in her program made Candice feel that her work was not valued and that the field broadly may not be interested in what she had to say. Conversely, having a Black woman mentor helped Lenox see her worth as a Black woman, a student, and a future professional because "other people see my worth who are in great positions [and] use that worth to build me up." Further, mentors who encourage their mentees to stand firm in their beliefs and not be swayed by attempts to whitewash their research are those who critically support the whole of the woman—a notion that Lenox provided: "[Mentors should be] very supportive of the cultural needs, as well as the psychological needs, and of course professional development. . . . particularly [because] the Black woman [sometimes] gets left out of those conversations about things that are meant to help her." Candice stated that a good mentor helps show their mentee how not to take on the weight of their research, which Candice struggled with while researching race studies.

Other critical needs listed by the participants include having established pathways for people of color to connect. Candice and Soraya expressed desires to engage with faculty outside of their programs or even departments, since their English departments overall were only slightly more diverse than their specific programs. They felt that connecting with Black women faculty in other programs, given that their own programs had few or no Black women professors, would have helped prepare them for careers as Black women faculty. Similarly, Comfort told us that Black women graduate students need a mentor who will show them how to navigate the racism that they will face. While ideally this type of support would be available within programs, as programs would have multiple Black women and faculty of color internally, a short-term solution that the women in this study propose is having internal mentors who can advise their mentee on things like how to reach out to faculty across campus, or systems for connecting students for cross-campus and interdisciplinary support.

Conclusion

The findings from this study resonate with those of previous research, which indicate that Black women graduate students value and crave mentorship. Despite their desire for connection, they often find themselves isolated and, as a result, must forge their own paths as they navigate the challenging experience of graduate school, made more difficult by racialized and gendered discrimination. Compounding the difficulties is the dearth of Black women faculty in the participants' programs, who might be cyclically discouraged by the ways that institutions fail to create and engage space for Black women faculty perspectives. Soraya shared that for the first several years of her doctoral program, she "did not know of any Black women assistant professors." She and others reported that they were consistently directed to the work of Jacqueline Jones Royster when seeking Black feminist scholarship in the field, regardless of whether or not Royster's work was relevant to their particular research questions. Outside of the field, the only Black scholar their faculty referenced was bell hooks. The work of each of these women has, of course, been hugely influential to the field's approach to language, literacy, and pedagogy. However, they are far from the only notable and worthwhile Black female scholars. Faculty's inability to name other Black female scholars indicates a lack of engagement with Black scholars' work, which was reflected in the course curricula for most of the participants' programs. The participants consistently reported having, maybe, one class that deeply explored the works of Black and brown scholars. Most often, work by scholars of color was relegated to one or two days, deemed largely irrelevant to the overall course material, and further contributed to the women's sense that the stories and perspectives of Black women and other people of color were not valued or considered not complex enough to warrant further study.

Lenox discussed her experience with having Black scholars presented as one-dimensional. Speaking of her experience with her external mentor, she shared that "I believe, had I not had that mentoring experience, I would have settled on seeing myself just one way. And although I loved what I did in a master's degree . . . I like the idea of seeing myself in multiple ways, in and outside of academia." Having a mentor shaped her ability to perceive herself and her work in a positive, multifaceted way. Her experience reflects our research on the desire for, role, and impact of a mentor. Although the definitions of "mentor" fluctuate, ours is informed by our research as someone who supports the whole of their mentee and empowers her in fulfilling her potential (Haggard et al.; Minnett et al.). Our participants shared that their ideal mentors would be motivating, collaborative guides who provide insight into their field. They hoped that these relationships would be multi-directional, engaging, and celebrate what makes them unique—from research interests to identities. These testimonies shed further light on what our research has evidenced: that Black women graduate students' need for mentorship is unique in perspective and form but common by many other measures. This means that their Blackness does not exclude them from the essential nature of mentorship and simultaneously brings beautiful difference and perspective that deserves to be nurtured. Our study leads us to the same conclusion others have reached: that mentorship is beneficial for all graduate students, and its scarcity creates incredible obstacles over which they must climb to succeed.

Our participants highlighted the ways in which they strove to fulfill their mentoring needs, particularly through outsourcing when internal opportunities were limited. Outsourcing, like in Lenox's case, may become a lifeline necessary to persist. Resource allocation in graduate programs may or may not include intentional mentoring opportunities for students, whose success, satisfaction, and ability to continue in their programs may very well hinge on such resources. Black women entering graduate spaces may have even less access to mentoring support. Data from this study reveal that, even when support and resources are available within a program, Black women students may not feel welcome or safe to explore those options, or they may not attend to their unique needs and perspectives. There is an unspoken standard of whiteness, coded as generalization, color blindness, or exclusion that Black women graduate students often must combat to obtain access to support and opportunities. They are often left to do this alone, without proper mentors. Outsourcing—seeking out alternative resources—thus became a form of resistance for our participants during their unique experiences in PHWIs.

"Paying it forward" and unintentional mentorship became a form of resistance as well. Comfort discussed the unintentional ways that mentorship manifested within academia. She said that

> For those of us who think that we're not mentors, I would say always remember that there are people who are watching us and watching the way we move. And may be drawn to us because they wish that they could have that type of confidence. And I think that Black women need other mentors around them who will continue to instill confidence because much of our persona is to be strong.

Many of our participants expressed the responsibility and joy of "paying it forward" in mentoring others. Their lack of mentorship, particularly from other Black women, encouraged them to be open and intentional in helping other Black women see their worth, identify their values, and create their own experiences in programs and as students. Essentially, having a model helps others model as well. Becoming a mentor may be seen as a mode of resistance just as self-created networks of Black women students who support one another within the whitewashed, underrepresented, and sometimes hostile environments of their graduate programs can be (Minnett et al.; Apugo, "'We All We Got'"; Henderson et al.; Apugo, "Black Women"). Mentoring in this way emphasizes our participants' values of mutually beneficial relationships and actively celebrating their Blackness. As mentors, whether formal or informal, Black women "pay it forward" in honor of the outsourced support that they sought and the internal, institutional support that they were denied.

While the informal networks and workarounds that these Black women created were and are valuable, we would like them to be less necessary. We call for individual programs and the field of rhetoric and composition collectively to create additional and varied pathways to mentorship for Black women in the field. Some possible ways to approach these pathways are listed below:

Individual Programs
1. Actively recruit and retain Black women and other scholars of color to your graduate programs and faculty.
2. Adjust faculty service loads/obligations to allow time for more sustained mentorship between faculty and students.
3. Ensure mentorship can be appropriately represented and valued in faculty annual evaluations to incentivize faculty to dedicate time to mentoring students.
4. Work with other departments and programs to establish mentoring and support across academic units. This may be particularly useful given the interdisciplinary nature of much research in rhetoric and composition.
5. Provide students with information about Black- and/or women-serving groups on campus and in the area (e.g., Black Grad Student Association).

Field & Scholarly Organizations
1. Leverage existing resources such as graduate student-focused subgroups like WPA-GO and the CCCC Graduate Student Standing Group to build targeted support for Black women and other students of color.
2. Conduct climate surveys to gauge participants' experience with the organizations and scholarly conventions.
3. Facilitate cross-institutional relationships between Black women scholars to help connect graduate students with trained and dedicated mentors from other institutions.
4. Create more ways for graduate students to connect outside of annual conventions.
5. Provide mentorship training and guidelines for those interested in mentoring others, including training on effective interracial mentoring relationships.
6. Value Black women's (and others') collaborative work in a way that acknowledges the different and often increased labor required in collaborative projects and the communal creation of knowledge.

Many mission and position statements from our field's scholarly organizations commit support for diverse scholars. For example, in its strategic governance statement, CCCC expresses a desire to "enhance participation by members who represent a diversity of races, cultures, languages, identities, institutions, and institutional roles" ("Strategic"). The International Writing Centers Association is dedicated to "Supporting social justice, empowerment, and transformative scholarship that serves our diverse communities" ("Purpose"). Both these and other organizations in the field signal their support for inclusive practices through mission statements and other, more specific statements, such as the CCCC "Statement on Language, Power, and Action" and the "WPA-GO Statement on Anti-Racist Assessment." Yet our study reveals that very recently, and most likely even currently, Black women graduate students in the field have been under-supported and undervalued. We believe the experiences of these five women are indicative of a larger problem in the field, documented anecdotally in the work of Black women students and scholars for decades. We call for the actions above as well as a more robust review of mentorship and professional development resources and programs in the field and for an intentional commitment to supporting Black women and other minoritized scholars in the field. The scholars in this study have provided clear guidance on what this support might look like; thus, we also call for programs to more carefully engage and listen to Black women. Refusing to do so is counter to our discipline's professed commitments to racial justice and intersectional inclusion.

Works Cited

Alcalde, M. Cristina. "Colleges Must Redefine Leadership." *Inside Higher Ed*, 16 Dec. 2021, www.insidehighered.com/advice/2021/12/17/colleges-should-support-women-faculty-color-leaders-opinion#.

Apugo, Danielle. "Black Women Graduate Students on Whiteness and Barrier Breaking in Leadership." *The Urban Review*, vol. 53, 2021, pp. 424–42. doi.org/10.1007/s11256-020-00552-4.

—. "A Hidden Culture of Coping: Insights on African American Women's Existence in Predominately White Institutions." *Multicultural Perspectives*, vol. 21, no. 1, 2019, pp. 53–62. doi.org/10.1080/15210960.2019.1573067.

—. "'We All We Got': Considering Peer Relationships as Multi-Purpose Sustainability Outlets Among Millennial Black Women Graduate Students Attending Majority White Urban Universities." *The Urban Review*, vol. 49, 2017, pp. 347–67. doi.org/10.1007/s11256-017-0404-2.

CCCC Statement on Language, Power, and Action. CCCC, 2022, cccc.ncte.org/cccc/language-power-and-action.

Charmaz, Kathy, and Linda Liska Belgrave. "Qualitative Interviewing and Grounded Theory Analysis." *The SAGE Handbook of Interview Research: The Complexity of the Craft*, edited by Jaber F. Gubrium, James A. Holstein, Amir B. Marvasti, and Karyn D. McKinney, 2nd ed., SAGE Publications, 2012, pp. 347–66. doi.org/10.4135/9781452218403.n25.

—, and Robert Thornberg. "The Pursuit of Quality in Grounded Theory." *Qualitative Research in Psychology*, vol. 18, no. 3, 2021, pp. 305–27. doi.org/10.1080/14780887.2020.1780357.

Garrett, Stacy D., Michael Steven Williams, and Amanda M. Carr. "Finding Their Way: Exploring the Experiences of Tenured Black Women Faculty." *Journal of Di-

versity in Higher Education, vol. 16, no. 5, 2023, pp. 527–38. doi.org/10.1037/dhe0000213.

Grant, Cosette M. "Advancing Our Legacy: A Black Feminist Perspective on the Significance of Mentoring for African-American Women in Educational Leadership." *International Journal of Qualitative Studies in Education,* vol. 25, no. 1, 2012, pp. 101–17. doi.org/10.1080/09518398.2011.647719.

—, and Juanita Cleaver Simmons. "Narratives on Experiences of African-American Women in the Academy: Conceptualizing Effective Mentoring Relationships of Doctoral Students and Faculty." *International Journal of Qualitative Studies in Education,* vol. 21, no. 5, 2008, pp. 501–17. doi.org/10.1080/09518390802297789.

Haggard, Dana L., Thomas W. Dougherty, Daniel B. Turban, and James E. Wilbanks. "Who Is a Mentor? A Review of Evolving Definitions and Implications for Research." *Journal of Management,* vol. 37, no.1, 2011, pp. 280–304. doi.org/10.1177/0149206310386227.

Henderson, Tammy L., Andrea G. Hunter, and Gladys J. Hildreth. "Outside within the Academy: Strategies for Resistance and Mentoring African American Women." *Michigan Family Review,* vol. 14, no.1, 2010, pp. 28–41. doi.org/10.3998/mfr.4919087.0014.105.

Kynard, Carmen. "Administering While Black: Black Women's Labor in the Academy and the 'Position of the Unthought.'" *Black Perspectives on Writing Program Administration,* edited by Staci M. Perryman-Clark and Collin Lamont Craig, NCTE, 2019, pp. 28–50.

Miller, Scott L., Brenda Jo Brueggemann, Bennis Blue, and Deneen M. Shepherd. "Present Perfect and Future Imperfect: Results of a National Survey of Graduate Students in Rhetoric and Composition Programs." *College Composition and Communication,* vol. 48, no. 3, 1997, pp. 392–409. doi.org/10.2307/358405.

Minnett, Jari L., ArCasia D. James-Gallaway, and Devean R. Owens. "Help A Sista Out: Black Women Doctoral Students' Use of Peer Mentorship as an Act of Resistance." *Mid-Western Educational Researcher,* vol. 31, no. 2, 2019, pp. 210–38.

Patterson-Stephens, Shawna M., Tonisha B. Lane, and Louise Michelle Vital. "Black Doctoral Women: Exploring Barriers and Facilitators of Success in Graduate Education." *Higher Education Politics and Economics,* vol 3, no. 1, 2017, pp. 157–80. doi.org/10.32674/hepe.v3i1.15.

"Purpose and Values Statement." *International Writing Centers Association.* writingcenters.org/about/.

Reid, E. Shelley. "Mentoring Peer Mentors: Mentor Education and Support in the Composition Program." *Composition Studies,* vol. 36, no. 2, 2008, pp. 51–79.

"Strategic Governance Vision Statement, November 2012." *Conference on College Composition & Communication,* Nov. 2012, cccc.ncte.org/cccc/about.

Walkington, Lori. "How Far Have We Really Come? Black Women Faculty and Graduate Students' Experiences in Higher Education." *Humboldt Journal of Social Relations,* vol. 39, 2017, pp. 51–65.

Wilson, Betty L., Brittany Davis, Brandi Anderson, Parthenia Luke, Christian Gorchow, and Agnes N. Nzomene Kahouo Foda. "'Tone It Down': The Whitewashing of Black Women Doctoral Students' Research and Scholarship at Predominately White Institutions—Implications for Social Work Doctoral Education." *Journal of Social Work Education*, vol. 59, no. 3, 2023, pp. 699–714. doi.org/10.1080/10437797.2023.2179147.

Winkle-Wagner, Rachelle. "Having Their Lives Narrowed Down? The State of Black Women's College Success." *Review of Educational Research*, vol. 85, no. 2, 2015, pp. 171–204. doi.org/10.3102/0034654314551065.

WPA-GO Anti-Racist Assessment Task Force. "WPA-GO Statement on Anti-Racist Assessment." *Council of Writing Program Administrators,* 17 July 2020, wpacouncil.org/aws/CWPA/pt/sd/news_article/313021/_PARENT/layout_details/false.

Talisha Haltiwanger Morrison (she/her) is associate professor of writing and director of the OU Writing Center at the University of Oklahoma. She is co-editor of *Writing Centers and Racial Justice: A Guidebook for Critical Praxis.* Her work has also appeared in journals such as the *Writing Center Journal* and the *Journal of Multimodal Rhetorics.*

Malina Anderson (she/her) is a recent rhetoric and composition MA graduate from Michigan State University and former rhetoric and writing studies undergraduate at the University of Oklahoma. She now works in environmental justice storytelling for a city development nonprofit. Her research passionately focuses on Indigenous and Black environmental belonging in community storytelling and policy rhetoric.

Addressing and Overcoming Barriers in the First-Year Writing Classroom: The Story of an International Graduate Teaching Assistant of Color

Jainab Tabassum Banu

The autoethnographic paper explores my experiences as an international female graduate teaching assistant of color teaching first-year composition courses in a predominantly White majority English-speaking classroom at a large Midwest university. I share my own experiences as I faced multiple implicit barriers while addressing and contextualizing the issues related to World English(es) and race. I applied an anti-racist pedagogy to my teaching and implemented my preconceived knowledge about the history of colonization in relation to language to overcome the barriers. In the process, I handled delicate discussions about my non-American accent and other Englishes with my students in the classroom. Also, I had one-to-one conversations where my students felt relieved to share their ideologically constructed ideas about race. In this article, I address and discuss the incidents where I faced obstacles and share my strategies for overcoming them. These barriers are recursive in a writing teacher's life. Therefore, I believe my paper is valuable for those international graduate students who are committed to pursuing their higher studies in English in the U.S., and who must go through the professional teaching assistantship phase in a predominantly English-speaking writing classroom environment.

Upon entering the first-year writing classroom at a large Midwest university, I held certain expectations regarding the acceptance from my White English-speaking students and my ability to claim my space as a multilingual female writing instructor of color. On the very first day, one of my students asked me, "If English is not your first language, how come you teach English?"

This inquiry momentarily undermined my self-assurance; the educational setting became an uneasy milieu for me, and I experienced a brief period of uncertainty regarding my ability to persevere in both the pursuit of knowledge and the facilitation of learning within an environment where my international identity lacks validation. However, the experience of imposter syndrome paradoxically facilitated my personal rejuvenation. Exhibiting a dearth of confidence in the presence of my students had the potential to contradict my pedagogical strategies and jeopardize my professional identity as an educator.

The apprehension of losing my assistantship loomed over me and instilled a reluctance to relinquish my scholarly endeavors. As a newcomer to the realm of U.S. academia, accompanied by my graduate student husband and three children from a South Asian country, I embarked upon the very first semester of navigating both the academic and sociocultural landscapes by engendering a sense of unfamiliarity with respect to my identity as a writing teacher and a South Asian woman of color. I agree with Jamaica Baldwin that "To be a body and a teacher simultaneously, to be a brown body, a cis-woman, and a teacher simultaneously, in a predominately White setting is to live on the cusp" (3). Numerous occasions prompted introspective conversations within myself, as I pondered the rationale behind forsaking the security of my homeland and embarking on this journey. The hurdles I encountered extended beyond a singular dimension, encompassing challenges related to language proficiency, racial identity, gender dynamics, religious affiliation, and the unique circumstance of my maternal role. Jessica McCaughey characterizes the last facet as the "underrepresentation of graduate student mothers in PhD programs." All these barriers further highlighted the multifaceted nature of my experiences as a writing teacher. The intersectionality of these barriers compounded, creating a formidable obstacle that potentially impeded my ability to cultivate a secure, inclusive, and amiable coalition within my writing classroom.

Rather than succumbing to increased anxiety in the face of these challenges, I approached my pedagogy as an empowered space for transformative action and aimed at overcoming any potential barriers that could arise within my teaching environment. I was inspired by bell hooks' *Teaching to Transgress* and Paulo Freire's *Pedagogy of the Oppressed*, which greatly shaped me as an anti-racist feminist pedagogue. I fostered a proactive mindset within myself, which served as the foundation for implementing an intersectional approach rooted in translingual and anti-racist pedagogies. Despite instructing a student body that lacked diversity, I remained committed to cultivating an inclusive classroom that embraced linguistic and cultural variations. I encouraged my English-speaking students to realize that their multidialectal linguistic positionality is humbly and gladly accommodated in my class. Monolingual people who might not realize that they can be multidialectal can also implement translingualism in writing or speaking or any form of communication. After all, "The English language at the beginning of its recorded history was already divided into distinct regional dialects" ("Students' Right" 7). When there is a lack of diversity in a population, the lack of diverse perspectives becomes an inevitable issue. Consequently, my purpose was to establish a dynamic learning environment that nurtured the cultivation of diverse perspectives, facilitated challenging discussions, and fostered a culture of mutual respect. Recognizing the barriers at hand, I consciously elected to confront and surmount them progressively.

Addressing Barriers

English Is My Second Language

Upon realizing that my language had become a subject of discourse, a pertinent question emerged within me: Did my students possess an expectation of being instructed by a White, English-speaking teacher? When my student asked me how I taught English while being taught in it as a second language user, I initially responded to his question by saying that the historical context of being colonized by the British Empire from the 17th to the early 20th century played a significant role in shaping our perspective on English language education. The profound impact of colonization on our educational system resulted in the prioritization of the English language as one of the primary languages for our children to learn. My mother tongue is Bengali, but I have been learning English since I began my formal education in kindergarten. Over time, I honed my linguistic skills and acquired a solid command of the English language that enabled me to teach it to both non-native speakers and, subsequently, native users. Through persistent effort and dedication, I developed the necessary expertise and competence to effectively impart my knowledge and facilitate language learning among diverse groups of learners. To contextualize my response, I encouraged him by saying, "in fact, you can learn and master Bengali to teach Bengali to the Bengali speaking students. If I can do it, you can too".

Facing language-related challenges, I had two choices: conform to Standard American English (SAE) and lose my cultural identity, or challenge linguistic norms and embrace my role as an international writing teacher. Clearly, I opted for the latter, recognizing that assimilating an unfamiliar identity detached from my roots would prove more arduous than confronting and overcoming the barriers I encountered. Seeking advice, I turned to my mentor, who suggested using texts that encompass a fusion of World Englishes.

Text Selection for First-Year Writing Course

In first-year writing courses, we use Lisa Arnold's *Writing Critically* alongside texts by writers from diverse linguistic and cultural backgrounds. Students often emulate the sample texts' voices while incorporating their own ideas. Exposure to varied authors helps them build confidence in developing their unique voice. To support this, I generally include multilingual authors of color who blend and switch codes in their writing, inspiring students to explore their own expressive styles.

For example, while reading Gloria Anzaldúa's "How to Tame a Wild Tongue," students know the importance of situating one's linguistic identity unapologetically in written texts. When I taught this text in the past, my monolingual but multidialectal students experienced several roadblocks caused by linguistic alienation. Some of them expressed their desire to Google a few Chicano Spanish words to know more about the text's meanings. Some felt reluctant to do so because, for them, the text appeared as a "tour guide" (Matsuda 482). Similar things happened when I taught Kaveh Akbar's "How I Found Poetry in Childhood Prayer." As a Muslim individual, I had the advantage of possessing knowledge and understanding of several Arabic words. Hence, I was able to explain the meanings to my students and enlighten them about the existence of languages other than English for conveying one's thoughts. By utilizing these materials, I was able to assert my own linguistic identity and embrace my multilingual existence within the predominantly English-speaking classroom. This approach not only challenged the conventional notions of language hierarchy but also fostered an environment that celebrated linguistic diversity and encouraged students to value a broader range of language expressions.

During the initial weeks of the semester, I introduced my students to the "Literacy Narrative" assignment, using Deborah Brandt's "Sponsors of Literacy." Brandt explores how literacy sponsorship is influenced by factors such as access, socioeconomic background, and appropriation. By employing human examples in her essay, she effectively demonstrates how literacy experiences vary based on individuals' diverse backgrounds and identities. To illustrate the impact of different socioeconomic circumstances on literacy, I delved into the stories of Raymond Branch and Dora Lopez, shared in Brandt's essay. Raymond, hailing from a privileged background, had access to computer literacy, while Dora, from a struggling bilingual family, lacked exposure to the same resources. Consequently, Dora's skills in bilingualism became her primary form of literacy development.

Building upon this discussion of bilingualism, I transitioned into bell hooks' "Language Teaching New Worlds/New Words." I wanted my students to know how important one's own language is for the sake of one's identity and existence. I wanted them to read and understand the gravity and weight of Anzaldúa's words when she writes, "if you want to really hurt me, talk badly about my language" (81). Hooks repeatedly refers to Adrienne Rich writing "This is the oppressor's language yet I need it to talk to you" (223), so that they know how important it still is to know the colonizer's English to turn it into a weapon of resistance. I included hooks' essay to help my students understand how polemically bell hooks used English to talk back to racial, linguistic, and cultural oppressions. These texts ensure linguistic justice while enabling a core understanding of how English language should be used in order to make the writer feel heard. This is my way of blending pragmatic and progressive pedagogies through selecting and assigning texts.

As my students grappled with the concept, particularly when confronted with the statement that "Standard English is not the speech of exile. It is the language of conquest and domination; in the United States, it is the mask which hides the loss of so many tongues" (hooks 223), I encountered resistance among them. They felt uncomfortable. One of my students said to me that my spoken English sounded different as if I had just learned to speak in this language. I felt offended but had to restrain and process my emotions. I thought I did not sound like an amateur, but I certainly sound different from native English speakers. However, I thought I had "a responsibility to teach students how to critically question Standardized English, to understand why it has more prestige than other dialects" (Dennihy 205).

In the positionality statement, "This Ain't Another Statement. This is a DEMAND for Black Linguistic Justice," teachers urge students to reject standard academic English as the norm, which reflects White Mainstream English. As a multilingual instructor, I embrace linguistic diversity in my classroom and foster critical language awareness. I remained myself–an unapologetically confident multilingual teacher who can write in two languages, speak in four, and dream in many!

Race Is a Taboo

Yet, the struggle was on. To clarify the hierarchical linguistic imperialism of Standardized English, I referred to the idea of racism. While teaching bell hooks' essay, my intention was to convey the notion that as multilingual users, both a couple of my students and I employed the language of the "oppressor" to subvert "hegemonic power dynamics" (167) and create a "counter-hegemonic discourse" (175). As part of my pedagogical approach, I sought to establish a contextual framework before delving into the text. Thus, I posed the question to my students, "Are you familiar with the history of racism in America?" Anticipating a well-informed response, I held a preconceived notion that American students would be open to discussing social inequalities. However, I was taken aback when one student responded that they knew but did not want to talk about it. This unexpected reply left me with a sense of surprise and disappointment, as it challenged my assumptions about the willingness of my American students to address and confront issues like racial inequality.

Before coming to the U.S., I did not know the state-based variations of racial issues. The Black Lives Matter Movement had a global impact and captivated the attention of people worldwide. Nevertheless, I had not previously recognized that the perception and extent of the topic's viability could differ across different states or regions. I had this belief that American young people were open and candid enough to discuss and engage in the conversation about racial matters. As soon as I started teaching at a Midwest university in a predominantly in a mostly White society, outside of academia, I was called a "fucking illegal alien," "you sick people" and a few other names for my skin color and accent. Whenever I resisted, I was told by people who witnessed the abuse that "everyone has the right to their own opinion." I asked myself, "then why can't I shout back? Don't I have the right to my own opinion? Why would they 'assume' me to be an illegal alien?" I was told to "shut up and ignore" these social situations and focus on my research and teaching. When I faced a similar, yet less violent atmosphere in the classroom, I understood that "Race is considered a taboo topic for discussion" (Tatum 5) in a White populated space. It was an awkward moment, but indeed a wake-up call. I knew I had to escape the situation for the time being but could not really avoid the subject in the long run.

I asked my students the next day if they read about racism or racial history in their middle or high schools. The answer was mostly negative. I am aware of the House Bill no. 1508 passed in 2021 that says that "A school district or public school may not include instruction relating to critical race theory in any portion of the district's required curriculum under sections 15.1 - 21 - 01 or 15.1 - 21 - 02, or any other curriculum offered by the district or school" (HB 1508). It was an act to prohibit teaching critical race theory in the public schools where race is under-theorized. Upon relocating to the United States and enrolling my children in one of the public schools, I observed a disconcerting pattern in the picture books they borrowed and brought home from the school library: a notable absence of Black characters, both in significant and minor roles. This partial erasure of Black representation in children's literature raised deep concerns within me. Many of my students had limited exposure to the nation's racial history. Learning from my children's exposure to the picture books available at their school libraries, I now understand why my mostly White students did not want to discuss race in the class.

Since my mentor encouraged me to focus on text selection, I assigned them to read Gloria Anzaldúa's "How to Tame a Wild Tongue." The following day, I encountered a disheartening situation as more than half of my students arrived in class without having read the assigned text. This lack of preparedness was a significant obstacle to fostering meaningful discussions and engaging with the course material effectively. Instead of accusing them of not reading the assigned text, I investigated the reason behind their unwillingness to read it. It was unusual for me as my students mostly came to the class prepared.

My students struggled to understand Chicano Spanish, a linguistic variety proudly used by Anzaldúa. My goal was to create discomfort, encouraging critical engagement with the text. Through Anzaldúa's work, they explored her skillful navigation of linguistic barriers and unapologetic use of her "home" languages (Anzaldúa 78). This exploration underscored the existence of an unequal and hierarchical relationship between various English varieties (Canagarajah, "Place of World English" 1619). My aim was to combat implicit linguistic bias, ensuring it didn't shape their perspectives or influence their understanding.

To navigate it further, I encouraged my students to use mixed languages in their papers. To clarify, I set an example when they got confused by my instructions. I used Bengali words and mixed them into my English sentences. For example, I said, "I used to give a lot of 'adda' with my students and colleagues back in Bangladesh." In Bengali, *adda* means a casual or informal conversation that takes place between two or more light-minded individuals." My students were fascinated to learn a new word in a different language which can be potentially used along with English. My students kept asking me to say something in Bengali and were thrilled to exhibit their own multilingual exposures. Many of my students learned an additional language in their schools. Though they thought they had forgotten many words and their meanings, they were surprised to find out how strong their own memories were.

Out of twenty-two students in one section, I had two Somali students who migrated to America at a very early age. I also had one student who knew Spanish and English. He was primarily English speaking, but he knew the basic level of Spanish. I learned a few Spanish and Somali words from them when they left my class saying, "Professor, have a lindo día (Spanish language for a nice day)" or "Professor, see you berrito (Somali language for tomorrow)." The exchange was rewarding. I do not follow a numeric order to label a language as the language paradigm may shift anytime for anyone. English, for me, is an "additional" language. Several students are fluent in speaking more than one language, but not really competent in writing and reading in other languages. I did not want to mark this ability as a lack; rather, I wished to accommodate their speaking skills in other languages in my classroom discussions. I ensured students' verbal involvement, only spoken versions of multilingualism or multidialectalism work well. I was willing to stay patient, respectful and empathetic to my multilingual students who aspire to be heard in an academic context. I usually recite five lines from one of my favorite poems, "Speak" by Faiz Ahmed Faiz, as a motivational tonic to boost students' verbal participation:

> Speak, your lips are free,
> Speak, it is your own tongue,
> Speak, it is your own body,
> Speak, your life is still yours.
> _____
> Speak, speak, whatever, you must speak!

Our translingual ventures were not limited to verbal conversation only. The literacy narrative and commentary assignments let them play with words of different languages. One of my Muslim students said, "You are the first Muslim teacher I have got after coming to the States from Kenya. And it feels liberating. Now, I can write a few Arabic verses with Somali language in my English essay." I realized that my religious identity, alongside my linguistic identity, played a vital role in helping restore my students' vocal expression.

Looking back, the topic of race as an integral aspect of one's writerly identity presents a challenging yet crucial conversation to engage in with my first-year writing students, given that writing is intricately linked to one's sense of self (Roozen 50). In *Teaching Racial Literacy*, Mara Lee Grayson asserts that a student's perspectives on race are often shaped by their living conditions and sociohistorical-cultural contexts, even if they do not consider themselves racist (81). It is essential for White students to develop empathy for people of color to gain a deeper understanding of their own racialized identities (Grayson 82).

Given the general discomfort among my students regarding discussions on race within the classroom, I took the initiative to engage in individual conferences with each student. In one of the conferences, a White student of mine shared her childhood experience with the concept of race and how her ideology was constructed by her grandmother. She said that she had a Black neighbor with whom she loved to play. Her grandmother strictly told her and her cousin not to play with him only because he was Black. Her idea of race is shaped by her grandmother. I was glad that she found the comfort zone with me and shared her long-established viewpoint and her desire to get rid of the stigma. I individualized my students' experiences and delicately dealt with texts stemming from racially charged issues.

The Danger of Tokenization

After discussing race and racial issues, Kaveh Akbar's narrative, "How I Found Poetry in Childhood Prayer," posed an additional hurdle for me and my own religious identity. My intention was to demonstrate how individuals' racial, religious, and cultural identities can foster code-meshing and potentially dismantle the supremacy of white Language. When I began teaching his essay, I experienced a "danger of tokenization" (Masterson 117). As a Muslim individual, I found it easier to articulate the Arabic verses and words in the article, as they were written using English fonts. The article commences with the phrase *Bismillahir Rahmanir Rahim* (In the name of God the merciful), which I am familiar with as it is commonly uttered at the beginning of various tasks such as eating, writing, or beginning any task. Certain terms like *wuzu* (ablution) and *ruh* (soul) are explained in English, while others such as *namaz* (prayer) and *janamaz* (prayer) are not explicitly defined but can be understood within the contextual framework of the text. Nonetheless, having no or a few Muslim students in the class, discussing the social, cultural, geographical, and even religious aspects became challenging but vital. Challenging, because I had to repeatedly and explicitly say that I was a writing teacher and not an Islamic preacher. Otherwise, there was a risk that my students might misunderstand my intentions and perceive me solely as an advocate for Islam, rather than recognizing my role as a multicultural writing instructor.

Nevertheless, coming from a sub-continent rich in diverse religious perspectives, I had a relatively good hold on Hinduism and Buddhism too. My aim was to let my students know that my religious identity mattered to me, but it was the knowledge of different cultures and religions that enriched an individual. Interestingly, I could showcase my knowledge of Hinduism when I was almost tokenized as an Islamic preacher. One of my very hardworking students, unfortunately, could not meet the deadline of submitting his midterm portfolio. He said that he had to work full-time that week, and so he missed the deadline. He opined, "Professor, it's all about money." I felt a moral responsibility to guide him without really sounding suggestive. Therefore, I took shelter in the knowledge of Hinduism. I said, "you know, in Hinduism, there are 33 cores of gods and goddesses. Among them, Goddess Laksmi is the goddess of wealth and money whereas Goddess Saraswati is worshiped as the goddess of knowledge, music, and wisdom. Most of the time, we forget to devote ourselves to Goddess Saraswati and run after Goddess Laksmi. My dear students, chase Saraswati, trust me, Laksmi will follow you." Upon hearing all this, my students were wowed by the analogy and appreciated my knowledge of a different religion and culture. They became more open and more tolerant towards different voices. Since I am a mother of three young children, I have a habit of storytelling which I sometimes implement in my composition classes. Stories from different cultures connect people of one culture with another. I believe that my exposure to different cultures through texts and embodied experiences helped me become a more open and accommodating teacher in America.

Bringing Intersectional Pedagogy into My Classroom

Employing an intersectional pedagogy of translingual approaches, CLA (Critical Language Awareness) pedagogy, and anti-racist pedagogy, I was able to navigate the aforementioned sensitive conversations effectively. Importantly, my intention was not to accuse or burden my students with the historical wrongdoings of White European settlers towards Native Americans and African tribes. Instead, I aimed to foster a sense of responsibility and encourage my students to critically examine race, explore their own identities, and challenge social inequalities through their writing.

The concepts of translingualism, translingual writing, and translingual pedagogy are not fairly new. However, as Paul Kei Matsuda writes, the term "translingual writing is still in search of its own meaning" (478). Apparently, translingualism is applicable for multilingual individuals. However, monolingual people might be multidialectal too. That means, translingualism encompasses codes of all kinds—be it language or dialects, be it spoken or written, be it verbal or non-verbal. Moreover, as Suresh Canagarajah suggests, "writing is multimodal" ("End of Second Language Writing" 440) which even includes signs, emoticons, symbols, images, layouts, patterns and other visual or auditory aspects into the realm of languages. Everything, apparent or non-apparent, takes part in the meaning-making process.

Furthermore, if language is a means of communication, the body must claim its stature of being a primitive form of language in its own right. In that case, gestures, postures, eye contact, and even breathing become languages. That is to say, language is ingrained in both verbal and non-verbal and written and spoken forms of communications. When all languages or codes are blended to make a meaningful communication, the speakers, writers, readers and listeners experience code-meshing. Vershawn Ashanti Young gives a compelling definition of code-meshing which I take as a definition of translingualism: "Code meshing blends dialects, international languages, local idioms, chat-room lingo, and the rhetorical styles of various ethnic and cultural groups in both formal and informal speech act" (114).

After considering the plurality of possible human languages and Young's idea of code-meshing, I argue that translingualism is a phenomenon which allows individuals to use their body, mind, sounds, and fonts to comfortably blend and express themselves in speech, writing, or signs. We often enroll students with accessibility issues who require more than written and spoken forms of communication. To me, any form of communication can be called translingual in its communicative approach if they mesh and make sense to express an individual's needs and feelings. In a way, the translingual approach ensures a safer place for users of all languages. As Horner et al. write,

> a translingual approach argues for (1) honoring the power of all language users to shape language to specific ends, (2) recognizing the linguistic heterogeneity of all users of language both within the United States and globally; and (3) directly confronting English monolingualist expectations by researching and teaching how writers can work with and against, not simply within, those expectations. (305)

Through my course, I created a translingual learning zone and helped my students be more tolerant, heterogeneous, and negotiable about language uses. I aimed to foster a pedagogical practice that helped students develop their own voice and feel confident and comfortable about it.

However, in the current situation when AI is almost replacing human writers, I wished for my students to succeed in academic and professional lives. Therefore, I cultivated critical language awareness in my writing class by adapting to both pragmatic and progressive pedagogies. A translingual approach allows an instructor to practice both styles. As Shawna Shapiro writes, "A translingual approach, similar to a CLA approach, treats language differences as an asset" (9). The blend of pragmatism and progressivism helps instructors to "make decisions about how, whether, and when to push against standardized norms" (Shapiro 10). When students write life writing or autobiographical narratives, they can resist standard English and incorporate multiple languages and dialects to claim their own unique writerly voice. On the contrary, when students practice academic writing or research-based writing and aim to get published in mainstream publication platforms, they understand the power of standardized convention of English language and emulate the genre of researched writing and write accordingly.

Since most barriers stemmed from language in the beginning, I intended to create a more conducive atmosphere for discussing linguistic and racial issues. I refrained from reiterating bell hooks' statement that "We take the oppressor's language and turn it against itself. We make our words a counter-hegemonic speech, liberating ourselves in language" (227) and instead opted to share a narrative of a colonial encounter, commencing with Columbus's invasion of America in 1492. It was crucial for me to avoid assigning blame to the present for the past or burdening the present with responsibility for the future. I sought refuge in the historical context of the English language. I emphasized that England itself had been subject to colonization by Rome, Normandy, Germany, and others countries which impacted the formation of the English language. I highlighted that English had not always enjoyed superiority over other languages but had evolved as a tool of colonization, eventually becoming a weapon of resistance. By acknowledging the fluidity and diverse versions of English, I aimed to foster acceptance among my students.

To explore the significance of language and its connection to personal identity, I designed a writing prompt for my students. The prompt posed the question: "What does your language mean to you? How do you relate your spoken language to your sense of self?" To my pleasant surprise, I discovered that their responses reflected a newfound tolerance and respect for other languages and World Englishes. One student shared how their language has been central to their selfhood since childhood, emphasizing that speech is deeply tied to personal identity. Another student highlighted language's universal importance, noting that accents—like mine—reflect cultural backgrounds and contribute to individual uniqueness. They expressed respect for linguistic diversity, recognizing that each person's way of speaking holds its own meaning and significance. Through this exercise, my students grasped the concept that English is a plurilingual language, encompassing diverse norms and standards. They recognized that "English as a plural language embodies multiple norms and standards. It is a multinational language, not owned by a particular group" (Canagarajah, "Place of World English" 1619).

I agree with Canagarajah when he writes that "Teachers don't have to wait till these policies trickle down to classrooms. They have some relative autonomy to develop textual practices that challenge dominant conventions and norms before policies are programmatically implemented from the macrolevel" ("Place of World English", 1618). So, I created my classroom as "a policy site" (1618). Within my classroom, I established a multilingual learning environment by implementing a pedagogical approach that embraces multiple languages. A key aspect of my instruction focused on cultivating audience awareness, recognizing that writers must possess a thorough understanding of their intended readership. This awareness allows them to tailor their composition. They eventually realized that not all essays required the use of jargon and sophisticated expressions to effectively communicate with their target audience.

In my writing class, one of the most vital lessons that I teach is audience awareness. Since first-year composition courses have students from various majors, the topics of writing are also diverse. Being a non-technical reader myself, I ask my students, especially those who choose to write on technical topics, to explain the jargon words or technical terms when they write for non-technical audiences. To make the classroom situation more comfortable and hilarious at times, I used the definition of books one day as performed in an Indian cinema called *3 Idiots* directed by Raj Kumar Hirani. The protagonist of the movie once defined books by saying,

> Instruments that record, analyze, summarize, organize, debate and explain information that are illustrative, non-illustrative, hard bound paper bag jacketed, non-jacketed, with foreword, introduction, table of contents, index that are intended for the enlightenment, understanding, enrichment, enhancement and education of the human brain through sensory route of vision . . . and sometimes touch.

My students were bewildered and did not know how to react to this longer definition of something they could not immediately guess. When I clarified that it was the definition of books, they all laughed out loud. I aimed to convey to them that the simplicity of language is what we embrace in writing.

I encouraged my multidialectical students to embrace their own versions of English, which may not conform to conventional standards but are appropriate for the specific context and purpose of their compositions. As a result, when they composed their commentary papers, some of them chose conversational tones and some chose research-based styles to write. For the conversational style of writing, the translingual approach, as I explained before, played a vital role in preparing my students to write for diverse audiences, including individuals like me who are multilingual. By promoting a sense of freedom and openness in writing for a broad range of readers, my students were able to craft engaging literacy narratives and insightful commentary papers. The implementation of multilingual pedagogy facilitated an enjoyable and liberating experience for my students, as they appreciated the freedom to express themselves authentically and cater their writing to various multilingual audiences.

One of the major reasons behind the joy and liberation of writing in my class was that they knew I do not judge their ideas from my own personal standpoint. One of my students wished to write her commentary paper on abortion and state law. I was aware of the ongoing pro-life/pro-choice debates around the topic. However, she had a very credible position as a writer due to her own personal experience with her topic. I felt the need to foster an accommodating writing environment for her because I believed that writing is also a healing process. She came to me one day and asked me about possible positions that she could come up with. I never imposed any writerly position on my students and rather encouraged them to feel confident and comfortable with their own unique voices. When she received my non-judgmental assurance, she collected credible sources for her paper and wrote a blog-style commentary. The writing process liberated her from the remaining agony that she had been bearing for years. Usually, the writing program I teach in offers the new writing instructors two sections of a first year writing course to teach. The first-year writing course, which I referred to in this manuscript, is designed to help students write narrative and research-based essays. Before students embark into their actual reading materials and writing assignments, they read "Framework for Success in Postsecondary Education" to prepare their minds for learning.

"Framework for Success in Postsecondary Education" places openness as a cognitive practice under the subsection of "habits of mind." I always wondered how much openness my students have had before they join any writing classroom and how much openness they require in the writing process. Students must be open-minded to accommodate other languages and accents, especially from their course instructors.

The CCCC statement "This Ain't Another Statement! This is a DEMAND for Black Linguistic Justice!" urges writing teachers to not conform to White language supremacy in their writing classes. As far as the statement is concerned, based on demand 1, I stopped "using academic language and standard English as the accepted communicative norm which reflects White mainstream English." Consequently, my students were able to transcend their apprehensions surrounding the expression of their personal experiences and perceptions through writing. For example, in the literacy narrative essays and blog-style autoethnographic commentary papers, my students personalized their subjects and used direct statements from their real-life situations. These linguistic choices really made a huge difference in cultivating the thoughts of becoming a writer from the state of being a student.

In her work on the politics of language, Martha J. Cutter defines Standardized English as "the grammatically correct language of 'consensus' normally taught in [U.S.] schools." I must confess the reality. Multilingual GTAs (Graduate Teaching Assistants) frequently experience a sense of inadequacy and uncertainty regarding the standardization of their voices. Doubts regarding their linguistic abilities often emerge within them. Elizabeth Baez recognizes that embracing one's own voice throughout the writing process is vital, regardless of whether one is an undergraduate student, a graduate student, or an emerging English faculty member of color. Drawing from my prior academic and educational background, I concur with Amanda Sladek, who noticed that a considerable number of her students expressed a desire to attain proficiency in standardized English for higher grades with a preconceived notion that their writing would be assessed based on their ability to produce standardized English sentences. This proficiency served as a benchmark that multilingual non-native English speakers like us aspired to achieve, with the goal of employing English akin to native speakers. I came to the realization that "enforcing standardized English disproportionately affected the grades of students of color, multilingual students, and working-class students" (Sladek 106). I agree with Sladek's assertion that "language standards are artificially developed; no variety of English is linguistically superior or inherently correct" (107).

According to Sladek, it is beneficial to adopt a pedagogical approach that refrains from evaluating all student writing solely based on standardized English conventions. Instead, actively promoting code meshing and inviting students to articulate their language choices "in their writing" can foster a heightened awareness of their own linguistic practices (127). When I assured my students that their writing would not be judged based on standardized linguistic norms, my multilingual and multidialectical students felt more comfortable and confident with their writerly voices.

Talking Through the Discomfort

Once I had established a supportive environment where my students embraced and respected my English, I proceeded to dismantle the racial barrier by conducting individual conferences with each student. The individual conferences I organized served a dual purpose: firstly, to provide support tailored to each student's specific needs regarding their assigned tasks, fostering a sense of value and agency in their voices; and secondly, to gain valuable insights into their respective cultures, societies, and generational perspectives. These conferences facilitated an open exchange of ideas and knowledge between myself and my students, promoting mutual understanding, and creating a space for meaningful learning experiences. During a conference, one of the more reserved students shared a deeply personal story, revealing her mixed Native American and European American heritage. She spoke about the challenges she faced growing up, explaining how her paternal grandfather had ingrained in her and her siblings the belief that speaking their Native language would bring punishment. She also shared her frustration with not learning about her own culture and history in school, and how this fueled her fight for the inclusion of Native American history in the school curriculum. The experience was profound and resonated deeply with me. I admired her bravery in addressing the systemic erasure of certain racial histories from education and was inspired by her commitment to studying Political Science to advocate for change in the future. At that moment, it became my responsibility to encourage her and affirm my own racial identity within the context of a predominantly White writing classroom. It was an opportunity to assert our shared experiences and reaffirm the importance of inclusivity and representation in academia.

In a meaningful conversation about race, I engaged in a heartfelt dialogue with another White student in my class. During our conversation, it became evident that some of my White students carried race-related memories from their past. One student opened about the influence of her grandmother on her understanding of race and racial issues. She recounted a childhood incident where her grandmother forbade her and her cousins from playing with a Black neighbor's son based on superficial appearances that did not align with their own. This revelation highlighted the lasting impact of early socialization and the importance of addressing and challenging such ingrained biases in the pursuit of fostering a more inclusive and equitable society. Beverly Daniel Tatum writes, "Because of the prejudice and racism inherent in our environments when we were children, I assume that we cannot be blamed for learning what we were taught (intentionally or unintentionally)" (3). Given that my students have reached the age of eighteen and above, it is reasonable to assume that their adult selves are now better equipped to "recognize that we have been misinformed, we have a responsibility to seek out more accurate information and to adjust our behavior accordingly" (Tatum 3). As a teacher, I stood in such a position in the power nexus from where I could credibly begin the conversation. As an educator, I recognized the unique position of power and influence which allowed me to initiate and facilitate these crucial conversations with credibility and integrity. It was my duty to create a safe and inclusive environment where students could engage in meaningful dialogue, challenge misconceptions, and foster personal growth and development.

However, I understand engaging in discussions about taboo subjects, such as racism, can evoke a range of complex emotions for both students and teachers in a classroom context. Therefore, I made a conscious decision to approach the topic by contextualizing it within the framework of colonial history. This theme emerged naturally during our discussions on World Englishes and the use of different vocabularies. By creating a safe and inclusive learning environment, I empowered my students to contribute to dismantling the structures of inequality and injustice.

Conclusion

International Graduate Teaching Assistants (IGTAs) undoubtedly encounter various barriers related to language, race, ethnicity, religion, and gender in their teaching experiences. However, I firmly believe that these barriers can be overcome through sincere and responsible approaches. It is crucial for incoming IGTAs to realize that college composition courses extend beyond simply teaching various genres of writing. Instead, these courses provide an opportunity to understand the world, appreciate the diversity among individuals, and cultivate respectful and responsible coexistence.

By addressing these barriers with sincerity, IGTAs can create an inclusive and supportive learning environment. This entails acknowledging and validating students' linguistic backgrounds, embracing multilingualism, and encouraging students to express themselves in their own voices. Additionally, fostering open discussions about race, identity, and social inequalities can help students develop a deeper understanding of these issues and promote a sense of empathy and inclusivity. The route is a two-way road which benefits both students and teachers. Therefore, it is important for IGTAs to recognize the transformative power of writing courses in shaping students' perspectives and fostering critical thinking. By going beyond the surface level of teaching writing genres, IGTAs can empower students to become active participants in a global society, equipped with the necessary skills to engage respectfully and responsibly with diverse communities. By actively dismantling barriers and promoting a nurturing learning environment, IGTAs like myself can make a meaningful impact on their own educational journeys and contribute to a more inclusive and equitable educational landscape for the students. From the position of a writing teacher, I must say that "To teach writing and critical thinking under the umbrella of capitalism without teaching social justice is negligent" (Baldwin 6). Therefore, I am glad I did not keep quiet. I acted and turned the barriers into a charged site of transformation for myself and also for my students.

Works Cited

Akbar, Kabeh. "How I Found Poetry in Childhood Prayer." Lit Hub, 2017. lithub.com/kaveh-akbar-how-i-found-poetry-in-childhood-prayer/.

Anzaldúa, Gloria. "How to Tame a Wild Tongue." *La Frontera/ Borderland*. Aunt Lute Books, 1987, pp. 75–113.

Arnold, Lisa. *Writing Critically: Genres and Rhetorical Choices*. Fountainhead P, 2019.

Baldwin, Jamaica. "Pedagogy as Risk: A Manifesto." *Writing on the Edge*, vol. 30, no. 2, 2020, pp. 3–9.

Brandt, Deborah. "Sponsors of Literacy." *College Composition and Communication*, vol. 49, no. 2, 1998, pp. 165–85.

Canagarajah, Suresh. "The End of Second Language Writing." *Journal of Second Language Writing*, vol 22, no. 4, 2013, pp. 440–41. doi.org/10.1016/j.jslw.2013.08.007.

—. "The Place of World Englishes in Composition: Pluralization Continued." *The Norton Book of Composition Studies,* edited by Susan Miller, 2009, pp. 1617–42.

Cutter, Martha J. *Lost and Found in Translation: Contemporary Ethnic American Writing and the Politics of Language Diversity*. U of North Carolina P, 2005.

Dennihy, Melissa. "Beyond English: Linguistic Diversity in the College English Classroom." *MELUS*, vol. 42, no. 4, 2017, pp. 192–212. doi.org/10.1093/melus/mlx066.

"Framework for Success in Postsecondary Writing." Council of Writing Program Administrators, National Council of Teachers of English, and the National Writing Project. files.eric.ed.gov/fulltext/ED516360.pdf.

Grayson, Mara Lee. *Teaching Racial Literacy: Reflective Practices for Critical Thinking*. Rowman and Littlefield, 2018.

"House Bill No. 1508," 202. sos.nd.gov/files/uploaded_documents/1508.pdf.

Horner, Bruce, Min-Zhan Lu, Jacqueline Joyce Royster, and John Trimbur. "Language Difference in Writing: Toward a Translingual Approach." *College English*, vol. 73, no. 3, 2011, pp. 303–21. doi.org/10.58680/ce201113403.

hooks, bell. "Teaching New Worlds/New Words." *Teaching to Transgress: Education as the Practice of Freedom*. Routledge, 1994, pp. 222–27.

Matsuda, Paul Kei. "The Lure of Translingual Writing." *PMLA*, vol. 129, no. 3, 2014, pp. 478–83. doi.org/10.1632/pmla.2014.129.3.478.

Masterson, Kelly. "Expanding Perspectives of Feminism in the Composition Classroom." *Composition Studies*, vol. 44, no. 2, 2016, pp. 116–33.

McCaughey, Jessica. "'This Seismic Life Change': Graduate Students Parenting and Writing During a Pandemic." *Peitho*, vol 24, no 2, 2022.

Sladek, Amanda. "Student-Centered Grammar Feedback in the Basic Writing Classroom: Towards a Translingual Grammar Pedagogy." *Journal of Basic Writing*, vol 41, no 2, 2022, pp. 106–34. doi.org/10.37514/JBW-J.2022.41.1.05.

Shapiro, Shawna. "Why Do We Need CLA Pedagogy?" *Cultivating Critical Language Awareness in The Writing Classroom*, Routledge, 2022.

"Students' Right to Their Own Language (with Bibliography)". *Conference on College Composition and Communication*, 2006. cccc.ncte.org/cccc/resources/positions/srtolsummary.

Tatum, Beverly Daniel. "Talking About Race, Learning About Racism: The Application of Racial Identity Development Theory in the Classroom." *Harvard Educational Review*, vol. 62, no. 1, 1992, pp. 1–25.

"This Ain't Another Statement! This is a DEMAND for Black Linguistic Justice!" CCCC position statement. July 2020. Retrieved from cccc.ncte.org/cccc/demand-for-black-linguistic-justice.

Young, Vershawn Ashanti. "Should Writers Use Their Own English?" *Iowa Journal of Cultural Studies*, vol. 12, no. 1, 2010, pp. 110–18.

Jainab Tabassum Banu is a PhD candidate and graduate teaching assistant in the department of English at North Dakota State University. She is a transdisciplinary scholar with a rhetorical focus on feminist disability studies and life writing and pedagogical focus on AI and writing pedagogy.

Where Chance and Invention Collide: Scrap Writing in the Composition Classroom

Danielle Koupf

For years, I have collected and shared fragments of found text, which I call "scrap writing." When teaching a course on handcrafted rhetorics, I invited students to hunt for their own scraps and present their findings. For this scrap writing project, each student had to embrace chance in their invention process, since no one could predict where or when they would stumble upon scrap writing. At the same time, each student drew upon their own personal resources, interests, and history to complete the project. Students' invention processes thus demonstrated a mix of unpredictability and personal agency consistent with recent materialist and externalist thought. This essay explores how chance and personal agency collide in much writing and research and therefore contributes to ongoing theorizing of invention in rhetoric and composition.

Since 2009, I have collected scraps of found writing and have encouraged my friends and family to do the same. In this endeavor, I join other scrap collectors who share their finds via websites like *Found Magazine* and r/FoundPaper on Reddit. Scraps are typically anonymous, unintentionally placed, handwritten, and not mass-produced. I call my finds *scrap writing*, as the term *scrap* highlights that these bits and pieces are decontextualized: parts of an original whole that has become fragmented over time as it has lost one rhetorical situation and found another. When I look back upon my collection of over 100 scraps, I am reminded of the places I have lived and visited and the spots where I chanced upon each scrap: a sidewalk in Wichita; a hotel outside Kansas City; a shopping cart in Winston-Salem. I am reminded of both the physical and the emotional worlds I have inhabited throughout the project, the colleagues and friends who have supported it along the way, and the inspiration I drew from other websites as far back as my college years. Finding each scrap felt like a random and unforeseen discovery even while, paradoxically, it also felt like a direct result of my intentional circulation among people and places. Having long been interested in invention as both chancy discovery and intentional creation (Miller; Simonson), I am intrigued that my project of hunting for and sharing scraps connects these two varieties of invention.

I share my own experience as a scrap collector because I seek to investigate the briefer yet similarly complex experiences that my students had when they embarked upon their own scrap writing projects. Before I examine student work in this essay, I contextualize scrap writing among recent treatments of invention, agency, and chance and describe the pedagogical environment in which I presented the assignment. I then highlight the mix of unpredictability and personal agency that underscored three student projects in an upper-level handcrafted rhetorics class: each project, though seemingly driven predominantly by chance, upon deeper examination clearly emerged out of the student's personal history and context, too. Through their projects, I learned more about my students' lives and interests, as each student brought to bear upon the work their previous and concurrent experiences and knowledge.

I contend that scrap writing serves as a reflection of the composing process, always featuring a mix of agencies. With scrap writing, I offer a concrete example of external, distributed theories of invention, which Laura R. Micciche encapsulates here, addressing writing in general: "Writing isn't a private activity, one that happens only in classrooms, heads, a room of one's own, or at kitchen tables, nor is it a set of linear tasks or a unimodal endeavor. It is elliptical, immersive in diverse environments, dispersed, ordinary (not rarified), mediated, ongoing, and coexistent with other activities" (493). This essay emphasizes the nuances of rhetorical invention, which I embrace as a nexus of discovery and creation dispersed across time and space and inflected by both chance and personal agency. Importantly, my theorizing here is influenced significantly by my own chancy encounters with students, colleagues, and other scrap collectors; I share and comment upon experiences that resisted planning and systematic study.

Hunting for Scraps: Theorizing Invention, Agency, and Chance

In my previous work theorizing scrap writing (Koupf), I argued that the lifecycle of a scrap features several varieties of invention, including creation and discovery, plus sharing, response, and republication. I demonstrated that a text is first created, then let loose upon the world, intentionally or not. Eventually, someone (re)discovers the text and identifies it as a scrap, cut off from its original context. This individual then creates a new contribution by sharing the scrap with others, who participate in continued invention by responding to the scrap with questions, interpretations, and comments. Finally, the scrap may be republished in a book or another collection, allowing it to reach a new audience. Chance permeates the lifecycle of a scrap, as many factors beyond anyone's control affect its creation, distribution, and discovery.

To conceptualize this chancy, uncertain work (and pleasure), consider the similar task of exploring an archive, a task that several scholars in rhetoric and composition have associated with the word *serendipity* (Gaillet; Skinnell). Accounts of archival scholarship and pedagogy help illuminate in scrap writing a persistent uncertainty combined with playfulness, perplexity, chance, and curiosity (Carey). Encountering archival treasures, including scraps and fragments of text, may lead finders to conduct further research into the questions such treasures pose. In my class, the scrap writing project required students to make something with their scraps—a gallery in which to compile, display, and write about their findings.

Such acts of compiling, repurposing, and displaying invoke a model of rhetorical invention reliant upon what already exists. This model supports the overlap of discovery and creation that I recognize in much collage and remix. Yet it also describes writing more generally. The celebrated nonfiction author John McPhee acknowledges that "Ideas are where you find them" and claims, "Even more so, however, new pieces can shoot up from other pieces, pursuing connections that run through the ground like rhizomes. Set one of these progressions in motion, and it will skein out in surprising ways, finally ending in some unexpected place" (11). Writing, especially with found and reused materials, involves making something new out of something old, making connections that lead in unpredictable directions.

Invention thus extends beyond a mental activity, moving into the physical environment. Kristopher M. Lotier argues that scholars began consistently theorizing invention as this external phenomenon around 1986, and externalist theories are "now everywhere—or pretty close to it" (160). He addresses a recent rebuttal from Phillip K. Arrington, in which Arrington describes invention as *always* having been somewhat external (Lotier 162). Arrington suggests that despite this fact, "the ability to discern, select, and combine what lay outside cannot even now, for all our technological wizardry, jettison a discerning human agent to perform these inventive acts" (Arrington 563, qtd. in Lotier 162). Lotier's response is worth quoting at length because it anticipates complications that arise when theorizing invention in dispersed endeavors like scrap writing. Lotier writes:

> I certainly agree that inventional thought has always been "external . . . to some extent." Even so, I would contend that the tropes of hunting and finding imagine the mind as a self-sufficient entity that can survey the external world without needing to rely upon it. A fully external account of invention would deny the distinction between hunter, hunted, and landscape by presuming that the hunter in question (i.e., the mind) exists only as a function of the other two. Similarly, working from an externalist perspective, I would frame the ability of Arrington's "discerning human agent" to discern as a function of language, symbols, and other external objects. To say as much isn't necessarily to "jettison" the human agent altogether but to re-think its nature (and its agency). (162–163)

Since I often describe the search for scraps as hunting and the scrap finder as a hunter, these passages from Arrington and Lotier are relevant to scrap writing. Obviously, scraps are external to the human mind, existing physically in various environments. The hunt for scraps can be more or less deliberate: in my class, students had an assignment to complete and therefore intentionally looked for scraps, whereas in day-to-day life, an individual may bump into a scrap unexpectedly. In both cases, Lotier might suggest that the human agent still must discern the scraps, and thus, I suppose there is a joint venture between the human and the scrap—along with many other factors of time, place, and environment that collaborate to make the encounter occur at all. This formulation is consistent with new materialist rhetorics, which fall beneath the umbrella of Lotier's externalism. As Leigh Gruwell explains, "New materialist rhetorics emerge from the larger critical turn toward the material, which positions agency as both collective and more-than-human. For rhetoric, the consequences of such a conceptual shift are massive: no longer the product of independent human agents, rhetoric is instead a continual process that emerges from the intra-actions of human and nonhuman agents (who themselves are in a continual process of becoming through their intra-actions)" (15). I agree with Lotier, then, that we need not abandon the individual but rethink its nature and agency. A combination of preparation, chance, and discernment seems at play.

This combination of agential factors undergirds an example of rhetorical invention that I believe sheds light on scrap writing—Sheryl I. Fontaine and Susan Hunter's 1993 collage essay "Rendering the 'Text' of Composition." The authors juxtapose disparate scraps of composition scholarship, offering no argument of their own but instead allowing different writers' voices to speak for themselves. In their introduction to the collage, Fontaine and Hunter declare, "we now hope that a written presentation of voices, unmediated by commentary and unattached to their speakers' names, will cause the voices to loose their boundaries, spilling their words into those clustered around them in both predictable and unexpected ways, creating a potentially endless play of meanings" (396). They ascribe agency to the voices on the page. They furthermore describe their process in a way that I find emblematic of the scrap collector's work:

> Sitting in our offices surrounded by books, journals, photocopies, and notes, we were overwhelmed with the magnitude of our task. We returned to books and essays we'd read years ago, laying them alongside more recent publications. As we did so, we bracketed and highlighted the most striking sections, experiencing surprise at what we'd forgotten, at what we had once discarded, at both the tonal

and atonal sounds we heard from the discipline. The selections we made—lines, paragraphs, pages—are relatively arbitrary but also are undoubtedly influenced by our own personal and professional histories, our own process of negotiation, and our combined attention to the sounds of the discipline. (396)

They acknowledge, "Certainly, other individuals would have selected different voices, would have heard different questions" (396). It is this interplay of apparent chance and personal agency that I explore with scrap writing. Like Fontaine and Hunter, I see myself and other scrap hunters surrounded by text—not just works of composition scholarship, but also lost and discarded, forgotten and abandoned pieces of writing. Scraps wait to be found in both predictable and unpredictable places.

Teaching Scrap Writing: Cultivating Creativity, Uncertainty, and Chance

A unit on scrap writing seemed a natural fit for my handcrafted rhetorics class because scraps are clear examples of material culture and tactile rhetoric. As Cydney Alexis and Hannah J. Rule explain, since the 1970s, interdisciplinary work in material culture studies has "validated the 'low-art,' ordinary, everyday artifact as worthy of scholarly study" (5). For example, Lesley Bartlett's ethnographic fieldwork with students in Brazil identified material cultural artifacts that students carried with them to develop their identities as literate individuals: pencil cases, printed matter, bookmarks, and words left behind on a chalkboard—a scrap of sorts. Bartlett's work contextualizes scraps and other writing objects as material cultural artifacts tied to literacy practices. Scraps exhibit unique character not only because they contain handcrafted messages, but also because they can be felt and sensed. Scrap hunters find scraps in physical settings and engage with what Estee Beck calls "a sixth mode of multimodality—the tactile, or the bodily forces used to create with all the accompanying sensations, pressures, and resistances our bones, muscles, and fibers use to make things" (2). Multimodal composition has embraced material, tactile, and physical realms, thanks in part to Beck's recognition of this sixth mode and David Michael Sheridan's call for incorporating "3D rhetoric" into composition pedagogy.

    I took up Sheridan's call when designing my handcrafted rhetorics course around three projects in making and curating digital and material objects. In this course designed for interdisciplinary writing minors, first taught in 2019 and again in 2021, students learned how to make things by consulting the campus makerspace, viewing online tutorials, and workshopping their ideas and progress together. Sonia C. Arellano argues that non-discursive practices such as quilting qualify as research (20–21), and this claim provided a foundation for the course. I divided the semester into three units, each driven by a major project requiring a proposal, process journal, presentation, and reflection. The first project tasked students with learning to make something they previously did not know how to make. Students built furniture, learned to knit and embroider, created digital environments with software, and crafted decorative items with the 3D printer and laser cutter. The second project challenged students to find, collect, and display scrap writing. It combined alphabetic text with 3D rhetoric because scraps contain words alongside images, textures, and materiality. For a third "craftivist" project, students created objects to raise awareness of or provoke discussion about social causes. In a final essay, they surveyed their experiences with all three projects to reflect substantially on handcrafted rhetorics and their connections to writing. Each project prompted students to embrace chance and pursue invention, yet the scrap writing project posed the most uncertainty. Simply put, none of us knew what could be found.

Throughout the course, the structure of each project supported my concern for process over product. I consistently assigned more weight to process elements than to final products. Likewise, in this essay I am interested in students' processes while pursuing their scrap writing projects, so I mostly examine their proposals and reflections rather than showcasing their final scrap galleries.

Jody Shipka emphasizes the importance of accounting for writing process, for tracking "the complex and highly distributed processes associated with the production of texts (and lives and people)" (*Toward* 13). She supports composition projects that are open to unpredictability and require complex decision-making, including one called "Lost and Found" that resonates with my project. Shipka asked students "to collect and analyze an assortment of found texts and create a context in which, and audience for which, the texts assume meaning when viewed in relation to one another" (*Toward* 91). Like the scrap writing project, Shipka's task offers some guidelines yet does not lead in one expected direction; it, too, is open to chance, favors open exploration, and encourages students to exert their own agency.

To prepare for the scrap writing project, students read about scrap writing and viewed scraps that I had collected, alongside samples shared and discussed online. Since students had already completed their first project of the semester, they were accustomed to the scaffolding I provided, which began with informal brainstorming in class, proceeded to a proposal and process journal, and concluded with a scrap gallery, an oral presentation, and a reflection. I offered students the option to investigate writing that was not strictly anonymous or unintentionally placed but still akin to scrap writing (such as graffiti, flyers, and personal notes) because I was concerned that scraps would be too difficult to find within a brief timeframe. Yet most students opted to hunt for scraps as I had initially defined them.

I hoped to ease students into the task of finding scraps by leading them on a scrap hunt around campus. We chose to wander the courtyard outside our academic building, the library stacks and study spaces, and the student center and post office, all places that we had predicted might offer a scrap or two. Much to my delight (and surprise), we quickly happened upon a handful of examples that could qualify as scraps, some of which found their way into students' galleries: orders and receipts from dining options on campus, jottings left behind on whiteboards in study spaces, and notes tucked inside library books. As we walked, we continued to brainstorm spaces conducive to finding scraps. We interacted with the environment in a new way, breaking down barriers to the awkward work of picking up discarded papers. I hoped that by practicing scrap hunting together first, students would later find it less intimidating and embarrassing to look for and pick up scraps on their own. After all, scrap hunting requires interacting with the environment in an unfamiliar, even unnatural way: entering unusual places; stopping to pick up, examine, and photograph scraps; and thus opening oneself to potential discomfort on a campus that favors conformity. Following our scrap hunt, students wrote proposals for their projects, which tended to evolve over time, as chance collided with planning.

Perhaps our trial scrap hunt readily yielded scraps because they are more common on a college campus than I had thought. Or, perhaps we cultivated a beneficial chance encounter by going out in search of scraps and looking closely for them. Such beneficial chance encounters, moments of serendipity, are so satisfying because they are unplanned and unexpected—yet artists, writers, and researchers often seek to cultivate them. Brad Gyori describes how artists chase kismet: "Filmmakers, writers, musicians, and painters often value these chance occurrences too much to leave them entirely to chance. So, somewhat paradoxically, they develop strategies for creating kismet on demand" (238). Likewise, my experiences searching for scraps over the years have attuned me to locations that are likely to contain scraps, such as used bookstores, libraries, and grocery stores. I have learned where to spot stray scraps (on the ground, in corners, in books, and on shelves) and have developed strategies for finding them.

Could my students and I experience serendipity even when we planned our scrap hunts? Given that they were pressed for time, juggling multiple responsibilities, and seeking to complete the project for a grade, students had to develop strategies for finding scraps to satisfy class requirements. Gyori describes three strategies (remixing, rebooting, and deconstructing) that can help artists and writers craft serendipity in their work. He promotes incorporating these practices into scholarly research to encourage true discovery (245). Likewise, Judy Holiday acknowledges that lengthy research projects always involve some uncertainty, chance, and serendipity:

> Everyone who has taken on an extended research project probably knows that it's impossible to know precisely where that research will ultimately lead. "Maintaining chaos" alludes in part to the idea that research projects have lives of their own. This is one of the great rewards of research: becoming friends with uncertainty and immersing oneself in a project that develops in ways that cannot be anticipated. (248)

While completing dissertation research, Holiday came to understand serendipity differently by paying more attention to it: "Instead of perceiving serendipity as a random instance of good luck, subject to chance, I began to focus on what I now know as its secondary definition, that is, the 'faculty of' or 'aptitude for' making fortunate discoveries" (249). Like Gyori, Holiday distills strategies for cultivating serendipity, including reading widely and indiscriminately and being attuned to one's passions, body, and gut responses. These same strategies can connect scrap hunters with scraps. In devising strategies for finding scraps, scrap hunters connect invention, personal agency, and chance much like in more conventional research projects like those that Gyori and Holiday document.

To demonstrate how scrap writing projects are governed both by chance and by deliberate invention, I supplement my own experiences collecting scraps with commentary from my students' process writing and reflections. I show how each project developed out of students' personal worlds: the other courses, responsibilities, interests, and experiences that seemed to collide haphazardly with the assignment and ultimately yielded rich and inventive creations. In doing so, I pursue an inquiry that Patricia A. Sullivan poses while reflecting upon her students' personal writing: "What if we thought of the literacies and knowledges our students already have, when they come to us, as having the potential to teach us? What might we learn from reading our students' personal writing if we thought of ourselves as students and scholars of their lived experiences, their literacies, their culture?" (46). Like Sullivan, I see this project as an opportunity to observe how students' individual spheres intersect with scrap writing. I seek to grasp how students exert personal agency while hoping for a serendipitous discovery. Students' reflections show how scrap writing impinged upon and poached from their lives beyond our writing classroom.

Scrap Writing Intersects with Three Students' Individual Spheres

Juliana's Writing Center Scraps

Juliana, a senior engineering major and interdisciplinary writing minor, collected the handwritten notes that Writing Center tutors keep during their appointments with students. A Writing Center tutor herself, Juliana took great care to obtain permission to collect and then share these notes on a private Instagram account that she opened to friends, classmates, fellow tutors, and me. Any notes with identifying information, such as student names, would not be used for the assignment, so that all notes would remain as anonymous as possible. Juliana explained her rationale for her approach to this project by writing in her proposal, "Due to the shorter time frame for this project, I wanted to pick a location that I knew had interesting scraps for me to collect and display." Though Juliana was more deliberate and intentional in her search for scrap writing than I have been in my own search, I find her approach careful and nuanced. She critically evaluated the means available to support her project and then used her resources inventively. She enlarged the notion of scrap writing that I had initially presented by moving beyond my own definition, which emphasized chance encounters with completely anonymous, unintentionally placed texts. Instead, Juliana found plentiful examples of somewhat decontextualized, semi-anonymous writing open to interpretation and response. Even though her scraps were not exactly stumbled upon but meticulously collected, they evinced key characteristics of scrap writing in that they included ambiguous notes and drawings that could prompt questions and interpretations (and thus invention) from viewers. Furthermore, her scraps contained brief, fragmented notes and doodles, another characteristic consistent across all the examples of scrap writing that students collected. Finally, Juliana would not have encountered many of these scraps herself had she not endeavored to collect them, given that tutors ordinarily discarded them after appointments.

Juliana collected many scraps and therefore had to make rhetorical choices about which to include in her Instagram gallery. She explained her process in her reflection:

> As I sifted through the scraps I collected, I would think to myself "Is there anything on this note that immediately grabs my attention? What?", or "Does this note cause me to ask questions?", or "Can I theorize anything about the tutoring session from this note?". Through asking myself these questions I was trying to see if the scrap resonated with, or puzzled me. If I reacted strongly enough to a scrap, I thought that my audience would also be likely to react to the scrap, which would provoke comments and engagement. Therefore, the act

of running the Instagram account showed me that all of the writing center notes counted as scrap writing, but some scraps were simply more intriguing than others. These were the scraps that I tended to gravitate towards and included in my final gallery since I thought they would spark the most engagement.

In this comment, Juliana shares a heuristic that she developed for sorting through the scraps that she collected and reflects on which scraps might prompt invention for both her and her audience. She demonstrates a rhetorical understanding of scrap writing and shows that collecting scraps involves invention and displaying them invites invention. Additionally, Juliana linked her selection process to our course theme of handcrafted rhetorics, recalling a conversation we had early in the semester about handcrafted rhetorics being personal and personalized, ordinary and everyday, rather than mass-produced and widely available. In her proposal, she wrote, "The handcrafted element of this process will be the scrap [. . .] selection process. In class we talked about handcrafted rhetoric being inherently personal. Thus, I will select scraps to post that personally resonate with me, which makes my choices about the arrangement of my gallery inherently personal and handcrafted." There are hand-selected, handcrafted, and rhetorical elements to this project, which selects and displays one-of-a-kind scraps found in a context of personal interest, value, and familiarity to Juliana.

In planning her project, Juliana evaluated her available resources and determined how her everyday activities already intersected with scrap writing. She thus made do with the scraps that came her way to yield a fruitful project. After selecting a context in which to collect scraps, she exerted personal agency, via her self-designed heuristic, to choose scraps from the somewhat random lot gathered from multiple Writing Center tutors. The scrap writing project called upon students, like Juliana, to strategize how they could work inventively within constraints imposed by the assignment's guidelines. Students frequently must find an available, even convenient way, to complete writing assignments; in doing so, they may draw upon preexisting or concurrent knowledge, resources, and experiences.

Juliana's familiarity with the Writing Center prompted her to explore the tutors' notes in the first place, but several factors enhanced the chanciness of these notes and their content. The range of students coming to the Center and the various, unpredictable writing assignments they brought with them meant that Juliana could not anticipate what notes her tutors would make and submit. Further, each tutor had an individual approach to writing notes, which often included doodles (e.g., a series of snails and slugs) and odd phrases taken out of context (e.g., "European colonial meddling"). In her efforts to collect ample scrap writing, Juliana combined her personal agency and deliberate decision-making with the chanciness of her fellow tutors' notetaking tendencies. Guided by her rhetorical awareness and our collaborative class environment, she practiced a distributed mode of invention that the other projects also evinced.

Charity's Genre Inquiry

Charity, a junior sociology major and interdisciplinary writing minor, used the scrap writing project to enhance and reinforce the genre studies she was undertaking in another writing class and therefore also engaged in distributed invention across academic contexts. She explained in her proposal, "when we were walking around campus looking for scraps, I really liked the idea of context and genre. I feel as though scrap writing can be looked at as a genre in and of itself, but at the same time, I kind of look at it as a very condensed version of other genres. I am thinking about using this project to explain something about context and genre." Evident here is a mix of direction and uncertainty, owing to the chanciness of scrap hunting. "My only concern," Charity continued, "is that I will collect scraps, but then they won't be usable for the purposes of my project so I won't end up with as much as I would like to have." This articulation sounds unique to scrap writing with its requirement that scrap hunters adapt to what is available in their surroundings, yet it also echoes concerns that students frequently share about generating adequate material, whether from internal or external sources. Overall, though, scraps seem scarcer, harder to find, and more ambiguous than more conventional writing sources.

Charity did modify her plan: she originally set out to find scraps in different locations on and off campus but came back from various sites empty-handed. She then adopted an openness to possibility, less constrained by location: her process journal shared, "Initially I was only looking out for scraps that I thought would fit into the theme I was trying to create. However, I couldn't find anything that fit where I thought it would so now I am just finding any scrap anywhere. I figure any of them might be useful, and even if they all aren't, I'd find something usable in what I will collect." She chose to collect any scraps that crossed her path, and in her scrap gallery, she placed each scrap alongside a related, established genre for comparison. She recounts, "I finally came to the decision to find scraps, see how many I could compare to recognizable genres and create an argument, or at least start a discussion on the ways that scrap writing can be considered its own genre, but sometimes comes out of previously established genres." Charity's presentation invigorated our study of both scrap writing and genre and owed much to the awareness of and interest in genre that Charity brought with her from other writing classes with other instructors. Her project leaves open the question of whether scrap writing is its own genre, a question that is beyond the scope of this essay but is worth attention. It is noteworthy, too, that for some scraps, Charity could not think of a related genre—for instance, a dollar bill with "Praise the Lord Jesus" written on it and a historical timeline with accompanying notes left on a whiteboard.

Charity succeeded in "at least start[ing] a discussion" on scrap writing and genre but was limited by time constraints and the materials that came her way. She ultimately embraced an aleatory process, explaining in her final reflection, "I just kind of went about my usual day and kept an eye out for scraps rather than going out to find them" and "I was looking for and inserting scraps until the day I completed the gallery." Throughout the project, Charity seemed to learn that she could not force the finding of scraps (with, say, a visit to the grocery store with the purpose of gathering scraps), and she seemed to grow more comfortable embracing chance. In her reflection, Charity underscores the interplay of intention and luck inherent to any scrap hunt. Individuals can go out in hopes of finding scraps, can pay greater attention to their surroundings in pursuit of scraps, but are ultimately constrained by chance.

With this project, I did not want to send students on a wild goose chase, yet I have found my students to be persistent and to make much of what they do find. Perhaps because scraps are scarce, or seem to be hiding, they evoke a lot of feeling when found. Charity expresses a close connection to her carefully curated finds:

> Over the course of this project I built a relationship with the materials (scraps) that I had never forced myself to create with any other form of writing before. Looking at the scrap writing I collected, I found myself looking deeper into the possibilities of the writing I had found rather than just the meaning of it like I normally would. I didn't want to just look into what it says but what it could say, or what I could convince others it's saying.

Scraps are artifacts of our individual worlds, and I can attest to their power to alter our moods and even our worldviews, as Amarah, a third student in our class, also recognized.

Amarah's Personal Scraps

Amarah was greatly affected by scrap writing. In fact, throughout her reflections, she reiterated that the concept altered her worldview. A sophomore studying communication and writing, Amarah already enjoyed writing and doodling with pen and paper, and her project accounted for the connections between the scraps she found and the "scraps" that she herself produced. On the website she crafted for her scrap gallery, Amarah presents five scraps collected on campus, followed by images of her own notebook pages covered in notes and doodles. She wrote in her final reflection that to make the project more interactive, "I decided to include some of my own 'scraps' that I found in one of my notebooks and have my classmates examine those to see what they could infer about me." In this way, Amarah would prompt her audience to engage in invention through interpretation and response.

As both a concept and a method, scrap writing intersected with Amarah's individual world, in which rhetoric, writing, and handwriting were already major concerns. Even in her proposal she noted, "Since this unit has started, I have not only noticed more scraps than before, but I also take more mental notes about the things that I write and why, no matter how small or large the piece is. This is the beginning of how scrap writing and collecting has altered my worldview." And in her final reflection, she observed, "Completing this project has certainly opened my eyes to this genre, and it has also provided valuable information towards some of my previous inquiries about more abstract aspects of writing." I wish to underscore here that, while scrap writing was initially a new idea for students, upon further inspection it actually overlapped with inquiries and practices that were quite familiar to them and the spheres they inhabited.

Reflecting further on how scrap writing transformed her worldview, Amarah explained:

> Before taking on this project, I only considered other people's notes as trash that had very little significance to me, and I honestly did not feel like it was my business to engage too deeply with what they left behind. However, as I started collecting scraps for this project, I began to value them much more, not just because I needed them to complete my work, but also because they allowed me to gain insight into the lives of complete strangers, which I think is fascinating.

She continued, "As a matter of fact, my greatest takeaway from this unit is being able to better understand the underappreciated rhetorical significance of scrap writing. [. . .] Writing in this genre allows us to analyze pieces that may delve into more private, or even trivial aspects of people's lives in a way that other forms of writing cannot achieve." Amarah became especially intrigued by the ambiguity inherent to scrap writing, the interpretation involved in interacting with it, and the individual thought processes that scraps can reveal. Her project recalls Shipka's fascination with found texts and objects gathered from estate sales and yard sales: with video, Shipka seeks "to begin finding ways of giving voice, life, and new potentials for meaning to these strangers and their largely silent life materials" ("On Estate Sales").

Drawing from her other coursework, Amarah also connects scraps to everyday rhetoric and communication and to rhetorical invention:

> The ambiguity of scrap writing is so critical to our understanding of rhetorics because it informs us of the different ways in which people write, process, and live. This, in effect, opens up possibilities for the various rhetorical strategies to be interpreted in different ways. I just think it is fascinating how people bring their own ideas and lifestyles into rhetoric, and scrap writing does a really good job of depicting how that shapes our world.

Here, like Juliana, Amarah identified a mode of invention wherein something is inventive because it inspires response from an audience, whether that response be puzzlement or interpretation. And for her, rhetoric itself is inventive, allowing people to "bring their own ideas and lifestyles" into it. In these remarks, Amarah combines takeaways from her scrap writing project with her prior understanding of writing and rhetoric, as gleaned from personal literacy practices and educational experiences. The chanciness of scrap writing thus collides with Amarah's individual sphere: her prior knowledge of and experiences with writing, rhetoric, and communication.

Like her classmates, Amarah described her own inventive practice as both a deliberate process and a product of happenstance. Notice how these sentences from her proposal reveal this mixed sense of agency:

> I believe the collection process will be the most challenging of this project because of the uncertainty of the scraps. *Even though I will be actively looking for them, I will most likely have to stumble upon them by happenstance* in order to obtain them. I have been looking in places on the ground across campus, but I have not come up with too many pieces yet. I have collected a note for the [dining staff] and a page of math notes in a lounge trash can, but that is all that I have so far. *Moving forward, I will probably have to be more intentional about where I choose to search for the scraps instead of hoping to come across them somewhere on campus.* (emphasis added)

As students learned firsthand, they could plan their hunts for scraps, favoring highly trafficked areas where stray papers tend to collect (e.g., libraries, cafeterias, classrooms, and bookstores), but they could not plan the finds themselves. In other words, students had a desire to be intentional about the project, as they were used to doing as students, but ultimately, they could not predict their findings. They had to embrace chance to achieve their goals.

Scrap Writing in the Composition Classroom

Students have consistently surprised me by taking up scrap writing in unique, unexpected ways distinct from my own efforts. I attribute these results in part to the fact that these students have searched for and collected scraps in contexts different from my own. Yet I also recognize the significance of students' previous and coexisting experiences and coursework, which encouraged them to make nuanced connections. For instance, Juliana, Charity, and Amarah connected scrap writing with rhetorical concepts such as invention, interpretation, genre, handwriting, and everyday communication. Introducing scrap writing into composition classes can reinforce course concepts and take instruction in new directions. Just as individual scraps can prompt invention for viewers, the concept of scrap writing can be a source of invention in the composition classroom.

Identifying the strands of thought and happenstance that contributed to students' scrap writing projects has reinforced for me the value and significance of factors and environments beyond my classroom. Students' lives outside the course played important roles in how they planned, executed, and assessed their projects. As such, the randomness inherent in finding scraps intersected significantly with personal agency and history. Thus, the scrap writing project can remind instructors that students come to our classes with their own experiences, interests, and knowledge and that they can use these resources toward inventive ends. Furthermore, this project reinforces for rhetoric and composition scholars just how complex invention is, incorporating not only discovery and creation but a mix of agencies stemming from individual and collective hopes, desires, and interests and from external materials and environments. Studying scrap writing helps us to recognize and reevaluate the chancy complexities of teaching and researching writing and rhetoric.

Works Cited

Alexis, Cydney, and Hannah J. Rule. "Introduction: The Material Culture of Writing." *The Material Culture of Writing*, edited by Cydney Alexis and Hannah J. Rule, Utah State UP, 2022, pp. 3–17.

Arellano, Sonia C. "Quilting as Qualitative, Feminist Research Method: Expanding Understandings of Migrant Deaths." *Rhetoric Review*, vol. 41, no. 1, 2022, pp. 17–30.

Bartlett, Lesley. "To Seem and To Feel: Situated Identities and Literacy Practices." *Teachers College Record*, vol. 109, no. 1, 2007, pp. 51–69.

Beck, Estee. "Discovering Maker Literacies: Tinkering with a Constructionist Approach and Maker Competencies." *Computers and Composition*, vol. 58, 2020, pp. 1–16.

Carey, Craig. "Archival Play: The Magic Circle of Fragments, Finding Aids, and Curious George." *Pedagogy*, vol. 21, no. 3, 2021, pp. 455–479.

Fontaine, Sheryl I., and Susan Hunter. "Rendering the 'Text' of Composition." *JAC*, vol. 12, 1993, pp. 395–406.

Gaillet, Lynee Lewis. "Fortuitous Happenstance: Serendipity in Archival Research." *Serendipity in Rhetoric, Writing, and Literacy Research*, edited by Maureen Daly Goggin and Peter N. Goggin, Utah State UP, 2018, pp. 59–69.

Gruwell, Leigh. *Making Matters: Craft, Ethics, and New Materialist Rhetorics*. Utah State UP, 2022.

Gyori, Brad. "Creating Kismet: What Artists Can Teach Academics about Serendipity." *Serendipity in Rhetoric, Writing, and Literacy Research*, edited by Maureen Daly Goggin and Peter N. Goggin, Utah State UP, 2018, pp. 237–46.

Holiday, Judy. "Coordinating Chaos and Befriending a Fuzzy Focus: Reflections of a Serendipitist." *Serendipity in Rhetoric, Writing, and Literacy Research*, edited by Maureen Daly Goggin and Peter N. Goggin, Utah State UP, 2018, pp. 247–56.

Koupf, Danielle. "Scrap Writing in the Digital Age: The Inventive Potential of Texts on the Loose." *enculturation*, vol. 28, 2019, www.enculturation.net/scrap-writing.

Lotier, Kristopher M. *Postprocess Postmortem*. The WAC Clearinghouse and UP of Colorado, 2021.

McPhee, John. *Draft No. 4: On the Writing Process*. Farrar, Straus and Giroux, 2017.

Micciche, Laura R. "Writing Material." *College English*, vol. 76, no. 6, 2014, pp. 488–505.

Miller, Carolyn R. "The Aristotelian *Topos*: Hunting for Novelty." *Rereading Aristotle's Rhetoric*, edited by Alan Gross and Arthur Walzer, Southern Illinois UP, 2000, pp. 130–46.

Sheridan, David Michael. "Fabricating Consent: Three-Dimensional Objects as Rhetorical Compositions." *Computers and Composition*, vol. 27, 2010, pp. 249–65.

Shipka, Jody. "On Estate Sales, Archives, and the Matter of Making Things." *Provocations: Reconstructing the Archive*, Computers and Composition Digital Press, 2015, ccdigitalpress.org/book/reconstructingthearchive/shipka.html.

Shipka, Jody. *Toward a Composition Made Whole*. U of Pittsburgh P, 2011.

Simonson, Peter. "Reinventing Invention, Again." *Rhetoric Society Quarterly*, vol. 44, no. 4, 2014, pp. 299–322.

Skinnell, Ryan. "Setting Out for Serendip: Of Research Quests and Chance Discoveries." *Serendipity in Rhetoric, Writing, and Literacy Research*, edited by Maureen Daly Goggin and Peter N. Goggin, Utah State UP, 2018, pp. 117–28.

Sullivan, Patricia A. "Composing Culture: A Place for the Personal." *College English*, vol. 66, no. 1, 2003, pp. 41–54.

Danielle Koupf is associate teaching professor in the writing program at Wake Forest University. She has published journal articles in *Composition Forum* and *enculturation* and has contributed to edited collections such as *Keywords in Making: A Rhetorical Primer* and *Teaching Critical Reading and Writing in the Era of Fake News*.

Generative Artificial Memories: Teaching AI Text Generators as Rhetorical Memory Devices

John J. Silvestro

In response to the public release of and subsequent academic panic about ChatGPT, compositionists largely focused on two concerns. They focused on text-generator-engaging composing processes and on developing students' critical literacies for text generators and their development. This essay proposes extending and merging these pedagogies through the metaphor of rhetorical memory devices. Rhetorical memory devices offer a metaphor through which first-year composition students can learn about the development of text generators and then use their knowledge of that development as part of their composing processes. To articulate a text-generators-as-memory-devices pedagogy, this essay articulates a theory of memory devices, emphasizing how they center the deliberate storage of information for subsequent compositional support. Next, the essay outlines text generators' development processes and connects those processes to the theory of memory devices and their development. The essay then proposes framing text generators as memory devices that store human memories and then regenerate them to support specific compositional acts. To confirm this metaphor of text generators as memory devices, the essay then reviews a case study of writers using text generators. Finally, the essay outlines an approach through which writing instructors can introduce and engage text generators through the metaphor of memory devices.

In response to the public release of ChatGPT and the ensuing panic about the end of academic writing, composition scholars leapt into action. Composition scholars developed pedagogies for engaging Natural Language Generator Large Language Models that operate through Generative Process Transformers, like ChatGPT, Google Gemini, and Microsoft Copilot—henceforth titled "text generators." Prominent examples of these responses include the special issues on text generators of *Composition Studies* and *Computers and Composition* and the edited collection *TextGenEd: Teaching with Text Generation Technologies*, all of which were published within a year of ChatGPT's public release. Across those texts, and others, compositionists developed a range of approaches for engaging text generators in composition courses, often for writing courses. Many scholars, though, focused on differing pedagogical concerns.

Several composition scholars studied how writers were already composing with text generators. Some scholars studied how students initially used the technologies as part of their writing processes (Bedington et al.; Pigg; Vetter et al.). Others proposed new writing processes that expanded process theories to incorporate text generators (Graham; Knowles). These scholars either built upon emerging writing processes or proposed writing processes that incorporated text generators. This focus foregrounded the pedagogical need to equip writing students to compose more deliberately with text generators or, at the very least, enable writing students to understand how they could incorporate text generators into their composing practices.

Other scholars examined the development of text generators as technological systems that have consequential socio-cultural effects (Gallagher; Silvestro). These scholars sought a clear-as-possible understanding of how text generators operate and, in turn, impact individuals and communities.

Others articulated frameworks that equipped students to understand the systems and then use that understanding to examine the harms they engender against marginalized communities (Aguilar; Byrd; Jimenez). These scholars aimed to develop students' critical literacies around the algorithms, coding, and data that undergird text generators—literacies that equip students to grapple with the effects and harms of these systems. This focus signaled the pedagogical need for writing students to understand how text generators function and then use that understanding to grapple with text generators' emerging socio-cultural effects.

Each focus gives voice to a significant pedagogical need in the wake of ChatGPT's popularization: writing students need better processes for composing with text generators while also having frameworks for critically engaging text generators and their larger effects. More bluntly, writing students—and their instructors—need *both* focus areas. Writing instructors need approaches to engaging text generators that enable them to provide students with a deeper understanding of how these systems are developed and then equip students to use that understanding to shape how they use text generators as part of their writing processes. Writing students need approaches that enable them to connect any critical literacies they develop around text generators with the ways they compose, either with or without text generators. To suggest a merged approach, this essay proposes that writing instructors frame text generators as memory devices.

Other scholars have already outlined memories as a useful metaphor for critically engaging text generators. In "'Places to Stand,'" Salena Sampson Anderson explores the datasets that undergird text generators. She articulates how text generators are developed on massive troves of writing largely scraped from websites and social media platforms and thus are incredibly contextual, flawed, and narrow. Text generators then use a mixture of algorithms and training processes to develop models of the writing in their datasets—models that later structure the writing that the text generators output. Anderson notes that the most significant element of text generators is that they "traffic in humanity's shared experience—our stories, our art—to generate their compositions" (2). She argues that text generators could be framed like medical devices as they are constructed around human materials, like blood transfusions. Thus, Anderson argues that text generators should be engaged as fundamentally human systems, built around the flaws and limitations of human memories (9).

Focusing more on the compositional possibilities of text generators, Alan M. Knowles's "Machine-in-the-Loop Writing" examines the ways text generators can be engaged through each of the rhetorical canons. He argues that the canon of memory can be a useful framework for examining a text generator's outputs for their accuracy. The canon of memory can serve as a reminder to critically review any information in a text generator's outputs. For Knowles, memory offers a means to expand writing processes to involve inspecting text generators' outputs (5–6).

Anderson's framing of text generators as developed through human memories and Knowles's articulation of the canon of memory as a means for critically engaging text generators' outputs suggests a foundation for a conjoined framing of text generators. Text generators can be understood as vast databases of human memories—with all the flaws, gaps, and biases that are inherent to human memories (Anderson)–that writers can regenerate into associations that attempt to closely mimic pre-existing texts. The generated outputs will be limited by the gaps, flaws, and overemphasis in the database of human memories (Anderson; Silvestro). When analyzed through the rhetorical canon of memory, text generators can be framed as externally developed memory devices for calling forth imperfect memories on how to approach various writing situations.

Specifically, this essay proposes framing text generators as memory devices in writing courses. While seemingly a little-needed rhetorical memory approach given its initial articulation as a tool for memorizing speeches, memory devices have a long history and have recently been recovered for critical engagements around data and writing practices (Johnson; Silvestro). Notably, Stewart Whittemore in *Rhetorical Memory* presents his research into the ways several writers at a software company developed a range of memory practices to handle the vast organizational and technological information they needed to manage and incorporate into their writing (18–19). Thus, memory devices offer an approach and metaphor for considering the ways memories are stored and then regenerated to support specific rhetorical processes. This essay proposes that memory devices can thus provide a useful pedagogical approach for equipping writing students to connect critical literacies about text generators with their composing practices.

To outline how to teach text generators as memory devices in writing courses, this essay first outlines a theory of rhetorical memory devices rooted in the deliberate storage of information to be used in support of various composing practices (Carruthers; Whittemore; Yates). Next, this essay uses the memory device theory to critically examine the development of text generators. The essay argues that by engaging text generators through the metaphor of memory devices, students can recognize and critically consider the central role of data and human training, also known as human memories (Anderson), in the development and subsequent functioning of text generators. To articulate how framing text generators as memory devices also connects with contemporary, text-generator-engaging composing practices, this essay reviews the findings from a case study of thousands of writers composing with text generators. The study demonstrates how, when engaged through the metaphor of memory devices, text generators can be understood as generating "memories" that support writers as they try to invent ideas and write in specific styles. The essay concludes with an outline as to how writing instructors could develop students' understanding of memory practices, equipping them to use that understanding to critically examine the development and functioning of text generators and make decisions about when, how, and why to use text generators in their composing processes.

A Theory of Memory Devices

Developed as one of the five canons of rhetoric that individuals work through to compose a speech, the canon of memory equips rhetors to store information that will be later retrieved during other parts of the composing process (Carruthers; Yates). Numerous rhetoric scholars have developed different memory approaches that enable better storage and/or usage of information for composing practices (Carruthers; Johnson; Whittemore). One of the first memory devices was the memory palace.

According to Frances Yates in her seminal study on the history of memory, *The Art of Memory*, memory palaces were initially articulated by the unknown writer of *Rhetorica ad Herennium* and later refined by Cicero (6–9). These scholars all drew from the myth of the poet Simonides, who survived a freak accident and later used his memory of where people sat at a table to help identify the bodies (Yates 28; 1–2). Out of this myth, the writer of *Rhetorica ad Herennium* articulated strategies for remembering that would aid rhetors while they composed. In general, a memory palace practice involves mentally creating associations between parts of one's speech with familiar spatial environments. Individuals can then call forth those associations while they deliver their speech by imagining themselves walking through the spaces. The act of mentally walking through the imagined spaces triggers the associations they developed and thus provides speakers access to the stored information (Yates 18–21). From its outset, memory devices were developed and deployed to help rhetors

- **store** information for future composing situations
- **support** compositional practices by providing ready access to stored information

For the initial concept of memory devices, they were developed to enable orators to store information that would later support the delivery of their speech—enabling the orators to recall parts of their speech and the arrangement of their speech, as the structure of the speech was embedded in the memory device. From their inception, memory devices have served the dual purposes of storing information and then providing that information as a support for other parts of the composing process.

Memory devices were subsequently extended to serve other composing practices by rhetorical theorists during the tenth, eleventh, twelfth, and thirteenth centuries. As Mary Carruthers outlines in her influential study *The Book of Memory*, the canon of memory, and memory devices in particular, took on increased pedagogical significance between the tenth and thirteenth centuries. During this time, rhetors found themselves swamped with information as manuscripts proliferated and became a dominant focus of advanced pedagogy and composition practices. So, students were taught to develop memory devices through which they could store critical pieces of information and then access that information when they needed to compose. Students were taught highly regimented memorization techniques to store information and passages so that they could recall said information and passages at will (84–87).

In the face of previously unfathomable access to information, rhetors between the tenth and thirteenth centuries turned to memory devices to help them store the information that they felt they needed to support their compositional practices. During this era, memory devices were developed to support invention and style. Students were trained to store information, passages, and quotes so that they could later use them as the foundation of their compositions. They also stored numerous passages to later draw upon and recreate their style (Carruthers 39–40). Once again, memory devices centered on guiding students to deliberately store information so that they could later use that information to support other phases of their composing process.

Whittemore's research into writers at a software company demonstrates that memory devices are still used by writers to deliberately store information that will later support specific compositional practices. In his study, he learns that writers deliberately store information through a variety of techniques—including post-it notes, Word documents, personal databases—to aid their composition practices, such as delivering points during meetings, inventing useful documents, and stylizing writing for specific audiences (201–203). Whittemore summarizes the importance of the rhetorical theory of memory to contemporary writing practices: "Rhetorical theory holds that the process of retrieving and adapting existing knowledge to the exigencies of shifting communication situations is absolutely essential to the creative process by which communicators determine what to say and how to say it to meet the needs of their audiences" (19).

In the past decade, scholars have further theorized twenty-first-century uses of memory devices by identifying the ways that various technological systems have come to function as memory devices for writers, particularly systems that store data and then provide that data in assorted ways during the composing process. In his book *Architects of Memory*, Nathan R. Johnson reiterates how memory devices have long served as critical tools used throughout the composing process. Drawing a connection to contemporary memory devices, Johnson writes that memory palaces in ancient Greece were viewed in much the same way that "tablets and phones are discussed as supplements to memory [in the twenty-first century]" (22). Memory devices have taken a range of forms—mental, physical, and, increasingly, digital—yet they always serve the general purpose of providing access to intentionally stored information to be accessed throughout the composing process.

Johnson focuses on a set of memory devices that he titles memory infrastructures. Memory infrastructures are the archives, collections, and databases that provide information and resources for performing rhetoric, such as archives, websites, and databases. They are the storehouses of information developed by individuals, organizations, and/or communities to establish the claims and information critical to the individual, organizations, and/ or communities (Johnson 4). Individuals regularly draw from memory infrastructures to enact rhetoric. Individuals compose with the information that they, others, organizations, and/or communities intentionally stored, and in so doing, align with the values, norms, and histories of those individuals, organizations, and/ or communities. Memory infrastructures are both storage devices, in that they contain intentionally stored information to be accessed later, and inventional resources, in that individuals draw from, reference, and/or acknowledge them as they compose. Thus, Johnson argues that critical rhetorical decisions are made about what information to store in memory infrastructures and how to store it—decisions that, in turn, shape the compositions individuals can subsequently perform with the infrastructures (13–14).

Building directly on Johnson's work, I, in "Remember Then Recommend," outline how the concept of memory infrastructures can be applied to algorithmic systems. I articulate how, much like with the public archives and digital databases that Johnson positions as memory infrastructures, algorithmic systems involve the deliberate storage and recall of information for inventional purposes. I argue that many algorithmic systems have become incredibly influential over contemporary composing processes (e.g., spell checker algorithms). Thus, what gets stored in and then output by algorithmic systems configures much of how and what individuals using the algorithmic systems write (63–64). I call for critical attention onto the data sets undergirding the algorithmic systems that have become a part of contemporary writing practices. Writers need critical understandings of algorithmic systems' data sets to understand how those systems influence how and when they can compose with them (84–85).

In sum, memory devices offer a metaphor through which individuals can critically examine the storage of information and then critically consider how that information can later be deployed to support various phases of the composing process. Memory devices connect the act of rhetorically storing information with the act of composing with said information, offering a way to understand how the decisions to store something are connected to the support role that the device will eventually serve. Regarding the writing process, memory devices have supported seemingly every phase of it. They were originally developed to support arrangement and style, enabling the recall of the structure and approach of a speech. They have also supported invention, equipping medieval rhetors to cite, summarize, and connect important information and texts at will. More currently, memory devices offer a metaphor through which one can critically engage data-centering technologies for the ways they can support the composing process, such as spell-checker algorithms, digital archives, social media platforms, or, as this essay aims to suggest, text generators.

Memory devices can function as a metaphor for engaging text generators, particularly in writing courses. Given their focus on the storage of information, memory devices offer a way to call students' attention to a text generator's data sets and training processes and to frame those datasets as fundamentally human and, thus, limited. Given their focus on how information can be used to support specific compositional phases, memory devices offer a way to value students' own writing knowledge, practices, and memories, and then contrast those with the potential uses of text generators. Developing this metaphor, though, requires a close examination of text generators and the role of data and human training in developing them.

Engaging Text Generators as Rhetorical Memory Devices

Building upon recent efforts to use the rhetorical canon of memory and theories of memory devices to examine algorithmic systems that function through datasets (Johnson; Silvestro), this essay proposes teaching text generators as memory devices. Engaging text generators in this way calls for critical attention to what data (or human memories, per Anderson) are stored within the systems and what compositional support roles they can play. More precisely, memory devices call for critical attention to text generators' development and functioning through datasets in order to understand what they can and cannot support during the composing process, which is a skill several composition scholars have already established as important for writing students to develop (Aguilar; Jimenez).

At base, most text generators are a combination of colossal datasets and dozens of algorithms that establish percentage-based associations between the data and then generate outputs based on those percentages. An initial set of algorithms repeatedly scans the colossal datasets, establishing associations or relationship percentages between the individual pieces of data. Data for text generators are tokens, which can be anything from individual letters to punctuation marks to parts of words to entire words. These algorithms establish a massive set of relationships between each individual token, noting how often each token appears next to every other token in the dataset. For example, in many text generators, the token "psychology" will have high relationship percentages with tokens like "behavioral" and "forensic," something like 99.9978%, and that same token will also have millions of other tokens with which it has a relationship percentage of 0.00001%.

Text generators then have secondary algorithms that extract tokens from a user's input, determining what tokens individuals want the text generator to generate around. Lastly, a set of predictive algorithms draws on the other two algorithms to generate outputs: they build upon the extracted algorithm's tokens to generate subsequent tokens that use the percentages from the associative algorithms to numerically "guestimate" what token should come next (Bender et al. 614-615; Crawford 96–97). However, the associative algorithms often have flawed association percentages between tokens. Two words might be overly connected in the dataset, leading the later predictive algorithms to frequently put the words together. To reduce issues like this, the predictive algorithms get further refined through various forms of training. The training involves different forms of evaluation for the outputs of the predictive algorithms. In one form of training, the system generates outputs that are compared with texts from its dataset. These comparisons further refine the association percentages, increasing some and decreasing others, bringing the predictive algorithms' outputs more in line with other texts in the dataset (Bender et al. 616-617; Crawford 97-98). Thus, the predictive algorithms only generate outputs that are more in line with the texts (or contextual and flawed human memories, per Anderson) already in their datasets.

The second form of text-generator training also centers human memories, as it involves human trainers who evaluate predictive algorithms' outputs. In this training, human trainers respond to pairs of randomly generated outputs. The human trainers determine which of the outputs are more acceptable. In effect, the trainers use their own literacies and memories of writing to influence the eventual text generator outputs. The human output evaluations further increase some percentages and lower others (Crawford; Ouyang et al.).

Most text generators bring about texts based on the relationships between the tokens in their datasets—relationships that have been refined through non-human and human training. This over-reliance on datasets is an issue, as all datasets have significant limitations. Many datasets either come from a specific set of writing from a particular group, such as the early text generator training dataset that was developed out of the publicly released emails written by former Enron Corporation employees (Crawford 102–103), or they come from collections of the publicly available writing on the internet that were collected by algorithms that collect nearly everything that it posted online, such as the millions of Reddit posts and tweets used to train foundational versions of ChatGPT (Ouyang et al.; Paullada et al.). Furthermore, the collected datasets overwhelmingly contain writing from White, middle-class groups from the Global North (Bender et al. 613). Put differently, text generators have been constructed around biased, limited, and otherwise highly contextual collections of writing, as Kate Crawford explains in *Atlas of AI*: "Skews, gaps, and biases in the collected text are built into the bigger system, and if a language model is based on the kinds of words that are clustered together, it matters where those words come from. There is no neutral ground for language, and all text collections are also accounts of time, place, culture, and politics" (103).

Drawing from Anderson's consideration of text generators, text generators can be understood to be built on vast collections of human memories, particularly the reactions to specific moments that were shaped by the historical, cultural, and physical location of the writers. Thus, the data in most datasets are limited, both by who originally wrote them and by the specific historical-cultural moments during which they were written, much like most human memories are limited. Text generators are also limited by their datasets, as a significant portion of the training done to refine outputs is done by comparing text generator outputs to texts from the original dataset, further inscribing the biases and limitations of the initial dataset (Bender et al. 613).

Text generators are also more generally limited by their algorithms and how they interact with datasets. First, text generators cannot productively engage with tokens that are either not prominent or not included in their datasets. If a word, phrase, or piece of information is not a token in a text generator's dataset, the text generator will struggle to generate texts with it (Bender et al. 618; Crawford 97). Second, because of the associative and predictive algorithms, text generators will generate false information. The falsifications arise for a myriad of reasons, including awkward token-relationship percentages, the inherent randomization of outputs, and the generator numerically inserting a random token, such as a letter or word, when it lacked relevant tokens in its dataset. These inherent errors and falsifications have been called "hallucinations" (Xu, Jain, and Kankanhalli).

As several composition scholars have already articulated (Aguilar; Jimenez), text generator's' biases, gaps, and falsifications pose considerable risks for writers. When working with text generators, writers will potentially be cajoled toward dominant discourses, unintentionally write with biases, and/or write with false and damaging information. These risks pose even greater harm for writers from underserved and marginalized communities.

Text generators' biases, gaps, and falsifications will more than likely cause significant challenges and harms for writers from underserved and marginalized communities—harms that will be spread throughout the writing process (Byrd; Jimenez). The potential effects of these harms can be seen in an experience that one individual in Carlo Perrotta, Neil Selwyn, and Carrie Ewin's study "Artificial Intelligence and the Affective Labour of Understanding" encountered. The individual, Gabrielle, who identifies as African American, experienced significant bias during her attempts to write with a text generator. Gabrielle participated in Perrotta, Selwyn, and Ewin's study, in which participants were asked to write with a text generator. The participants were assigned a prompt and had the text generator write a few lines that participants could then revise, expand, or regenerate. The participants, in effect, used the text generator for invention, arrangement, and style. For Gabrielle, the text generator immediately pushed her toward language, experiences, and emotions that felt completely misaligned with how she understood herself (1598). The text generator even exposed her to biased language against African Americans (1601). Perrotta, Selwyn, and Ewin explain that

> Gabrielle is now convinced that the system is following a precise notion of how the writing should unfold, deliberately obscuring some avenues and highlighting others that confirm specific biases. Indeed, her perception is that the system is hard-wired to operate along cul-

> tural tropes which are being imposed on her as the only acceptable and reasonable options. (1601)

The text generator exposed Gabrielle to biased language and failed to provide vocabulary, styles, memories, or arrangements that aligned with her experiences. Ultimately, Gabrielle felt obstructed by the text generator in her efforts to write in ways that aligned with who she is and what she wanted to write.

When engaged through the rhetorical concept of memory devices, text generators can be engaged as algorithmic systems that regenerate human memories: they use the statistical relationships between words and other symbols in their datasets and the feedback from human trainers to generate text. Put differently, they are memory devices. They use multiple algorithms to regenerate and reassemble the elements within their datasets based on users' prompting. Like other memory devices, text generators' strengths lie in what information is stored in them and how that information is stored; their limitations lie in the biases and gaps in what is and is not stored in them, as well as how they regenerate those memories.

It is these two aspects of memory devices that this essay seeks to frame text generators through. Text generators are constructed in a manner that evokes the development of memory devices: billions of texts are selected—or, more appropriately, are what is publicly available, free, and occasionally a copyright violation—and then stored (Bender et al.; Crawford; Paullada et al.). Next, algorithms scan the texts to develop associations between the words, phrases, and sentences in the datasets. What is stored will not necessarily be the exact product that is generated during the composition process, but it will have a significant influence over it. What is stored in the text-generator device has a significant influence over what is later made available through the device, which is a key consideration for the development and usage of memory devices. Teaching text generators as memory devices thus provides a critical awareness of what is stored in text generators and how that storage influences composing practices.

Such an approach raises questions about whether it aligns with the ways individuals actually use text generators: Do any writers use text generators in ways that align with notions of drawing from stored information at specific phases of the writing process? To address this question, this essay examines Erik Brynjolfsson, Danielle Li, and Lindsey Raymond's "Generative AI at Work," which is a multi-method study of how thousands of customer service agents used a provided text generator. Performed before the public release of ChatGPT, the study examined how agents used a text generator during a common writing task. Brynjolfsson, Li, and Raymond's study thus offers a sense of how agents used the text generator and which parts of the writing process it supported.

Existing Study of Writers Composing with Text Generators

When examined through the metaphor of text generators as memory devices, Brynjolfsson, Li, and Raymond's research study "Generative AI at Work" provides a fascinating understanding of how, why, and when writers use text generators. Their study confirms that what is stored in text generators can and does influence what aspects of the writing process they can support. In their study, the co-researchers examined how customer service agents worked with a further-trained version of ChatGPT during online customer-agent conversations.

For the study, the co-researchers got access to an early version of ChatGPT that they subsequently did additional output and human training on. The researchers' additional rounds of training aimed to make the text generator more useful to the customer service agents. For the additional training, the researchers had the text generator work through and test on thousands of effective customer service interactions. They also did an additional round of human training in which the human trainers prioritized empathy and accuracy in the generator's outputs. Lastly, the researchers developed an interface centered around the further-trained text generator. Designed to be used by customer service agents while they interact with customers through online chats, the interface would first receive an online-submitted complaint from a customer. The text generator would then generate, and the interface would display two potential responses to the customer's complaint. The two responses would appear underneath a blank textbox that the agent would use to write to the customer. The agent could then copy, adapt, or ignore the generated responses.

Using a range of human-subject research methods, Brynjolfsson, Li, and Raymond studied over 5,000 agents at the company, approximately half of whom used the text generator interface. The researchers surveyed the agents about how they felt about their work/writing, analyzed logs of the agents' use of the text-generator-equipped interface content analyses of the agents' written responses. Key to their study, the researchers then analyzed the agents based on how long they had been at the company and when they got access to the text-generator interface. The researches wanted to understand what effects the text generators had on individuals based on their experience level with the company and its writing work.

In their study, Brynjolfsson, Li, and Raymond discovered that the most noticeable impact from the text generators occurred with the newest agents, who had been at the company for in some cases less than a month and in others no more than three months. They found that the newer agents using the text generator did better in their work and had significantly faster response times, compared to newer agents who did not have access to the text generator. They found that the newer agents used the interface-generated suggestions 37% of the time and did so by copying or rewriting one of the two suggestions. In comparison, more experienced agents used text generator suggestions less than 30% of the time and rarely copied the suggestions (12–14). As Brynjolfsson, Li, and Raymond explain, "Access to the AI tool helps newer agents move more quickly down the experience curve: treated agents with two months of tenure perform just as well as untreated agents with more than six months of tenure" (2).

Based on their findings, Brynjolfsson, Li, and Raymond argue that their further-trained text generator provided the studied agents with some of the organization's tacit knowledge, or memories, for writing to customers. Their text generator provided an understanding and rhetorical awareness of how to engage their specific audience in a highly specific genre; specifically, the text generator provided agents with memories of how and what to write in the highly specific genre and context of technical customer service writing (Brynjolfsson, Li, and Raymond 12). The further-trained text generator could be understood as a memory device that provided agents with access to the organization's memory infrastructure (Johnson). These memories were most useful to the newer agents, who likely lacked both an understanding of the organization's memory infrastructures and hadn't developed their own memories or memory devices for this type of writing. More experienced agents likely had their own memories, memory devices, and understanding of the organization's memory infrastructure.

This study establishes two significant facets about text generators and how they can be engaged through the metaphor of memory devices. Text generators can provide writers with "artificial" memories of how to write in various contexts and genres, something most useful to individuals who are relatively new at writing in various contexts and genres. Brynjolfsson, Li, and Raymond repeatedly note that their system seemed to have minimal detectable impact on the writing of the most experienced agents (15–16). The co-researchers also note that for the newest employees, the writing gains leveled off after roughly three months of use (19). Text generators can seemingly provide writers with artificial memories of how to compose in specific situations. Thus, text generators can be engaged based on what is stored within them. By considering what is stored within them, text generators can be situated as a storehouse of rhetorical moves based on what writing is in the datasets and training that were a part of the generator's development.

The memory device metaphor underscores how what a text generator offers writers is useful when the data and training used to construct the text generators are relevant to an individual writer, based on the situation the writer engages. Brynjolfsson, Li, and Raymond stress that the text generator in their study was trained on an additional set of well-received chats from prior customer service interactions, and their text generator received an additional round of human training that prioritized outputs that demonstrated empathy and appropriate technical documentation (8). The text generator in this study was thus most useful to newer writers in the complex situation of online, technical customer service interactions, largely because of the additional data and training, or memories, added to the text generator.

Furthermore, if text generators are collections of memories, then they are collections of memories that are most useful in supporting specific parts of the writing process. In Brynjolfsson, Li, and Raymond's study, the memories were particularly useful for invention and style concerns. The text generator provided agents with a general sense of acceptable responses as well as applicable writing styles. More bluntly, the text generator offered the newer agents a starting point. The newer agents often needed a starting point in this unfamiliar rhetorical situation; so, the text generator offered that starting point. The text generator provided artificial memories of the arrangements, information, and styles that generally worked in this rhetorical situation. However, these memories were seemingly less useful to established agents, who likely have their own memories of and/or memory devices for this rhetorical situation, much as Whittemore's research suggests more established writers have.

Text generators can provide memories to writers that serve as inventional, arrangement, and/or style resources, shaping the writing process and the final text. The support they can offer is constrained by their datasets and the training done on them (i.e., the memories within them). Thus, writers, and particularly student writers, need metaphors that enable them to connect the data and training performed in the development of text generators to the ways they could use the text generator to support their writing processes. One approach that can accomplish this is a memory device metaphor, which can focus writing students on the data storage and compositional support that text generators can offer.

Teaching Text Generators as Memory Devices

For writing instructors, memory devices offer a metaphor for pedagogically addressing two of the biggest concerns that composition scholars have identified around text generators. Memory devices offer a metaphor through which the data and the training done on text generators can be critically engaged by situating them as human memories. Memory devices also offer a metaphor for identifying where and when to deploy those human memories to support the composing process. The memory device metaphor suggests a way to productively connect considerations of text generators' datasets and training

(Byrd; Anderson) with composing practices that involve those text generators (Graham; Knowles).

In writing courses, memory devices offer a metaphor for critically engaging the development of text generators and then using that critical understanding to identify when, how, and why stored memories can be used to support various parts of the writing process. A text generator's regenerated, "artificial" memories could be deployed by writing students as inventional resources by suggesting various ideas. The regenerated, "artificial" memories could also offer style approaches or examples, provide arrangements for genres and situations that writers are unfamiliar with, and provide ideas on how to write for audiences and situations that writers are unfamiliar with. The memory device metaphor itself equips students to determine for themselves the phases of the writing process that text generators can support based on their understanding of the data and training done to develop the specific text generator.

For writing instructors, there are several other equally useful composing processes for engaging text generators (Graham; Vetter et al.) and even other processes that center the rhetorical canons (Knowles). There are also several equally critical and impactful frameworks for engaging text generators and their effects (Aguilar; Jiminez). At base, the memory device pedagogical metaphor offers a way to supplement these approaches, such as connecting Antonio Byrd's call in "Truth-Telling" for students to think critically about the standardized English enforced by ChatGPT 4.0 with decisions about the challenges of then composing with the "memories" provided by ChatGPT 4.0 during one's writing process. The memory device metaphor also offers a way to connect and extend the pedagogical need to understand and develop critical literacies around text generators (Aguilar; Byrd; Jimenez) with the need to have students enact useful composing processes (Graham; Knowles). With this connection in mind, this essay thus ends with an outline of how writing instructors could teach text generators through the metaphor of memory devices.

An Approach to Teaching Text Generators as Memory Devices

First, writing instructors will need to make the rhetorical canon of memory a more prominent part of their courses. Instructors will need to engage with students' memories and memory devices and illuminate how both influence students' writing. Early in writing courses, instructors could guide students to consider what memories they draw from as they write.

Students could be asked to identify what memories arise as they compose or identify any specific memories that influence their writing process. Building upon the engagement with their "natural" memories, students should consider the "artificial" memory practices that they enact. They could be asked to identify memory practices like making post-it notes, writing lists in apps, taking pictures of classroom boards, or repeating information to themselves to make sure they later write with said information. Students could be asked to consider their "natural" and "artificial" memory practices either as part of literacy narratives or in reflections on the projects they did for the course. As part of these considerations, instructors should introduce the concept of memory devices. Instructors should emphasize that what is stored within a memory device then shapes what aspects of the composing process the memory device can support.

Second, following the consideration of rhetorical memory devices, writing instructors should introduce text generators. Instructors should explain that one way to engage text generators is through the metaphor of memory devices. Instructors should introduce text generators as a device through which countless numbers of memories have been stored and, in turn, (re)generate those memories to support compositional activities. Building upon their considerations of how they develop and deploy their own memory devices, students could be asked to research various text generators' datasets and training, examining them as forms of storage for future support. Instructors could have students research Common-Crawl datasets, human training of AI, and AI hallucinations. As part of this research, students could consider what "memories" (data) seem relevant to their writing practices and which "memories" do not.

Writing students can then use a memory device metaphor to understand that the data in text generators are "memories" from specific, and thus constrained, writers and situations (Byrd; Anderson). Biases and gaps will thus be an inevitable part of these memories. Text generators can thus be situated as algorithmic systems that have compiled billions of pieces of highly contextual writing and then developed ways to regenerate algorithmically-narrowed writing that mimics those highly contextual pieces of writing. Teaching text generators as such will likely require either some sort of mini-lecture from instructors or additional assigned readings on text generator development.

Furthermore, this work will likely need to be part of a singular engagement with text generators, requiring part of a class period dedicated to engaging with text generators. As part of this instruction, instructors will need to emphasize the very human data that is the foundation of text generators' outputs and how this data will inevitably have falsifications, gaps, and biases. Furthermore, instructors can emphasize how the data's flaws and biases often get enhanced by text generators' development processes (Byrd; Anderson). The flawed data and training affects all writers who work with text generators, either by being biased in some form against the writer or providing the writer with biases and falsifications that they might not recognize (Perrotta, Selwyn, and Ewin). Through this framing, students can develop an understanding of how text generators, like all memory devices, are demarcated by the information stored within them.

Third, writing instructors could ask students to identify writing situations during which they have stronger memories than a typical text generator. Instructors should have students investigate their own memories and memory devices, identifying what memories they have that might be more useful in many situations. Students could identify the situations, genres, and audiences that they individually have more relevant memories for writing toward. For example, students could consider how they likely have deeper, more useful memories on how to write to a friend group or email a professor. Students could make considerations like this when they work on specific, related elements of a writing project, such as considering the project's audience, genre, or context.

Fourth, writing instructors could ask students to identify writing situations where text generators might offer memories they lack and thus what writing work the text generator might support. Students could identify specific writing situations where text generators might be useful, as well as different points in the writing process when the text generator's "memories" might be useful to their writing process. Students could be asked to identify a part of a current writing project during which they would want to draw from a text generator's artificial memories. For example, students could prompt Google Gemini for an example body paragraph for an academic essay. As part of these considerations, students should be asked to search for the falsifications, biases, and limitations in the generated "memories." At the very least, students should be required to examine the text generator's outputs for any biases or hallucinations. The goal of these considerations would be for students to recognize what text generators can and cannot offer and then use that recognition to determine specific points in their writing processes that they believe text generators could usefully support, while also being aware of the risks of drawing from these artificial memories.

Memory devices offer writing students a metaphor for engaging text generators that equips them to better understand text generators' development, to contrast that understanding with their own writing practices, and to use that contrasted understanding to inform how, when, and why they use text generators. By engaging text generators through the metaphor of memory devices, students can engage the systems as another artificial memory device that enables them to deploy the data the systems are built on to support specific composing practices and thus require critical decisions to be made about when and why to use those memories. Most of all, the text-generators-as-memory-devices metaphor centers students: it frames text generators as devices that are useful for each student's personal contexts, needs, practices, and memories.

Acknowledgments

I would like to thank Sally Neidhard, Rich Shivener, the two anonymous reviewers, and the copy-editors for their feedback on this article.

Works Cited

Aguilar, Gabriel Lorenzo. "Rhetorically Training Students to Generate with AI: Social Justice Applications for AI as Audience." *Computers and Composition*, vol. 71, 2024, doi.org/10.1016/j.compcom.2024.102828.

Anderson, Salena Sampson. "'Places to Stand': Multiple Metaphors for Framing ChatGPT's Corpus." *Computers and Composition*, vol. 68, no. 1, 2023, doi.org/10.1016/j.compcom.2023.102778.

Bedington, Andelyn, Emma F. Halcomb, Heidi A. McKee, Thomas Sargent, and Adler Smith. "Writing with Generative AI and Human-Machine Teaming: Insights and Recommendations from Faculty and Students." *Computers and Composition*, vol. 71, 2024. doi.org/10.1016/j.compcom.2024.102833.

Bender, Emily M., Timnit Gebru, Angelina McMillan-Major, and Shmargaret Shmitchell. "On the Dangers of Stochastic Parrots: Can Language Models Be Too Big?" *FAccT '21: Proceedings of the 2021 ACM Conference on Fairness, Accountability, and Transparency*, 3-10 Mar. 2021, Canada, pp. 610–23, doi.org/10.1145/3442188.3445922.

Brynjolfsson, Erik, Danielle Li, and Lindsey Raymond. "Generative AI at Work." *NBER Working Paper Series*, no. w31161, Nov.2023, ssrn.com/abstract=4426942.

Byrd, Antonio. "Truth-Telling: Critical Inquiries on LLMs and the Corpus Texts that Train Them." *Composition Studies*, vol. 51, no. 1, 2023, pp. 135–42.

Carruthers, Mary. *The Book of Memory: A Study of Memory in Medieval Culture*. 2nd ed., Cambridge UP, 2008.

Crawford, Kate. *Atlas of AI: Power, Politics, and the Planetary Costs of Artificial Intelligence*. Yale UP, 2021.

Gallagher, John R. "Lessons Learned from Machine Learning Researchers about the Terms 'Artificial Intelligence' and 'Machine Learning.'" *Composition Studies*, vol. 51, no. 1, 2023, pp. 149–54.

Graham, S. Scott. "Post-Process but Not Post-Writing: Large Language Models and a Future for Composition Pedagogy." *Composition Studies*, vol. 51, no. 1, 2023, pp. 162–68.

Jimenez, Christopher D. "Teaching Social Identity and Cultural Bias Using AI Text Generation." *TextGenEd: Teaching with Text Generation Technologies*, edited by Annette Vee, Tim Laquintano, and Carly Schnitzler, The WAC Clearinghouse, 2023, wac.colostate.edu/repository/collections/textgened/ethical-considerations/teaching-social-identity-and-cultural-bias-using-ai-text-generation/.

Johnson, Nathan. R. *Architects of Memory: Information and Rhetoric in a Networked Archival Age*. U of Alabama P, 2020.

Knowles, Alan M. "Machine-in-the-Loop Writing: Optimizing the Rhetorical Load." *Computers and Composition*, vol. 71, 2024, doi.org/10.1016/j.compcom.2024.102826.

Ouyang, Long, Jeff Wu, Xu Jiang, Diogo Almeida, Carroll L. Wainwright, Pamela Mishkin, Chong Zhang, Sandhini Agarwal, Katarina Slama, Alex Ray, John Schulman, Jacob Hilton, Fraser Kelton, Luke Miller, Maddie Simens, Amanda Askell, Peter Welinder, Paul Christiano, Jan Leike, and Ryan Lowe. "Training Language Models to Follow Instructions with Human Feedback." *OpenAI*, 2022, cdn.openai.com/papers/Training_language_models_to_follow_instructions_with_human_feedback.pdf.

Paullada, Amandalynne, Inioluwa Deborah Raji, Emily M. Bender, Emily Denton, and Alex Hanna. "Data and Its (Dis)contents: A Survey of Dataset Development and Use in Machine Learning Research." *Patterns*, vol. 2, no. 11, 2021, doi.org/10.1016/j.patter.2021.100336.

Perrotta, Carlo, Neil Selwyn, and Carrie Ewin. "Artificial Intelligence and the Affective Labour of Understanding: The Intimate Moderation of a Language Model." *New Media & Society*, vol. 26, no. 3, 2024, pp. 1585–1609, doi.org/10.1177/14614448221075296.

Pigg, Stacey. "Research Writing with ChatGPT: A Descriptive Embodied Practice Framework." *Computers and Composition*, vol. 71, 2024, doi.org/10.1016/j.compcom.2024.102830.

Silvestro, John J. "Remember Then Recommend: Critically Engaging Spell Checker Algorithms and Other Text Recommender Systems as Memory Infrastructures." *College English*, vol. 86, no. 1, 2023, pp. 59–88.

Vetter, Matthew A., Brent Lucia, Jialei Jiang, and Mahmoud Othman. "Towards a Framework for Local Interrogation of AI Ethics: A Case Study on Text Generators, Academic Integrity, and Composing with ChatGPT." *Computers and Composition*, vol. 71, 2024, doi.org/10.1016/j.compcom.2024.102831.

Whittemore, Stewart. *Rhetorical Memory: A Study of Technical Communication and Information Management*. U of Chicago P, 2015.

Xu, Ziwei, Sanjay Jain, and Mohan Kankanhalli. "Hallucination is Inevitable: An Innate Limitation of Large Language Models." *arXiv*, 13 Feb. 2025, doi.org/10.48550/arXiv.2401.11817.

Yates, Frances. *The Art of Memory*. Bodley Head, 2014.

John J. Silvestro is associate professor at Slippery Rock University. He researches rhetorical conceptions of memory and how they can be used to engage critical literacies and conceptions of information. His scholarship has been published in *College English, Composition Forum, enculturation*, and *Reflections* and in multiple edited collections.

Fumbling Toward Co-Territorialized Spaces: Composition Pedagogy and Dual Enrollment

Joe Courchesne, Jennifer DiGrazia, and Wyatt Hermansen

This article explores the pedagogical possibilities and institutional tensions of co-taught dual enrollment (DE) first-year writing courses. Drawing on their teaching experiences in an early college program, the authors examine how DE fosters collaboration between secondary and postsecondary instructors. They argue that, with adequate professional development and institutional support, DE can promote curricular alignment and enrich writing instruction for future college students. Through classroom narratives and student reflections, the authors show how co-teaching challenges traditional hierarchies and illuminates the increasingly porous boundary between high school and college writing cultures.

Introduction

The introduction to *The Dual Enrollment Kaleidoscope: Reconfiguring Perceptions of First-Year Writing and Composition Studies,* an edited collection of critical scholarship about dual-enrollment writing, opens with a confession from the editors, Christine Denecker and Casie Moreland: "To be honest, we are not entirely sure how we feel about dual enrollment (DE)" (3). Given the potential for such programs to expand access to higher education, bolster flagging enrollment for many colleges and universities, and offer students chances to earn college credits, such ambivalence seems surprising. But Denecker and Moreland, along with many of the contributors to *The Dual Enrollment Kaleidoscope,* argue that the DE landscape is too varied and vast to generalize that the "steady migration of college composition courses into the high school experience" is an unalloyed good for FYW or for the students who stand to benefit from it. They point to valid concerns and questions about the quality of FYW curriculum in such programs and the territorial disputes that can arise when college courses move to high school.

Indeed, as FYW continues to drift beyond the boundaries of secondary institutions at an accelerating pace—the number of students enrolled in DE jumped by 8.8% between 2022 and 2023—DE "serves to hyper-illuminate struggles, inconsistencies, and ongoing challenges" of FYW instruction ("Undergraduate Enrollment Grows"; Denecker and Moreland 4-6). The tensions inherent in teaching FYW are pronounced in DE contexts, where its complexities are magnified. As DE grows in both popularity and significance, it compels us to join scholars like Denecker, Moreland, and others in critically engaging with its possibilities and pitfalls.

In that spirit, we share our experience teaching collaboratively in DE contexts not to extol its virtues uncritically, but to explore both the transformative possibilities and the pressing challenges of what Christie Toth describes as the increasingly "porous" space between high school and college. We reflect here on our experiences teaching FYW in a DE/early college enrollment (ECE) program from three perspectives (339). Jennifer and Joe—a tenured faculty member at Westfield State University and an ELA teacher at a public high school in the same region, respectively—co-taught four sections of FYW over the course of four years. Wyatt, also a tenured faculty member at Jennifer's institution, has co-taught with two different ELA teachers at two different high schools over six years.

In this article, which we co-write to mirror the collaboration we advocate for, we make the case for building and fostering partnerships that bridge institutional spaces while acknowledging the complexities we've encountered and highlighting the resources and strategies we believe these programs need to thrive. Our pedagogical approach to writing in our DE courses draws from the composition program at our four-year institution, which emphasizes inquiry into research questions that arise in students' areas of interest. Students' inquiries are scaffolded with research and result in each student producing a final project that is created for a public audience. Thus, students navigate increasingly complex choices focused on purpose, audience, and genre. In our dual-enrollment classrooms, high school teachers, with their understanding of their students and local contexts—including power dynamics, structures, and social networks—bring an invaluable perspective to the collaborative teaching of first-year writing. This effort, however, needs to be supplemented, strengthened, and supported through additional professional development to ensure it is both sustainable and transferable.

Drawing on scholarship in our field and our own co-teaching experiences as well as using excerpts from student work to illustrate our claims, we argue that the questions posed in *The Dual Enrollment Kaleidoscope* about DE in FYW—who teaches it, how authority is earned and leveraged in the classroom, who supervises and assesses student work—speak to a broader challenge in our field. This challenge was articulated by Steve Graham in 2019, when he asked how we can "put into action the forces needed to develop and successfully implement a coherent, well-constructed, and consistent vision of writing instruction that cuts across multiple levels" (297). We have found that within co-taught DE writing courses, there are opportunities for collaboration between high school and college instructors that wouldn't have existed otherwise. As we work together to co-facilitate our FYW courses—sharing students, pedagogies, classroom space, and navigating institutional systems—these opportunities can help us move toward a more "consistent vision of writing instruction that cuts across" high school and college levels (297).

When the ecosystem of DE is thoughtfully cultivated and maintained and co-teaching pairs are given opportunities to build relationships, DE FYW courses allow for secondary/postsecondary pedagogical collaboration that, in our experience, achieves several key outcomes: it helps to provide multiple audiences for students' writing, enables college and high school teachers to collaborate on assignments, helps instructors to communicate a clearer sense of college expectations for high school teachers, and offers college instructors valuable insights into the norms, values, and institutional systems that shape high school teaching. Denecker notes that as dual enrollment classrooms provide "a unique space where students simultaneously experience both high school and college expectations," they also create a space in which "the tensions and inconsistencies between secondary and post-secondary writing instruction" are thrown into sharp relief ("Transitioning Writers" 29). In having curiosity about those tensions and inconsistencies, high school teachers and college instructors can better understand their students and the overlapping literacy worlds they inhabit—and must navigate—throughout our courses.

We begin with some context about our ECE program and the institutional spaces we inhabit as part of that program. Through stories from our classrooms and analysis of our experiences, we hope to demonstrate the kinds of breakthroughs and possibilities that exist in the dual-enrollment space while also highlighting the particular advantages and challenges we face. We address the obstacles Joe faced while adjusting an 12th grade ELA curriculum to accommodate more composition pedagogy; we share stories about how Joe and Wyatt negotiated the shared power and responsibilities that are inherent to a co-teaching partnership; we explore the trial-and-error process that Wyatt experienced while settling into a productive relationship with their co-teacher. Most importantly, we conclude our work with a call to promote more opportunities for high school and college instructors to collaborate and engage with professional development (PD) that involves both high school and college composition instructors. We acknowledge that while this model of ECE FYW can be difficult to sustain, it provides an impetus for all constituents—students, teachers, coordinators, and administrators—to continue to ask important questions about the value of FYW and potentially enables conversations that could help to vertically align writing between high school and college contexts.

Our Institution's ECE Program

Dual enrollment programs take a number of forms. Some are hosted on college campuses and taught by either college faculty or high school teachers; if they are hosted on high school campuses, they are taught by either college faculty or high school teachers who are then remotely supervised by college faculty. The Deneker and Moreland collection outlines these approaches and some variations. However, none of the models presented in the collection align with our approach. Indeed, when we presented research about our collaboration at the 2023 CCCC in Chicago, several audience members commented that they hadn't heard of a program structured like ours.

Instructors in our ECE program travel from our university campus to local high schools to co-teach a year-long (or "stretch") Composition 101 course alongside local high school ELA instructors. Several days a week, college instructors are physically present in the high school classroom, providing direct instruction, mentorship, and support to help students bridge the gap between high school and college-level writing. Students in the program, who enroll during their junior year, are recruited by teachers and guidance counselors at their high school. Because each high school recruits the students, there is no uniform set of criteria for admission. These students benefit from intensive writing instruction that can be provided by two instructors who, while they represent different institutional contexts, are both working toward a common purpose of supporting those students as writers and learners.

Now in its eighth year, our institution's ECE program serves two primary goals: introducing local high school students to our institution and encouraging those who may not consider themselves "college ready" to pursue higher education. While the program aims to recruit students from diverse racial and economic backgrounds, we treat ECE participants as we do any first-year composition students, recognizing their varied writing experiences and levels of preparedness for college writing.

The program is structured to provide a gradual transition into college coursework. In their junior year, students begin the program by taking an introductory college course, typically history, taught at their high school. As seniors, they transition to our university campus, where they complete two additional college courses—one each semester. Students who successfully complete the program earn twelve college credits, applicable to our institution's common core of studies.

The success of our ECE program is shaped by our diverse experiences and expertise as educators. Jennifer, a tenured professor of composition in the English department, has over eighteen years of experience at our institution, including fourteen years as the WPA for the Program in Composition. She is white, middle-aged, cisgender, and queer. Wyatt, also tenured, is a white, middle-aged professor who identifies as non-binary and queer. Joe, a white, middle-aged high school teacher, has extensive classroom experience and recently earned an MA in English, focusing his graduate research on integrating composition pedagogy into high school ELA curricula.

Jen and Joe co-taught at an urban public high school about fifteen miles from the university, where the student population is predominantly Puerto Rican and from low-income families. As of this writing, the school is preparing to exit a nine-year state receivership implemented due to low test scores. Meanwhile, Wyatt has spent five years co-teaching with Kristen Biancuzzo—affectionately known on campus as "Mrs. B."—a veteran ELA teacher at a public high school in the same suburban town as the university. This school serves a predominantly white student population from a mix of middle- and working-class families.

These varied teaching experiences inform our program's collaborative approach, which fosters a strong partnership between high school and college educators. This structure not only addresses concerns raised in the Denecker and Moreland collection—such as unequal power dynamics between high school and college instructors (Lueck and Nordquist; McWain and Hoermann-Elliot), inconsistent administrative oversight (Jones), and challenges related to access (Mendenhall and Gelleher) and equity (Schneider)—but also creates opportunities for further dialogue and institutional collaboration. By bridging pedagogical, academic, and systemic divides between high school and college, our program serves as a model for strengthening cross-institutional teaching and learning.

At the heart of our ECE program is a commitment to partnership that benefits students and educators alike. By pairing high school teachers with college instructors in co-teaching arrangements, the program creates a dynamic environment where different pedagogical approaches and institutional contexts intersect. These collaborations extend beyond the classroom, evolving into professional relationships that lead to conference presentations, co-authored articles (including this one), and, most importantly, enriched learning experiences for students. The following reflections illustrate how these partnerships challenge us as educators and help us navigate the complexities of preparing students for the transition from high school to college writing.

Joe's Reflections: Challenging Pedagogical Regression

In his experience teaching in our ECE program, Joe encounters a strange paradox: college preparation often justifies high school practices, yet co-taught dual enrollment spaces highlight their disconnection from college. Joe believes a typical high school teacher justifies curricular choices by leaning on the "you'll need this for college" argument. In a co-taught dual-enrollment setting, no such plausible deniability exists: the skills students need for "college readiness" for writing are playing out in real time. What do you do when your "baby"—the curriculum that is comfortable, proven to engage students, and a labor of love—might not be as "college preparatory" as you thought?

This reality has to be confronted as two competing classroom foci begin to clash: a reading curriculum and a writing curriculum. Generally, high school teachers are not as well-versed in writing instruction as they are with literature. Teacher preparation programs generally foster this by training future secondary teachers to be literary experts at the expense of writing pedagogy and the study of rhetoric. Writing, they are taught, is important, but primarily as a means to assess students' understanding of the literature. Even when writing assignments are argument-focused, the emphasis remains on the writer's message and without consideration to rhetorical choices and concepts. As a result, the focus shifts from consideration of genre, style, audience, and purpose. Teachers are often satisfied when students meet the requirements of literary analysis without encouraging them to explore other important aspects of their writing.

As Nadia Behizadeh suggests in "Realizing Powerful Writing Pedagogy in U.S. Public Schools," when literature is de-centered and when composition gets a foothold in a high school classroom, writing achieves a place that it often otherwise does not have. One of Behizadeh's suggestions for implementing Powerful Writing Pedagogy (PWP) is that high school writing instruction should be informed by composition pedagogy. She suggests that it increases the "connection between authentic educational experiences and student performance," and that "active engagement in learning and knowledge production, disciplined inquiry into problems" adds "value beyond school" and supports student achievement (268-69). During his collaboration with Jennifer, Joe saw this "active engagement" in action in his students emerge both in their writing and reflection. As one student wrote,

> It doesn't just take one person and it doesn't just take one attempt, writing takes time and takes conversation between you and someone who you want to understand the writing. This was my first time writing to an audience rhetorically and it still seems like it got out because of the feedback I got from my peers and teachers.

This realization about the complexity and collaborative nature of the writing process likely would not have been reached in a traditionally literary-focused course.

So why might high school teachers resist making this instructional shift? To answer that, we also must also acknowledge a perceived expertise imbalance that Joe suspects makes high school teachers defensive and less likely to be open to these collaborations. In welcoming a professor to their classroom, a teacher's professional pride is at stake. Joe recalls a collaboration between his high school and a local community college. As a part of this collaboration, Joe and an English professor arranged to visit each other's classrooms. After this person visited his classroom, Joe was presented with an extensive list of suggestions that read more like he was being professionally evaluated than working with a collaborator. While he doesn't shy away from constructive criticism, the sense of condescension and the implication of a professional hierarchy was unmistakable.

While conducting his visit to the college, Joe found the classroom practice itself was effective. However, Joe did make note of the interesting contrasts between his working environment and the professor's: in the college course, students were working at their own pace and left when they were finished. The class consisted of eleven students and the professor reported that 25% of students had dropped the course since it began. So much of the professor's feedback to Joe was about advising him to give up control and tailor content to individual students. Joe connected this advice to the environment and context: these are pedagogical moves that become increasingly difficult in a classroom of thirty where students could not drop the course if they became overwhelmed. Joe left this exchange understanding the professor's context and challenges but confident they didn't fully understand his own.

This was not the case in Joe's partnership with Jennifer. The co-taught model meant Jennifer was in the high school setting twice a week, and very quickly, Joe's struggles became Jennifer's struggles. While Jennifer never compromised the integrity of the composition program or her own practice, she did understand the need to be adaptable and how the complexity of the environment and different student populations can impact a teacher's approach. While Joe was getting a refresher on composition theory, Jennifer was learning about both his community and school. The students benefited most from this partnership: they were appropriately challenged by the composition course while still feeling grounded in their familiar high school environment. Joe believes this co-teaching was essential for students: he believes it unlikely they could have adapted to the shift in approach and expectations without a guide, and he believes the composition course would not have been effective had it been solely taught by him.

So much of what we do in composition relies upon the idea that writing is a social act; we encourage students to engage in peer review, to take and give feedback, to understand that writing is not done in a vacuum. In their article, "Collaborative Authorship and the Teaching of Writing," Lisa Ede and Andrea Lunsford explain that "for teachers of writing . . . the most immediate need is for pedagogy of collaboration, one that would view writing as always shared and social; writers as constantly building and negotiating meaning with and among others" (438). Ede and Lunsford are discussing dynamics between students and an assumed single teacher. What happens when we have two instructors who are collaborating, both with one another but also with students, and who are both contributing to students' conceptions of meaning for a given text? The following section helps to demonstrate both tensions and benefits that can emerge from the interactions, types of classroom support, feedback, and evaluation of students that can occur with two instructors working toward a common goal.

Collaboration in Action: Jennifer and Joe

When Jennifer and Joe co-taught, Jennifer quickly learned from Joe that high school classes don't meet or function like college classes do. Consider student-instructor conferences. In college settings, FYW instructors can cancel a couple of classes to make room for conferences, but high school students are required to be in the classroom at specific times, and they need to be occupied. This dynamic makes one-on-one conferences with students difficult, but not impossible. This is where the collaboration between co-teachers is essential. In the three years Jennifer and Joe co-taught, through trial and error, they created an arrangement wherein Jennifer conducted conferences on the floor in the hall while Joe helped students revise previous work, supported them as they worked on their labor logs, or read articles and other student samples in anticipation of the next full class. He often found himself in the role of interpreter for Jennifer, as students worked to understand her comments and feedback, and they were challenged to think about their writing and their role as writers in more nuanced ways. When they received grades lower than what they had hoped for or than they thought they had deserved, Joe often found himself explaining how college expectations and grading standards differed from the ones they had come to expect in high school. Because he was closer to his own time in college than Jennifer, and he was simultaneously an ambassador of the college experience and their teacher, his ability to help students bridge the gap between high school and college proved invaluable.

When the class first sat in a circle and discussed the value of peer review as well as how to give effective peer feedback—an important skill that we carefully scaffold in our composition program—Joe often had to intervene, interpreting the moves of "Sayback," "Pointing" and "Questions" to which Jennifer had introduced the class. He often shared his own experiences receiving these forms of feedback, and he suggested that while the benefits of peer review were sometimes less immediately apparent, they came with time. While these are points that Jennifer also made, hearing them reinforced by another teacher—one they trusted and saw every day–often made all the difference and helped to dispel some of the need for instant gratification.

Peer review group formation was another challenge that required negotiation. Jennifer initially found peer review easier to manage in classes that took place in a traditional university setting, because most of the students are strangers to each other. Other students in the class were unfamiliar audiences, enabling writers to take risks and share work because everyone is in a similar place. She quickly learned that isn't always true in high schools where students have sometimes known one another for most of their lives. In a high school class, you are not working to build a community as much as you are entering one that already exists. As a newcomer, Jennifer didn't know the tangle of relationships that preceded their entry to the class. Until Jennifer and Joe learned to be strategic about forming peer review groups, they often saw students gravitate toward friends for safety. That doesn't create the best conditions for effective peer review, so Jennifer and Joe formed groups based on Joe's understanding of students' strengths and areas of need. Peer review and instructor feedback require time and energy on behalf of all participants. One of our former students reflects, "One thing that will stay in my head is that writing takes time. Before this class I knew writing took time, but never knew it took weeks to a month for a proper piece of writing."

While all three of us feel like the work we do and the conversations we have about individual students and how to reach them make for great opportunities, we recognize that we give up a measure of individual authority in a co-teaching arrangement. But in the process, we earn a shared authority that is often more powerful than what we sacrifice. That collaboration works both ways—or it should; high school teachers get to see what writing instruction at the college really does look like (as Joe will illustrate), and university instructors understand the conditions for teaching, writing, and learning for high school teachers.

Some of these differences are related to the roles we are assigned from our institutional context. As Joe reflected, we are learning that transferring the expectations of FYW to high school instructors requires more than sharing outcomes for a course. Annie S. Mendenhall and David Gehler, reporting on Denecker's research, suggest that high school instructors tend to focus on argument and reporting, while FYW college instructors seek to encourage students to use writing to open possibilities for inquiry, to create meaning in conjunction with other speakers or sources. Again, such a difference often requires students to understand and practice more nuanced writing and thinking valued in a college class than the more cut and dry (state your thesis and make sure to include a counter argument!) writing expected of high school students. Another student reflects: "I thought that this was going to be a waste of time and that I should just stay doing my regular high school classes but i take those thoughts back . . . This class has helped me become a college student without the stress and it helped me be less nervous to start college . . ."

The success of these collaborations often hinges on the strength of the relationship between co-teachers, and the administrators of ECE programs can help ensure that these relationships have opportunities to grow and flourish. As Mendenhall and Gehler suggest, "DE staffing . . . creates numerous professional development and student learning challenges that are complicated by the power dynamics inherent in the DE relationship" (133). One source of those unequal power dynamics is the issue of ownership, such as when the ECE partnership is enacted as institutional colonization by the sponsoring college or university. A vital component of a program like ours is that both institutions enact shared ownership of the program and enable shared responsibility between ELA teachers and college instructors. Yes, the physical space of such collaborations matters, but maintaining a partnership between teachers in the classroom should be supported by a partnership between institutions. This balance between institutional and interpersonal dynamics is central to understanding how co-teaching partnerships function in practice.

Wyatt: Reaching Equilibrium

This interplay became evident in Wyatt's first co-teaching partnership in the ECE program. Assigned to an 11th grade ELA class alongside a well-respected teacher at a vocational high school a few miles from the university's campus, Wyatt began their collaboration in a context that demanded flexibility and shared purpose. The partnership began smoothly enough: Wyatt was assigned to an 11th grade ELA class alongside a well-respected teacher at a vocational high school a few miles away from the university's campus. At "the Voke," as the school was called, students alternated between academics and career training, which meant Wyatt met with them biweekly on Tuesdays and Thursdays.

While some of the disjunction could be attributed to the schedule—it was difficult to maintain a strong sense of continuity with such sporadic course meetings—Wyatt quickly realized that, through no fault of either instructor, co-this teaching partnership would not be a fruitful one. Wyatt butted heads with their co-teacher over disagreements about issues ranging from the trivial—how much class time should be spent on certain activities, for example—to the significant, like grading criteria. Perhaps because the ECE program was in its first year and lacked the structured professional development opportunities it would later offer, Wyatt and their co-teacher were not provided structured or compensated time to collaboratively plan the course or build a strong working relationship. This experience underscores the importance of ECE programs providing financial support for instructors on both sides of the high school-college partnership. Such compensation is essential to ensure adequate time for course planning, professional collaboration, and the development of a cohesive curriculum.

After a year-long stint with Wyatt, that ELA teacher is now thriving in a co-teaching arrangement with a different instructor from the English department at the ECE host institution. Wyatt began teaching with Mrs. B at the other public high school in town, where they had valuable opportunities to build a collaborative relationship both before and throughout their first year. Wyatt and Mrs. B's teamwork has gotten them through tough situations as a teaching team. They taught together during the pandemic and periods of institutional upheaval, leadership changes, and systemic inconsistencies in the program that might have threatened the stability of a weaker co-teaching partnership. Wyatt and Mrs. B have become adept at working together and navigating the inevitable tension that can arise while traversing what Denecker calls the "uneven juncture where the paths of secondary and post-secondary writing meet" ("Transitioning Writers").

As they met Mrs. B at that uneven juncture, Wyatt brought to the partnership the knowledge of composition pedagogy and the demands of college writing to the high school classroom, but lacked familiarity with the particular demands of teaching ELA to 11th graders. Like Joe, Mrs. B got a primer in college composition pedagogy and had the added obligations of preparing students for standardized tests and college applications. Thus, in order to meet the demands of both institutions, Wyatt and Mrs. B must often meet in the middle. For example, when a state standardized test loomed at the end of the month, students voiced their concerns about several aspects of the exams. Students are required to pass the standardized tests to graduate, which means that many students—specifically students with disabilities—must settle for an equivalency certificate for fulfilling all other graduation requirements instead of participating in school-wide graduation. To address students' anxieties while working to enact composition pedagogy's focus on purpose, audience and genre, Wyatt and Mrs. B developed a writing assignment that allowed students to research possible audiences, identify stakeholders, and develop arguments for change. This assignment was rooted in principles of composition pedagogy but it also spoke to issues of direct relevance to students' high school experiences and hopefully helped them meet the state exam requirements.

High school teachers like Mrs. B navigate an unstable terrain of shifting curricular restraints, benchmarks, and standardized tests, making high school literacy harder to generalize than college literacy. Denecker refers to the "top-down pressure to rely on prescriptive pedagogies for instruction" such as the five-paragraph essay in high school English classes ("Transitioning Writers" 28). In fact, the state exam represents one such example. As Katie McWain observes, "high school teachers are surveilled by and made accountable to public stakeholders, including parents, administrators, voters, and legislators, in ways college faculty traditionally are not" (407). Wyatt experienced this surveillance first-hand while co-teaching with Mrs. B; often, a phone in the corner of the room would ring during class, interrupting the flow of a lesson with a student being summoned to the front office, maybe, or an administrator or faculty member would stroll in with a question or an update. College faculty often take for granted how protected their classroom spaces are from such interruptions. As a result of that surveillance and public accountability, high school teachers' day-to-day experiences at work—and, by extension, our students' learning experiences in high school—are subject to more scrutiny and intrusion and shaped by more complex forces than many college composition instructors realize.

As a high school teacher, Mrs. B drew on her deep connections to the local community as a high school teacher who often teaches siblings and cousins from the same families to bring valuable insight into the classroom projects. For example, while reading *Dreamland,* a 2015 book by Sam Quinones about the opioid epidemic, students in the class designed and created a documentary film called "Breaking the Silence," where they explored the local impact of the opioid crisis. Mrs. B's familiarity with the community and her investment in civic-based projects helped ensure the project's resonance and relevance to the classroom community and the broader town context, which enabled students to connect the academic work they were doing in their FYW class to a real-world issue.

Becoming more aware of the high school ecosystem was an important stage in the development of Wyatt's co-teaching relationship with her. Wyatt has found that the very complexity of this space—that it's not quite high school and it's not quite college; that Mrs. B and Wyatt operate from very different subject positions within very different institutions; that they have different perceptions of our students' needs—is what makes it such a rich site for coming together to better understand our students' literacy experiences.

Conclusion: ECE Quality over ECE Quantity

Denecker's metaphor of a Venn diagram underscores the "transformative power" of collaborative partnerships when supported by meaningful professional development and a mutual willingness to learn. This vision aligns closely with our own experiences in the early years of our ECE program, where FYW instructors successfully advocated for professional development opportunities that brought together teachers from both high school and college. These sessions, which sometimes included instructors from four different high schools and their university partners, created a space for rich dialogue about the purpose of dual enrollment, the value of secondary education, and the power dynamics inherent in these partnerships.

In these sessions, we spent time troubleshooting difficult classroom situations and brainstormed strategies for working more effectively with particular shared students. We discussed the value of secondary education and debated the merits of it for all of the students in our programs. To ensure equity, high school and part-time university instructors were compensated for their time spent participating in these professional development sessions, while full-time tenure-track faculty integrated this work into their regular salaried responsibilities. These efforts went a long way toward addressing the power dynamics highlighted by Mendenhall and Gehler, which can often strain co-teaching partnerships.

Unfortunately, the professional development opportunities that were so instrumental in fostering these relationships didn't last. Administrative turnover at both the high school and university levels led to the end of those opportunities, and they haven't been offered again since 2019. As noted in the beginning, one of our goals with this article is to encourage administrators at the high school and the university to support and reinstate those opportunities, as such time for collaboration creates opportunities for building and sustaining relationships. We believe our partnerships have endured and flourished largely because of those early PD sessions.

What we've learned from our collaborations across institutions is that, in their early days, collaborations need administrative support in the form of intensive PD that is currently lacking in our program. We are concerned that this is why our program hasn't been able to create and sustain new working collaborations between instructors who have expressed interest in joining the program. Effective PD can provide some of the important structural supports to facilitate the relationship-building that is required for effective partnerships. One such example is when a part-time comp instructor was working, by all accounts successfully, with a high school teacher as part of our program. However, she lacked critical support from our program, and we failed to see or comprehend the significance of a troubling situation arising with her classes. When her co-teacher of two years quit unexpectedly, leaving her to manage their once-shared cohort of students alone, the class floundered. She didn't have the necessary counterpart at the high school to help her navigate what Joe and Jennifer have identified is necessary to sustain a relationship with students or navigate the culture and systems of the schools. This includes insider knowledge about, for example, unexpected shifts in schedule that are not communicated to "outsiders" like Joe and Jennifer, and an understanding of students' relationships with and histories with one another. Due to failures on the part of the high school administration that struggled to provide her with a suitable replacement teacher, she ended up frustrated and quit. She lacked support from both high school and college administrators who failed to comprehend and address the situation. Instances like these place our university's relationships with participating high schools in jeopardy.

When supported with effective professional development and strong collaborative synergy, programs like ours can effectively support and facilitate dual-enrollment college writing courses. Students benefit not only from earning both high school and college credit but also from the guidance of two instructors who help shape their learning experiences. But the broader impact of such programs extends beyond individual student success.

As Graham suggests, writing instruction is most effective when it follows a coherent and well-constructed vision (283). Likewise, Behizadeh's concept of Powerful Writing Pedagogy underscores the need for meaningful, student-centered approaches. We believe this vision should extend across all schools, and while effective pedagogy must be responsive rather than rigidly prescribed, cross-institutional collaboration is essential for identifying promising strategies that meet the diverse needs of students.

What better way to enact this vision than by sharing physical spaces, working with real students, and negotiating pedagogical goals across institutional boundaries? Programs like ours create these opportunities, provided that teachers, students, and administrators commit to the shared work of fostering meaningful and equitable writing instruction.

Works Cited

Behizadeh, Nadia. "Realizing Powerful Writing Pedagogy in U.S. Public Schools." *Pedagogies: An International Journal*, vol. 14, no. 4, 2019, pp. 261–79.

Denecker, Christine. "Transitioning Writers across the Composition Threshold: What We Can Learn from Dual Enrollment Partnerships." *Composition Studies*, vol. 41, no. 1, 2013, pp. 27–50.

Denecker, Christine. "A Venn Diagram of Secondary-Postsecondary Teaching and Learning: The Transformative Power of Concurrent Enrollment Partnerships." *Concurrent Enrollment Review*, vol. 1, article 5, 2023.

—, and Casie Moreland, editors. *The Dual Enrollment Kaleidoscope: Reconfiguring Perceptions of First-Year Writing and Composition Studies*. Utah State UP, 2022.

—. "Introduction." Denecker and Moreland, pp. 3-16.

Graham, Steve. "Changing How Writing is Taught." *Review of Research in Education*, vol. 45, 2019. pp. 277–303.

Jones, Joseph. "Location, Delivery, and the Historical Divide between Schools and College English." Denecker and Moreland, pp. 52–70.

Lueck, Amy, and Brice Nordquist. "Dueling Enrollments: Historicizing the High School-College Divide." Denecker and Moreland, pp. 35–51.

Lunsford, Andrea A., and Lisa Ede. "Collaborative Authorship and the Teaching of Writing." *The Construction of Authorship: Textual Appropriation in Law and*

Literature, edited by Martha Woodmansee and Peter Jaszi, Duke UP, 1994, pp. 417–38.

McWain, Katie. "Finding Freedom at the Composition Threshold: Learning from the Experiences of Dual Enrollment Teachers." *Teaching English in the Two-Year College*, vol. 45, no. 4, 2018, pp. 406–24.

—, and Jackie Hoermann-Elliot. "The Optics of Observation: Exploring Tensions and Opportunities at the High School-College Composition Threshold." Denecker and Moreland, pp. 71–88.

Mendenhall, Annie S., and David Gehler. "When College Faculty Go To High School: Dual Enrollment and the Changing Scenes of 'First-Year' Composition." Denecker and Moreland, pp. 129–44.

Quinones, Sam. *Dreamland: A True Tale of America's Opiate Epidemic*. Bloomsbury Publishing, 2015.

Schneider, Barbara. "And Yet the Gap Persists." Denecker and Moreland, pp. 19-34.

Toth, Christie. "Unmeasured Engagement: Two-Year College English Faculty and Disciplinary Professional Organizations." *Teaching English in the Two-Year College*, vol. 41, no. 4, 2014, pp. 335–53.

"Undergraduate Enrollment Grows for the First Time Post Pandemic, despite Freshmen Declines." *National Student Clearinghouse*, 13 Oct. 2023, www.studentclearinghouse.org/news/undergraduate-enrollment-grows-for-the-first-time-post-pandemic-despite-freshmen-declines/.

Joe Courchesne has been an English teacher at both the secondary and college level for four fourteen years. Currently, he spends most of his time on the Springfield Technical Community College campus where he serves as coordinator for the early college pathway at Veritas Prep High School in Springfield, Mass. He also teaches Composition I at Westfield State University, Holyoke Community College, and Springfield Technical Community College. He is proud to serve as co-director of the Spring Leadership Institute for the Western Mass Writing Project.

Jennifer DiGrazia is an English professor and the current site coordinator of the Western Mass Writing Project at Westfield State University. She teaches multiple forms of composition, upper-division writing courses, queer lit classes, and supports emergent ELA teacher candidates with writing pedagogy. She is a former WPA for the composition program at WSU.

Wyatt Hermansen is associate professor of English at Westfield State University, where they coordinate the composition program and serve as faculty liaison for early college and dual enrollment programs. Their research focuses on composition pedagogy, the rhetoric of education policy, and the transition from high school to college writing.

Pandemic-Era Workload in the Online Writing Classroom: Lessons in Sustainability for the Future

Jennifer Sheppard

To investigate how online writing instructors' workloads may have shifted over the first two years of the COVID-19 pandemic, I conducted a study of faculty in a large public state university system. Almost two-thirds of participants reported positive experiences for their students and themselves, noting that these teaching environments catered to more diverse learning and teaching styles, offered greater flexibility, and were inclusive of a variety of personal circumstances. Despite these and other benefits, respondents also indicated substantial increases in their pedagogical, emotional, and professional development workloads. As a result, while respondents saw many advantages, they also shared the unsustainable impact working exclusively in online modalities had on their personal and professional lives. This article examines and highlights survey participants' online writing instruction (OWI) workloads in relation to existing scholarship to inform writing program sustainability and instructor satisfaction. As online offerings grow and we understand more about post-pandemic shifts in students, learning, and institutions, these experiences offer insight into realizing OWI's benefits without overburdening the instructors who sustain it.

Introduction

The first months of the COVID-19 pandemic saw an unprecedented, nearly universal transition to emergency remote teaching that tested even some experienced online writing instructors. Advice and training to support faculty could be found through campus IT departments, centers for teaching, professional organizations such as the Global Society for Online Literacy Educators (GSOLE) and the Online Writing Instruction Community, university writing programs, and social media. Anecdotally and through emerging scholarship in and out of composition (Auger and Formentin; Sheppard "Pandemic Pedagogy;" Griffiths et al.), though, it is clear that many faculty struggled with significant changes in their daily work lives. Recent research has reported that this was particularly intensified for contingent/non-tenure track instructors, as well as women, Black, Indigenous, and people of color (BIPOC), and multiply marginalized faculty across academia (Berheide et al.; Chen and Lawless; Xiao et al.). With little preparation for the rapid shift online—and amid increased care work (Beare et al.)—instructors scrambled in spring 2020 to adapt their teaching and learn new technologies. Two years later, even as the pandemic eased and faculty gained online teaching experience, reports of burnout had become widespread.

The project reported on here grew out of a hyperlocal assessment conducted by my writing studies department in summer 2020, which was aimed at understanding faculty support needs ahead of the first fully online semester. Analyzing responses from that specific local moment, I identified four key instructional needs: addressing heavier workloads, developing new pedagogies, attending to personal and professional well-being, and managing daily logistics (Sheppard "Pandemic Pedagogy").

To investigate how these issues evolved over the next two years of the pandemic, I surveyed faculty across English departments and writing programs in a large public university system. Participants self-reported significant increases in weekly work hours, course preparation time, professional development activities, and attention to students' overall wellbeing. While my findings— that workload increased substantially for most instructors and that many experienced a high level of burnout as a result—are hardly surprising, they call on writing programs and administrators to consider the professional, pedagogical, and personal toll of shifting instructional modalities. Although we have moved beyond the necessity of emergency remote teaching and programs are embracing the pedagogical benefits and expanded educational access that online writing instruction (OWI) can offer, we continue to discover more about how students, learning, and higher education institutions are changing post-pandemic. Participants' experiences provide important insight into how to support faculty and fully realize OWI's potentials moving forward. However, to do so, the field must prioritize equitable, sustainable workloads and inclusive professional development for faculty at all levels.

Survey responses echoed OWI workload concerns emphasized in previous research, including responding to more student writing (Griffin and Minter; Melonçon and Harris; Sibo), spending additional time developing digital materials and offering student support (Borgman and McArdle; Cicchino et al.; Cargile Cook and Grant-Davie; Hewett and DePew), and participating in often uncompensated professional development for learning new technologies and pedagogies (Jackson and Olinger; Melonçon; Warnock "Teaching the OWI Course"). The survey also highlighted additional pressures from the expanding reliance on contingent instructors, oversized classes, and teaching loads that exceed professional guidelines (Horning; CCCC Executive Committee; GSOLE Executive Board), and broader pandemic-related stressors. This article examines and highlights survey participants' OWI workloads in relation to existing scholarship to inform professional development, administrative decisions, and writing program sustainability.

Description of Study

The survey discussed here, reviewed and verified as exempt by the author's campus Institutional Review Board (protocol HS-2022-0029), investigated online writing instruction and the experiences of college writing teachers during the COVID-19 pandemic in academic years 2020–21[1] and 2021–22. Participants were recruited from English departments and writing programs in a large, linguistically-, racially-, geographically-, and socioeconomically-diverse public state university system in the western United States. The survey was open to tenure track faculty, lecturers on one or three-year contracts, contingent instructors, and graduate student teaching assistants who taught writing in any modality in the first two years of the pandemic. Respondents were asked to complete a Google Form consisting of 26 closed- and 10 open-ended questions that took approximately 15 minutes to complete. A total of 98 responses were received from participants at 19 of the 23 campuses in the university system.

This article focuses on responses to a subset of survey questions related to online instructor workload that addressed the following research questions:

- In what ways did the shift to online teaching because of COVID-19 impact the workload, pedagogy, and practice of college writing instructors?
- Given instructor experiences with OWI during the first two years of the pandemic, what can scholars and writing program administrators learn that would help to strengthen future online teaching and make it more sustainable for instructors and programs?

The survey used a mixed methods approach to gather demographic, quantitative, and qualitative data on teaching and professional development. This approach was well suited to investigating the complexity of educators' experiences. For example, quantitative questions captured self-reporting of hours worked but could not account for what additional teaching or training activities were undertaken. The qualitative component addressed these gaps, offering deeper insight into online pandemic teaching. As John Creswell and Vicki Clark note, "quantitative results can net general descriptions of the relationships among variables," while qualitative data "can help build [an] understanding of what it means" (9).

In beginning my analysis, I studied the auto-generated charts in Google Forms for participants' responses to demographic and quantitative questions. These visualizations helped to identify details such as years of teaching experience, usual course teaching loads and class sizes, and preferences for teaching modalities. They offered important but limited context.

For the open-ended questions, I conducted a content analysis using an emergent coding scheme that I developed iteratively. I started by writing short notes with initial observations to familiarize myself with the data. Next, I coded responses to identify recurring topics. In the first pass through the data, I assigned short, descriptive codes to all responses. In further passes, I refined these codes to ensure they were reflective of respondents' comments. Lastly, I examined the codes to identify broad but repeated themes. According to Virginia Braun and Victoria Clarke, this type of recursive thematic analysis produces themes that each have a single focus, build on one another but do not overlap, and connect to the research questions (66). I concluded by using these identified themes to report on survey participants' teaching, emotional, and professional development workloads.

Findings

Despite the many challenges reported in my data and elsewhere, 69%[2] of the 97 respondents who answered a question about teaching modality preference reported that they would favor teaching at least some of their classes in online or hybrid modalities given the option. In a follow up question, participants noted that these teaching environments catered to more diverse learning styles, offered students greater flexibility in scheduling, and were inclusive of a variety of student realities, including disabilities, the time and costs of commuting, childcare, and working. As one participant explained, "asynchronous classes offer students the most flexibility and independence" in navigating "obstacles to attending college." Another noted that "offering asynchronous writing courses is a matter of supporting diversity, equity, inclusion, and belonging." Some highlighted technological learning affordances, such as the "uniquely helpful" use of breakout rooms for more focused small group work. Another emphasized the value of hybrid classes, commenting,

> I noticed that many students who might not have chosen to speak up in an in-person setting were contributing rich, thoughtful ideas to online activities. However, I know that many students need or benefit from in-person writing instruction and conversations with peers. I think that hybrid classes have allowed me to keep many of the activities that encouraged engagement from students who might not have spoken up while at the same time giving us the face-to-face time that many students need.

Beyond benefits for students, many instructors also noted the professional and personal advantages of teaching online. These issues were especially significant for part-time instructors juggling multiple jobs, families, disabilities, and/or long commutes. As one respondent shared, "I have a better work/life balance than when commuting and I get more accomplished."

Despite these and other affordances of online and hybrid teaching, survey responses revealed three significant OWI workload challenges. First, participants reported substantial increases in hours worked per week as they developed new pedagogical strategies, prepared materials for digital delivery, and facilitated instruction and student interaction online. Second, at the same time instructors' pedagogical workload increased, so did their emotional workload, including reaching out to struggling students, working harder to create classroom community, and helping students navigate the many challenges of the pandemic. Third, while working more intensively in the classroom, many instructors also reported an increased need for or requirement to engage in professional development. Taken together, these responses point to significant challenges and the unsustainable toll that teaching exclusively online had on participants' professional and personal lives.

An Increase in Pedagogical Workload

When asked about workload changes during the study period, most respondents reported increases compared to previous in-person teaching. While some said workloads eventually leveled out with experience and development of reusable materials, 85% of 78 respondents estimated working at least four extra hours per week, and 48% reported working seven to eleven hours more. As many scholars (Melonçon and Harris; Sibo; Warnock, *Teaching Writing Online*) have suggested, upfront course planning, daily class preparation, and continual interaction with students through and about their writing makes teaching writing online particularly time-consuming. These findings were echoed in many survey responses, including the following: "Initially, the workload to transition from in-person to online was brutal. Too much to do in too little time. Anticipating what had to be designed and loaded online was mind boggling." Another noted that "[t]he pivot to online was hard. I'm glad we didn't have to stop instructing students, but the workload took a toll on me and my ability to take care of myself and my family." As participants' comments reflect, the sudden shift to online teaching, combined with writing instruction's existing workload, limited preparation time, and the need for technology and pedagogy training, led to increased instructional labor, especially early in the pandemic. Still, many faculty eventually learned to leverage online tools and pedagogies, despite the personal costs.

Even with ample preparation and support, online instructors face increased workloads, a trend highlighted over a decade ago in the CCCC 2011 *State-of-the-Art of OWI* report. While responding to student writing does not vary by modality, Lisa Melonçon and Heidi Harris note that other activities like responding to a higher volume of emails, commenting on discussion posts, and writing learning management system (LMS) announcements significantly increase the workload (427). As they note, online writing instruction is "text-heavy," requiring instructors to teach primarily through writing, which can be as taxing for them as it is for students. Although Scott Warnock suggests that an increase in written communication can support students' rhetorical development (*Teaching Writing Online*), it also risks overextending instructors unless balanced with a strategic redistribution of workload.

Data in the more recent CCCC *2021 State of the Art of OWI Report* echoed findings on instructor workload from the 2011 study. The authors not only noted the additional time commitments for course preparation and day-to-day response work in OWI but also spotlighted the responsibilities of LMS course shell and multimodal content design, managing online "ghosting" and classroom community engagement, and handling larger class sizes sometimes given because physical space is not a constraint to enrollment (171–179).

To understand where instructors experienced increased pedagogical demands beyond in-person workloads, I asked the following: What were/are the biggest challenges you face/have faced in teaching WRITING as an online or hybrid course (select all that apply)? Among the 95 respondents, the five main challenges were:

- 76% – Creating/delivering digital content (e.g., video lectures, slide presentations)
- 72% – Organizing/sharing content (e.g., LMS modules, calendars, digital materials)
- 72% – Managing course logistics (e.g., announcements, student check-ins, tracking work)
- 67% – Building student community and interaction
- 62% – Interacting with students (e.g., emails, discussion boards, Zoom meetings)

With 80% of participants having six or more years of teaching experience pre-pandemic, their responses highlight the added labor involved in shifting to online and hybrid modalities. Though many reported improved pedagogy across modalities and lighter workloads over time, the initial added demands clearly contributed to instructor burnout.

Further, with 57% of respondents teaching five or more course sections and 56% teaching 76 or more students per semester, it is unsurprising that so many expressed frustration and weariness in their extra workload. Additionally, while respondents taught a range of professional writing, rhetoric(s), stretch composition, WAC/WID, literature, and creative writing courses, the majority (76% of 98 responses) had teaching assignments consisting primarily of the intensive workload of first-year composition (FYC). Nearly all of the contingent and part-time instructors taught FYC exclusively.

Comments reiterated the unsustainable strain such administrative scheduling and institutional policies placed on OWI faculty:

- "I've essentially changed every aspect of my teaching practices during the pandemic. Teaching 5 classes online with a class of 25–30 students [each] has created stress and burnout."
- "I have worked harder than I ever have before. The amount of resources I had to shell out for instructional triage during the first year online is astronomical."
- "At our university, caps were brought up during the pandemic. This added to the workload we were already facing. . . . To have more is to subtract time from any other student in the classroom or to add to our already underpaid and undervalued workload. . . Freshman composition classes are already intense in regard to grading of essays and with the changes made by the administration, I feel unseen and exploited."

Despite the varied workload challenges of moving writing instruction online, many respondents found lasting opportunities for professional growth and student success. As one shared, "Even though it was a ton of work getting up to speed with teaching online, I learned an immense amount . . . and I now use some of the technology when I teach in person because of the benefits." Another noted, "[b]ased on what I have said [in response to earlier survey questions], it may not be clear that I enjoy and appreciate online teaching and learning tools. I am a BIG fan and I am advocating for continuing offering courses in online and hybrid modes." It is evident from these and similar comments that while the transition significantly overburdened workloads, many ultimately recognized lasting benefits in OWI.

An Increase in Emotional Labor

The experience of teaching online during the pandemic not only included the usual pedagogical, technological, and practical writing classroom concerns but also an extended set of issues tied to the emotional workload instructors faced. As one respondent reflected,

> It's pretty general but it was hard in a way that exhausts me to begin to try to articulate. Students were tired, emotional, disconnected, and worrying about issues much more grave than writing for school. I felt like if I could create community, maintain attendance, have fruitful discussions, and get most of the assignments turned in, I was

a great success. Getting just those things accomplished has drained me beyond belief.

Others highlighted the complexity, anxiety, and isolation they saw students struggle with, the impact this had on students' participation in course activities, and the efforts they undertook to support student success. As one participant explained, "I found engagement levels stayed fairly level, but only because I put enormous effort into creating engagement, interactivity, and connection." Likewise, another wrote, "I was spending a lot MORE time with the students who were NOT thriving online, and almost entirely missing the students who were genuinely excelling."

Additionally, a number of respondents highlighted that they were "teaching through trauma" and working with students from "marginalized and oppressed communities who were adding covid obstacles to their already complicated lives." As one respondent described, the carework of attending to these students "meant they needed more follow-up and support" and more time "to vent about how covid was impacting their academic careers." And, as another reflected, this work required teaching "one-on-one during the most fraught days, not because of class content [but] rather [because] students are living through trauma and have additional responsibilities that supersede their classwork."

Even before COVID emerged, the work of attending to students' emotional needs through and beyond their writing was a component of many instructors' teaching practices. As Amy Flick and Sommer Streud contend, emotional labor in composition "is omnipresent in the work we do as teachers, not only in our relationships with or responses to students, but in the decisions we make as teachers, the pedagogy we employ, the professional and political structures we encounter, [and] the evaluations we receive from students and superiors" (43). Perhaps because writing courses are often among the smallest classes in which students enroll during college or because instructors engage intensively with students' ideas through multiple iterations of their work or because the field has increasingly taken up pedagogies that honor diversity and work towards anti-racism and inclusion, our courses are frequently ones where students build relationships and seek support from their instructors. Heather Robinson defines this emotional labor or care work as "the activities that academic staff undertake to support students' learning and . . . emotional health and academic advancement. Care work focuses on the affective parts of teaching, service, and research, rather than the content of what we teach" (87). However, she argues that the extra work instructors invest in providing this level of care is often unrecognized by institutions in workload assignments and reappointment, promotion, and tenure processes.

While many respondents noted online courses offered students flexibility and connection, nearly all mentioned spending extra time to keep students engaged. The following comment is representative:

> Online learning existed long before the pandemic, and it works for many students. . . . With that said . . . I had more students go MIA more quickly into the semester than was previously typical. Emails went unreplied to. Work remained unsubmitted . . . there were a lot of students who just stopped. Period. On a more personal note, this has been draining, it has changed me, . . . and I am still recovering.

It is unsurprising that the emotional workload of faculty increased during the pandemic. Beyond the real health consequences that resulted from the virus itself, it disrupted nearly every aspect of daily life, including living arrangements, employment, finances, relationships, mental health, and more (Salimi et al.). Instructors were on the educational front lines as students, some returning to less-than-ideal living situations, navigated these challenges. These concerns came through in students' work (or lack of it), their levels of engagement, and their communications with instructors. Supporting students during such challenging times added significantly to instructors' workloads and took a personal toll on many.

As Brett Griffiths, et al. report in their study of community college instructors during COVID, "[w]hile respondents described institutional support for acquiring and implementing new technologies, they described a gap in support for instructors navigating the increasing demand for emotional labor associated with student-responsive teaching adaptations" (66). Similarly, Kari Kono and Sonja Taylor highlight the essential role faculty played during the pandemic in supporting students in and beyond the online classroom. Several of their faculty research participants emphasized "rich discussions and deep connections that they felt with students," but also remarked that "one aspect of care that was challenging for faculty was the extra time and emotional labor involved in trying to meet the various needs for all their students" (160).

Qualitative responses in my survey echoed findings by Griffiths et al. and Kono and Taylor. As one participant expressed,

> I was so hopeful at the beginning that this [instructional innovation] would happen. I thought people would do the kind of re-seeing of their courses that online pedagogy invites. And I think they did. . . . But the main message I hear isn't that they are excited to have discovered new pedagogies that will inform their teaching moving forward, [it is] . . . that they are tired and they have reached their limits of compassion and flexibility.

While the emotional labor participants experienced in their online and hybrid teaching was surely intensified by the quick transition to emergency remote instruction and the unique circumstances of the pandemic, it is inescapable in the work of writing faculty more broadly. As we return to more "normal" times, writing programs need to be attentive to online instructors' emotional workloads and the ways in which they might need added support.

An Increase in Professional Development Workloads

A third theme that emerged from survey responses concerned institutional support and professional development. Just over three-quarters (77%) of respondents completed some form of online instruction training before the fully online fall 2020 semester. Although the majority engaged in this additional workload, not all training and support was equally valued by faculty and not all received compensation for participation. These varied experiences offer important lessons for writing programs and administrators in professionalizing online writing instructors, considering the labor involved in these activities, and sustaining online offerings and programs.

Perhaps because of the rapid shift online, about 15% of participants found any training helpful regardless of format. However, 85% of 89 qualitative responses about training experiences offered detailed critiques. Least helpful were tech-focused sessions that largely ignored pedagogy (especially those centered solely on the campus LMS), asynchronous modules without peer interaction, and workshops on lecturing, testing, or exam cheating— topics many respondents found irrelevant. A common concern was the lack of composition-specific support, particularly in areas like community building, peer feedback, and managing synchronous or asynchronous discussions. Notably missing from much professional development, especially in retrospect, was attention to the broader context of how the pandemic and evolving sociocultural conditions were reshaping learning. Many respondents felt training was rooted in pre-COVID models of "good" online teaching, with little guidance for adapting to the shifting realities of students' and instructors' real-time needs.

At the same time, there were many bright spots in professional development. As I have written about elsewhere (Sheppard, "How the Pandemic Changed Us"), about 25% of respondents reported that the best support they had came from colleagues either through formal department or writing program presentations or through regular online meetings to share experiences, approaches, and materials with colleagues in the discipline. As one participant noted, "The most helpful resource for me was the support and experience provided by colleagues. Meeting with them to discuss everything from structuring Canvas pages to utilizing new online tools was a life saver." Another highlighted the value of "workshops developed and delivered within my department by writing studies faculty" because of their immediate applicability. Regular meetings with departmental colleagues who could share pedagogical strategies and day-to-day activities and who could commiserate when things did not go as planned were also popular.

Two additional themes in professional development arose in the survey findings. First, many participants reported being un- or undercompensated for their participation in professional development. One noted that they felt "really under-supported by my university with regards to pandemic-era teaching. We've had paid professional development trainings, but the compensation nowhere near made up for how much more time I've spent working to design and deliver quality educational experiences." Another wrote, "[t]he little amount we are supposed to get for reimbursement is woefully insufficient. I feel massively discouraged." This sense of frustration with under-compensation for work completed to develop online courses and pedagogies was palpable and recurrent.

Second, several comments indicated that once the pandemic subsided, they were required to earn formal certifications to continue teaching online. This was particularly true for participants who identified as non-tenure track faculty. One of these respondents described the situation this way: "I wish our collective experience counted for something. I've been prevented from teaching certain classes because I don't have 'credentials' to teach online, despite having been teaching online since Fall 2020." As with the issue of undercompensation, the dismissal of hands-on experience and prior professional development fueled a pronounced sense of dissatisfaction among many respondents.

These recurrent themes of devaluing experience, undercompensation for professional development, and lack of access to OWI-specific training reiterate findings reported in the *2021 OWI State of the Art Report*. Summarizing some key findings, those authors note,

> Training and preparation continue to be a problem for instructors teaching online courses. . . . Most training still focuses on using the learning management system. . . . Twenty-seven percent of respondents indicated that they did not receive any training specific to OWI. A majority of respondents who did receive training did not receive any payment (59%), which is comparable to the 2011 Report. (9)

While continuing professional development is critical as we reflect on COVID-era teaching and as new instructional technologies emerge, the devaluation of instructors' online teaching experience and the lack of compensation for this labor was a repeated frustration. Further, it is clear that participants valued access to writing-specific online instruction training, as well as opportunities to engage with knowledgeable, supportive colleagues rather than more generic forms of training often offered at institutional levels. Writing programs and departments must be attentive to these issues in ways that are more equitable for all stakeholders moving forward.

Takeaways

As these survey findings reflect, emergency remote teaching during the pandemic deeply affected many writing instructors. While OWI offered meaningful benefits for students and instructors, respondents also faced serious challenges to their personal and professional wellbeing. These experiences, shaped by the broader context of the pandemic, highlight the pedagogical, emotional, and professional development workloads instructors carried, and offer guidance for future research, teaching, and administrative support in OWI. As both emerging scholarship and anecdotal evidence suggest, higher education has not returned to its pre-pandemic state[3]. We must reflect on these changes and adapt across all teaching modalities.

Reducing Workloads

While the pandemic itself contributed to heavier online teaching workloads, writing programs and administrators now have an opportunity to support faculty in implementing more sustainable practices for OWI moving forward. This is especially vital for instructors who primarily teach online and those who may still be coping with negative COVID-era experiences (CCCC Standing Group 16). Over the past three decades, distance education and OWI scholarship have promoted diverse, strategic pedagogies that leverage digital tools and spaces. This includes variations of group projects (Darby and Lang), student-led facilitations (Dunlap; Warnock and Gasiewski), tactical mixes of assignment types (Snart), cohort-based feedback teams (Sibo), and boundary setting around instructor availability (Borgman and McArdle; Warnock "Teaching the OWI Course"). Embracing these best practices can ease instructor workloads while enhancing student engagement and support.

Beyond classroom strategies, programs and administrators can support more manageable workloads by adopting collaborative faculty models. Lisa Melonçon and Lora Arduser promote a department-wide communities of practice (CoP) approach to online course development (82), though Hutchison cautions against inequities in compensation that may burden contingent faculty (13). Similarly, Jennifer Burke Reifman suggests three sustainable strategies for OWI communities: adopting a "take-one, leave-one mentality to sharing curriculum;" using asynchronous tools like Google Docs, Discord, and LMS shells to enhance flexibility; and decentralizing leadership so "responsibilities don't fall on the same people repeatedly" (slide 11). These and other collaborative models not only reduce individual workloads but also foster knowledge-sharing and provide professional support for navigating the emotional labor inherent in teaching across modalities.

Several survey participants highlighted the value of formal and informal CoPs when asked about the most helpful OWI training and support. They pointed to self-sponsored co-working cohorts, departmental workshops, mini-conferences, and ongoing faculty discussion groups as key structures. Many emphasized that OWI professional development must be collaborative and continual as new tools and practices evolve. In any form, CoPs offer a valuable model for distributing workload and enhancing the sustainability of OWI.

Acknowledging and Reducing Emotional Labor

Although emotional labor is a common aspect of teaching, it became especially acute during COVID. As Giselle Auger and Melanie Formentin note,

> During the pandemic, listening to students meant listening to their anxiety, their fears of the coronavirus, job insecurity for themselves or their parents, concerns about grades and getting work done, inability to concentrate, and in some cases, food insecurity. Meanwhile, professors had to be empathetic while dealing with some of the same anxieties, maintaining standards of pedagogy, and learning how to deliver content remotely. (377)

While the pandemic was an extraordinary circumstance, Flick and Streud remind us that "invisible emotional labor is and has always been present, regardless of newly emergent circumstances like pandemics" (48). This labor not only consumes time but also creates a need for self-care and collegial support. Elizabeth Kleinfeld calls for resisting notions that emotional responses to trauma and grief are unprofessional. Instead, she advocates for developing professional support networks and approaching work with flexibility, compassion, and patience to sustain the vital care work faculty perform (313).

As writing programs pursue systemic improvements, such as advocating for equitable class sizes and inclusive pedagogies, they must also consider how care work factors into faculty assessment. Robinson argues that "[care] work in the classroom benefits more than just the students; it benefits our institutions because it supports student retention and graduation" (97). Acknowledging emotional labor in faculty evaluations—whether for continued employment, tenure, or promotion—helps document and validate this work. By building supportive structures, especially for OWI faculty who often lack informal in-person connections, and incorporating care work into assessment, programs can better support instructors, students, and the long-term sustainability of OWI.

Additionally, as I discuss below, care work is often disproportionately shouldered by women and BIPOC faculty, who are also overrepresented among contingent instructors (Lin and Kennette). To address this imbalance within OWI workloads, programs should prioritize equity-centered professional development. Sustained, online-specific efforts that emphasize inclusive pedagogy and culturally responsive teaching can center the lived experience of faculty, challenge bias, and foster a sense of community and belonging. In turn, this can support the wellbeing and longevity of instructors and the sustainability of online writing programs while also enriching student learning.

Creating an Accessible and Compensated Culture of Professional Development in Online Writing Instruction

While strategies like reducing daily online workloads and fostering inclusive professional communities can ease pedagogical and emotional labor, survey findings underscore another critical issue: how faculty access and are compensated for OWI professional development—particularly contingent instructors juggling multiple campuses or seeking full-time roles. Melvin Beavers captures this in his study of WPAs, noting that this "work helped to solidify what research (e.g., Hewett and Martini; Bourelle) in rhetoric and composition continues to reveal, that professionalizing part-time faculty, especially those teaching first-year writing online, is essential to student learning, and those faculty members' growth as teachers" (154). Yet his participants also recognized the "ethical implications" of requiring (or even inviting) faculty to train without temporal or financial compensation, even when it could lead to more permanent roles (161). To address this, Beavers advocates for "administrative rhetorical mindfulness" which calls for inclusive, budget-conscious approaches such as asynchronous training, elevating overlooked faculty voices, and attending to how intersectional identities affect access to development and advancement (165).

Beyond financial compensation, WPA support for equitable and sustainable workloads should include giving instructors greater choice in teaching modalities where possible. This flexibility can ease course preparation demands, offer better control over time, leverage instructor strengths, enhance professional satisfaction, and foster long-term resilience by avoiding repetitive teaching in a single format.

Limitations, Future Research, and Conclusions

These survey findings reveal the impact of the unexpected, large-scale shift to OWI during the pandemic's first two years, with clear increases in pedagogical, emotional, and professional development workloads. Despite the valuable insights participants offered, the survey has notable limitations. In addition to a small sample size focused on a specific geographic region and institution type, the study was not designed to assess the disproportionate impact of the pandemic on BIPOC faculty. As Anuli Njoku and Marian Evans note, "COVID-19 has also exacerbated inequities among faculty of color, especially Black women faculty, as a microcosm of the larger social context," who faced heightened physical, mental, and financial challenges (1–2).

The survey also did not gather data on respondents' gender or its intersections with race, class, or family status. Stephanie Lechuga-Peña, in her *Testimonio*, describes the overwhelming pressure of being a woman of color, a parent, the partner of an essential worker, and an untenured faculty member who had to manage caregiving, teaching, and scholarly productivity during the pandemic (15). These pressures were compounded by the often invisible service and care work disproportionately expected of BIPOC faculty (Choi; Supiano) and by biased teaching evaluations—already a flawed measure of teaching effectiveness—that were further distorted by pandemic-era modalities but still used in decisions about retention, promotion, and tenure (Kreitzer and Sweet-Cushman 16).

Additionally, while the survey did capture employment status to contextualize workload, it did not link this data to gender, race, or class, factors often critical to understanding faculty precarity. Prior research shows women and faculty of color are overrepresented in contingent roles (Boss et al.; Lin and Kennette), and scholars such as Lechuga-Peña, Berheide et al., and DiMartino have documented how the pandemic intensified these inequities. The survey demographics capture a wide range of employment classifications, but the design falls short in including broader identity data necessary to fully understand workload impacts and the efforts required to achieve more equitable labor conditions.

While this survey revealed significant workload challenges, many tied to the pandemic itself, it also showcased significant benefits of online writing instruction and the care, innovation, and adaptability of faculty. Participants highlighted how synchronous, asynchronous, and hybrid formats supported diverse learners, offered greater flexibility, and expanded access for both students and instructors in navigating systemic and institutional barriers. These findings captured a pivotal moment in OWI and point to opportunities for writing programs to foster a more sustainable and inclusive future for online teaching.

Notes

1. In this university system, all courses were taught online in the academic year 2020–21. In the following year, some campuses stayed online while others implemented hybrid models or returned to in-person instruction.

2. For ease of reading, all percentages have been rounded up or down to the nearest whole number. Not all survey participants responded to every question.

3. Many researchers have suggested that higher education students, faculty, and institutions will not return to the status quo that existed prior to March 2020.

Works Cited

Auger, Giselle A., and Melanie J. Formentin. "This Is Depressing: The Emotional Labor of Teaching During the Pandemic Spring 2020." *Journalism & Mass Communication Educator*, vol. 76, no. 4, 2021, pp. 376–93, doi.org/10.1177/10776958211012900.

Beavers, Melvin. "Administrative Rhetorical Mindfulness: A Professional Development Framework for Administrators in Higher Education." *Academic Labor: Research and Artistry*, vol. 5, no. 1, 2021, pp. 152–68, digitalcommons.humboldt.edu/alra/vol5/iss1/9.

Beare, Zachary C., Jessica Masterson, and Shari J. Stenberg. "To Reimagine . . . To Start Again: Pedagogy and Possibility in the (Post)COVID-19 University." *Pedagogy: Critical Approaches to Teaching Literature, Language, Composition, and Culture*. vol. 24, no. 2, 2024, pp. 157–67, doi.org/10.1215/15314200-11030744.

Berheide, Catherine White, Megan A. Carpenter, and David A. Cotter. "Teaching College in the Time of COVID-19: Gender and Race Differences in Faculty Emotional Labor." *Sex Roles*, vol. 86, no. 7–8, 2022, pp. 441–455, doi.org/10.1007/s11199-021-01271-0.

Borgman, Jessie, and Casey McArdle. *Personal, Accessible, Responsive, Strategic: Resources and Strategies for Online Writing Instructors*. The WAC Clearinghouse/UP of Colorado, 2019, doi.org/10.37514/PRA-B.2019.0322.

Boss, Ginny, Tiffany Davis, Christa Porter, and Candace Moore. "Second to None: Contingent Women of Color Faculty in the Classroom." *Diversity, Equity, and Inclusivity in Contemporary Higher Education*, edited by Rhonda B. Jeffries, IGI Global, 2019, pp. 211–25, doi.org/10.4018/978-1-5225-5724-1.ch013.

Bourelle, Tiffany. "Preparing Graduate Students to Teach Online: Theoretical and Pedagogical Practices." *WPA: Writing Program Administration*, vol. 40, no. 1, 2016, pp. 90–115.

Braun, Virginia, and Clarke, Victoria. "Thematic Analysis." *APA Handbook of Research Methods in Psychology, Vol 2: Research Designs: Quantitative, Qualitative, Neuropsychological, and Biologica*l. edited by Harris Cooper, Paul Camic, Debra Long, A.T. Panter, and David Rindskopf. American Psychological Association, 2012, pp. 57–71, doi.org/10.1037/13620-000.

Cargile Cook, Kelli, and Keith Grant-Davie, editors. *Online Education: Global Questions, Local Answers*. Baywood Publishing, 2005.

CCCC Committee for Best Practices in Online Writing Instruction (OWI). *The State-of-the-Art of OWI*, 2011, owicommunity.org/uploads/5/2/3/5/52350423/owi_state-of-art_report_april_2011.pdf.

CCCC Executive Committee. *Principles for the Postsecondary Teaching of Writing*, Conference on College Composition and Communication, 2023, cccc.ncte.org/cccc/resources/positions/postsecondarywriting.

CCCC Standing Group for Best Practice in Online Writing Instruction. *The 2021 State of The Art of OWI Report, 2021*, Conference on College Composition and Communication, sites.google.com/view/owistandinggroup/state-of-the-art-of-owi-2021.

Chen, Yea-Wen, and Brandi Lawless. "'I Felt Too Involved in Something that I Didn't Know How to Deal with': Navigating Emotional Labor as 'Immigrant' Women in U.S. Academia." *International Journal of Qualitative Studies in Education*, vol. 38, no. 1, 2024, pp. 127–40, doi.org/10.1080/09518398.2024.2365183.

Choi, Minkyung. "BIPOC Women Faculty in Community Colleges and the Expectations of Emotional Labor." *New Horizons in Adult Education and Human Resource Development*, vol. 35, no. 2, pp. 104–07, 2023, doi.org/10.1177/19394225231117159.

Cicchino, Amy, Kevin DePew, Jason Snart, and Scott Warnock. "Global Efforts to Professionalize Online Literacy Instructors: GSOLE's Basic OLI Certification." *Composition Studies*, vol. 49 no. 3, 2021, pp. 101–17.

Creswell, John W., and Vicki L. Plano Clark. *Designing and Conducting Mixed Methods Research*. 3rd ed., Sage, 2018.

Darby, Flower, and James M. Lang. *Small Teaching Online: Applying Learning Science in Online Classes*. Jossey-Bass, 2019.

DiMartino, Gina, "Burnout and Work Fatigue in Contingent Faculty During the COVID-19 Pandemic." National Louis University, EdD dissertation, *Digital Commons*, 2024, digitalcommons.nl.edu/diss/830.

Dunlap, Joanna. C. "Workload Reduction in Online Courses: Getting Some Shuteye." *Performance Improvement*, vol. 44, no. 5, 2005, pp. 18–25.

Flick, Amy, and Sommer Marie Streud. "Am I Doing this Right: The Emotional Labor of Confronting Inequitable Writing Assessment." *Academic Labor: Research and Artistry*, vol. 6, no. 1, 2022, pp. 36–59, digitalcommons.humboldt.edu/alra/vol6/iss1/5.

Global Society of Online Literacy Educators (GSOLE). gsole.org.

Global Society of Online Literacy Educators Executive Board. "Online Literacy Instruction Principles and Tenets." 2019, gsole.org/oliresources/oliprinciples.

Goin Kono, Kari, and Sonja Taylor. "Using an Ethos of Care to Bridge the Digital Divide: Exploring Faculty Narratives During a Global Pandemic." *Online Learning*, vol. 25, no. 1, 2021, pp. 151–65, doi.org/10.24059/olj.v25i1.2484.

Griffin, June, and Deborah Minter. "The Rise of the Online Writing Classroom: Reflecting on the Material Conditions of College Composition Teaching." *College Composition and Communication*, vol. 65, no. 1, 2013, pp. 140–61, doi.org/10.58680/ccc201324228.

Griffiths, Brett, Lizbett Tinoco, Joanne Baird Giordano, Holly Hassel, Emily K. Suh, and Patrick Sullivan. "Community College English Faculty Pandemic Teaching:

Adjustments in the Time of COVID-19." *Community College Journal of Research and Practice*, vol. 46, no. 1–2, 2021, pp. 60–73, doi.org/10.1080/10668926.2021.2010623.

Hewett, Beth L., and Kevin Eric DePew, editors. *Foundational Practices of Online Writing Instruction*. The WAC Clearinghouse/Parlor P, 2015, doi.org/10.37514/PER-B.2015.0650.

Hewett, Beth L., and Rebecca Hallman Martini. "Educating Online Writing Instructors Using the Jungian Personality Types." *Computers and Composition*, vol. 47, 2018, pp. 34–58, doi.org/10.1016/j.compcom.2017.12.007.

Horning, Alice. "The Definitive Article on Class Size." *WPA: Writing Program Administration*. vol. 31, no. 1-2, 2007, pp. 11–34.

Hutchison, Allison. "Technological Efficiency in The Learning Management System: A Wicked Problem with Sustainability for Online Writing Instruction." *Computers and Composition*, vol. 54, 2019, doi.org/10.1016/j.compcom.2019.102510.

Jackson, N. Claire, and Andrea R. Olinger. "Preparing Graduate Students and Contingent Faculty for Online Writing Instruction: A Responsive and Strategic Approach to Designing Professional Development Opportunities." Borgman and McArdle, pp. 225–42, doi.org/10.37514/PRA-B.2021.1145.2.13.

Kleinfeld, Elizabeth. "Strategies for a Sustainable, Equitable, and Humane WPA Practice." *The Things We Carry: Strategies for Recognizing and Negotiating Emotional Labor in Writing Program Administration*, edited by Courtney Adams Wooten, Jacob Babb, Kristi Murray Costello, and Kate Navickas, Utah State UP, 2020, pp. 313–14.

Kreitzer, Rebecca J., and Jennie Sweet-Cushman. "Evaluating Student Evaluations of Teaching: A Review of Measurement and Equity Bias in SETs and Recommendations for Ethical Reform." *Journal of Academic Ethics*, vol. 20, no. 1, 2022, pp. 73–84, doi.org/10.1007/s10805-021-09400-w.

Lechuga-Peña, Stephanie. "Navigating Pre-Tenure and COVID-19: A *Testimonio* of a BIPOC Junior Faculty Mother." *Affilia: Feminist Inquiry in Social Work*, vol. 37, no. 1, 2021, pp. 13–19, doi.org/10.1177/08861099211048432.

Lin, Phoebe S. and Lynne N. Kennette. "Creating an Inclusive Community for BIPOC Faculty: Women of Color in Academia." *SN Social Sciences*, vol. 2, no. 11, 2022, doi.org/10.1007/s43545-022-00555-w.

Melonçon, Lisa. "Contingent Faculty, Online Writing Instruction, and Professional Development in Technical and Professional Communication." *Technical Communication Quarterly*, vol. 26, no. 3, 2017, pp. 256–72, doi.org/10.1080/10572252.2017.1339489.

Melonçon, Lisa, and Lora Arduser. "Communities of Practice Approach: A New Model for Online Course Development and Sustainability." *Online Education 2.0: Evolving, Adapting, and Reinventing Online Technical Communication*, edited by Kelli Cargile Cook and Keith Grant-Davie, Baywood Publishing Company, 2013, pp. 73–90.

Melonçon, Lisa, and Heidi Harris. "Preparing Students for OWI." Hewett and DePew, pp. 411–38, doi.org/10.37514/PER-B.2015.0650.2.13.

Njoku, Anuli, and Marian Evans. "Black Women Faculty and Administrators Navigating COVID-19, Social Unrest, and Academia: Challenges and Strategies." *International Journal of Environmental Research and Public Health*, vol. 19, no. 4, 2022, doi.org/10.3390/ijerph19042220.

Online Writing Instruction Community (OWIC). owicommunity.org/.

Reifman, Jennifer Burke. "Sustaining Communities of Practice for OWIs: Emphasizing a Distributed System for Self-Care." *The Online Writing Instruction Community OWI Symposium*, 2021, owicommunity.org/uploads/5/2/3/5/52350423/01_jennifer_burke_reifman.pdf.

Robinson, Heather. M. "Time, Care, and Faculty Working Conditions." *Transformations: Change Work across Writing Programs, Pedagogies, and Practices*, edited by Holly Hassel and Kristi Cole, Utah State UP, 2021, pp. 87–104.

Salimi, Nahal, Bryan Gere, William Talley, and Bridget Irioogbea. "College Students Mental Health Challenges: Concerns and Considerations in the COVID-19 Pandemic." *Journal of College Student Psychotherapy*, vol. 37, no. 1, 2021, pp. 39–51, doi.org/10.1080/87568225.2021.1890298.

Sheppard, Jennifer. "How the Pandemic Changed Us: Training, Technologies, and Pedagogies in Covid-Era Online Writing Instruction." *Computers and Composition Online*, Spring 2023, cconlinejournal.org/dec_2022/sheppard_pandemic_owi_cco_site/index.html.

—. "Pandemic Pedagogy: What We Learned from the Sudden Transition to Online Teaching and How It Can Help Us Prepare to Teach Writing in an Uncertain Future." *Composition Studies*, vol. 49, no. 1, 2021, pp. 60–83.

Sibo, Alex. "The Literacy Load Is Too Damn High! A PARS Approach to Cohort-Based Discussion." Borgman and McArdle, pp. 71–81, doi.org/10.37514/PRA-B.2021.1145.2.04.

Snart, Jason. "Hybrid and Fully Online OWI." Hewett and DePew, pp. 93–127, doi.org/10.37514/PER-B.2015.0650.2.02.

Supiano, Beckie. "The Uneven Burden of Identity." *The Chronicle of Higher Education*, 31 May 2022, chronicle.com/article/the-uneven-burden-of-identity.

Warnock, Scott. *Teaching Writing Online: How and Why*. National Council of Teachers of English, 2009.

—. "Teaching the OWI Course." Hewett and DePew, pp. 157–87, doi.org/10.37514/PER-B.2015.0650.2.04.

Warnock, Scott, and Diana Gasiewski. *Writing Together: Ten Weeks Teaching and Studenting in an Online Writing Course*. National Council of Teachers of English, 2018.

Xiao, He, Supuni Dhameera Silva, and Danielle Teo Keifert. "'I Gave it All, Who Gave it to Me?' A Qualitative Study of Challenges Experienced by Faculty During the COVID-19 Pandemic." *Journal of University Teaching and Learning Practice*, vol. 21, no. 1, 2024, doi.org/10.53761/hn9nmd88.

Jennifer Sheppard is associate professor of rhetoric and writing studies at San Diego State University, where her research explores online writing instruction, multimodal rhetoric, and professional communication. Her work appears in journals such as *Composition Studies, Computers and Composition*, and *Research in Online Literacy Education*, as well as in collections like *Designing Texts* and *Concepts in Composition*. She is co-author of *Writer/Designer: A Guide to Making Multimodal Projects* (3rd ed., Macmillan Learning). At SDSU, she has served as graduate advisor and associate director of the lower division writing program, contributing to curriculum development and graduate mentoring.

Course Designs

AI & Writing: An Experimental First-Year Composition Course

Laura J. Panning Davies and Kate Navickas

"AI and Writing" is a collaboratively designed first-year writing course taught at Cornell University and SUNY Cortland. The course, designed as a semester-long inquiry, invites students to explore how generative AI affects writing and writers. Students experiment with generative AI writing tools (i.e., ChatGPT, Microsoft Copilot, Perplexity) in class and read researched articles about the ethics of generative AI and essays that examine central writing theories of process, revision, failure, and authorship. The assignments move from summary and response to a source-based writing philosophy, a close analysis of the class's writing philosophies, a researched op-ed argument, and a final reflection. The course is an experiment in the truest sense: both of us feel a mix of curiosity and skepticism about generative AI. We deliberately made room in the course for students to experiment with evolving generative AI technologies and explore emerging arguments, policies, and conversations about generative AI in writing studies. A central goal of this first-year writing course is to foster a critical AI literacy that helps students use generative AI ethically while also gaining knowledge about writing, writing and research practices, and their own writing and research identities.

Institutional Context

One novel aspect of this course is that we are teaching it to first-year writers in two very different institutional contexts: an Ivy League university and a public state regional university. These institutions, just twenty miles apart, have distinct missions and student populations, and we plan to further research how these institutional contexts affect students' perceptions of how generative AI affects writing and writers.

WRIT 1370, Kate's version of the course, is taught within the Knight Institute for Writing in the Disciplines at Cornell University. At Cornell, all first-year students are required to take at least one first-year writing seminar (FWS). Each fall, the Knight Institute offers over 200 FWS sections that are taught primarily by trained graduate students as well as faculty. WRIT 1370 classes make up a small subset of FWSes that are geared towards students who are less confident writers; these sections are housed within the Knight Institute's Writing Workshop program and taught by Knight faculty. While not institutionally labeled as a basic writing course, WRIT 1370 has a course cap of 12 students and more required conferences in order to better support students. About 70% of students self-select into WRIT 1370 with the help of several email and LMS notifications about the ways the course is different from a traditional FWS. The remaining 30% typically come through directed self-placement measures, including faculty conferences with students who seem to be struggling with the first few weeks of their FWS; we accept students into this class up to three weeks into the semester. With such a small class size and conferences with all students at least once a unit, WRIT 1370 supports students throughout the writing process with more one-on-one help, explicit attention to how writing works, and more flexibility (e.g., when necessary, lessening the assignment expectations for one student and meeting more regularly in conferences; or, working more closely with students one-on-one when significant absences occur).

Laura teaches at SUNY Cortland, a regional public state university in the State University of New York system (SUNY). She taught her version of the course in two different first-year writing courses at SUNY Cortland: CPN 100 (Writing Studies I) and ENG 110 (Introduction to Inquiry). CPN 100 is the first course in SUNY Cortland's required two-semester first-year writing sequence, and it has a course cap of 22 students. Students admitted to SUNY Cortland's honors program take ENG 110 in lieu of the two-semester first-year writing sequence (CPN 100 and CPN 101). ENG 110's course cap is 15 students. Both CPN 100 and ENG 110 fulfill students' SUNY general education requirement for written communication. The outcomes from both courses draw on the WPA Outcomes Statement for First-Year Composition (3.0), and both courses ask students to read complex, source-based texts and compose research-based arguments in a range of academic and public genres. The courses are designed as writing studios: students have daily reading and writing work; participate in whole-class and small-group reading, drafting, and revising workshops during class; and attend at least one individual conference with the instructor during the semester. Students' work is evaluated using a grading agreement that prioritizes revision, participation, experimentation, and students' growth as writers and readers.

Throughout the summer and fall 2024 semester, we met every two to three weeks, checking in about how students were engaging with the content, sharing and brainstorming plans for activities, and reflecting on challenges that arose. While these meetings became less frequent mid-semester, we found them to be uplifting, supportive, and fun. As experienced teachers, we rarely get the opportunity to brainstorm specific lesson plans with someone doing the same thing, especially at another institution. For this alone, we recommend collaborating with more colleagues on courses!

Theoretical Rationale

We sketched out the first draft of this course while waiting for our flights home at the Spokane International Airport after the 2024 Conference on College Composition and Communication. The day before, we both attended the panel "An Abundance of Humanity: Teaching Writing in the Age of Generative AI," composed of four University of Southern California professors reflecting on how generative AI writing technologies have impacted their teaching and their students' learning (Bankard, Clements, Condon, and McNiff). Jim Clements' provocative final talk of the panel, "There Are Positive Uses of ChatGPT (But It Doesn't Matter)," seized our attention. His presentation, based on students' written reflections of their experiences using generative AI, highlighted key differences between how students understood writing (as a way to gather and transcribe information for outside readers) and how the field talks about writing (as a way to do complex thinking and create new ideas). Our initial course design was in response to Clements' talk and the entire USC panel: instead of asking students to use generative AI for a single assignment or unit, as many on the USC panel did, we wondered what would happen if we created an entire course focused on generative AI and writing. If students were immersed in the field's conversations about the writing process, revision, failure, and authorship, would they respond differently to generative AI writing technologies?

Certainly, "An Abundance of Humanity: Teaching Writing in the Age of Generative AI" functioned as both exigence and motivation for our course design. By bringing in more explicit discussions of writing and learning in our course, we hoped to address the main critique discussed at that panel: students using generative AI did not value the writing process or understand the relationship between writing and critical thinking. Yet we believe that the assignment sequence we created sets this course apart from other courses focused on generative AI and writing. This assignment sequence asks students to create, curate, and analyze a class set of data; to practice sustained revision; and to explore writing theories and research in the spirit of the "writing-about-writing" pedagogical tradition (Downs and Wardle, "Teaching about Writing"). The assignment sequence positions students as active participants in the disciplinary conversation about how generative AI affects writers and writing—a conversation we argue is missing the perspective of students, especially first-year writers.[1]

Use of Student-Created Data to Notice Trends and Make Arguments

The component of this class that we are most excited about is the use of class-created data, which we facilitate in two specific ways: through the Writing Philosophies Case Study (Assignment 4) and by requiring students to use their in-class experiments with generative AI as evidence in their Writing Philosophies (Assignment 3) and Op-Ed (Assignment 5). In Assignment 3, every student composed their own writing philosophy in which they cited shared course readings and specific in-class activities during which they experimented with generative AI tools. In Assignment 4, students read and analyzed the entire class set of writing philosophies. First, students read the entire set and noticed basic similarities and differences (e.g., How many of your peers find writing with generative AI ethical or unethical? Can we categorize reasons?). Then, each student created a smaller data set to work from; we recommend 3–6 writing philosophies to start. We use *Writing Analytically's* tool "The Method" to help deepen students' analyses (Rosenwasser and Stephen). Within this smaller curated set, students located one interesting trend to analyze.

Also, as is briefly referenced in the included course calendar, students experimented with writing and generative AI tools at least once a week. Students worked in groups or as a full class to compose prompts in order to use generative AI tools for parts of the writing process. For example, students took a paragraph from a draft they had written and asked a generative AI writing tool different prompts, such as "edit this," "elevate the language," "act like a tutor," or "revise this." As a class, we read examples from students' in-class experimentation and reflected on what the generative AI tool did, the process and success of prompt revisions, and the ethics of each particular prompt. Students were then asked to use both forms of data—the Writing Philosophies Case Study (Assignment 4) and the generative AI in-class experiments—with outside sources to compose an Op-Ed, a public-facing argument, about an AI issue of their choice (Assignment 5).

The use of student-created data in these assignments is supported by calls to include primary research in first-year composition courses (FYC). Doug Downs and Elizabeth Wardle advocate for primary research as a "noteworthy feature" of their writing-about-writing curriculum. They write, "Conducting primary research helps students shift their orientation to research from one of compiling facts to one of generating knowledge" ("Teaching" 562). Likewise, Thomas Sura adds primary research to a writing course sequence to foster "more robust research identities." Such scholars advocate for limited primary research, like surveys, interviews, or small textual analysis projects. We hope the Writing Philosophies Case Study (Assignment 4)[2] extends this list by adding studying a class-created data set. Like other cases for primary research in FYC, we believe this assignment fosters greater student authority with their research projects and "mixes the personal and the public and values the imagination as much as the intellect" (Davis and Shadle 422). It is important that students see themselves as researchers, especially first-year students who are too often "excluded from conversations that result in the academic making of knowledge," as James P. Purdy and Joyce R. Walker suggest (24). Additionally, though, when students are working with their peers' texts as data, they tend to bring a different rigor to their analyses, careful not to overstep in their claims. We also noticed they are much more careful with references to the author; that is, they want to represent their peers' work in ways that are accurate, responsible, and even kind. Further, this assignment fosters community: students are excited (and, of course, nervous) to work with their peers' texts and to discover how others will use their own.

Sustained Revision

This course also draws on foundational disciplinary theories of process and revision. We see the course as an exercise in sustained revision: each assignment carefully links to the next, and students revise their thinking about writing, generative AI, and their own writing philosophies as they move through the assignment progression. This structure attempts to move students beyond seeing revision as a "stage" in a linear writing process and instead view the process of revision as more dynamic and continuous; as Ann E. Bertoff suggests, revision is a "dimension" of writing (21–22). This sustained revision helps students practice revision as expert writers, as Doug Downs writes, "revising, or the need to revise, is not an indicator of poor writing or weak writers but much the opposite—a sign and a function of skilled, mature, professional writing and craft" (67). This understanding of revision as essential instead of remedial or optional is a new concept to many first-year writers, and it often flies in the face of their past experiences with revision.

What we hope that students learn through the course progression is that revision does not need to be contained to a discrete writing assignment or task. Yes, students participate in peer review sessions for their assignment drafts, but the revision continues beyond that assignment in the entirety of the course inquiry. For example, up until the Op-Ed (Assignment 5), the assignments all draw from the same widening set of shared class readings and ask similar questions but from different angles. The quick first assignment asks students to summarize and synthesize three short passages from class readings they will eventually read fully and summarize in depth. This recursivity is intentional and important, as it helps students practice what "expert readers" do: students come back to a text over and over again, revising their understanding of the source itself as well as their own evolving ideas about how generative AI affects writers. The Writing Philosophy (Assignment 3) asks students to put these same readings into conversation with their own experiences–again, reworking their beliefs to put a personal experience in conversation with theory. Once they start analyzing their peers' philosophies (Assignment 4), students inevitably re-evaluate their own ideas within the context of the set of philosophies, allowing their ideas to evolve and be reworked to account for others' experiences and conflicting accounts. This scaffolding relies on asking the same questions in different contexts while adding new readings and outside experiences. Essentially, the inquiry revolves around one question: "What does it mean to be a writer using AI?" Extending the scope of revision beyond individual assignments gives students the "time and space for further consideration of a writing problem" (Downs 66).

In addition to their revision of their ideas about AI and writing, students' understanding of revision itself shifts. As we experiment with asking AI to "revise," we discuss what students and AI think "revision" means. Both typically understand revision, at least initially, as attending to surface-level features, including editing, improving vocabulary, and rephrasing sentences. Indeed, in Kate's class, students discovered significant differences in how AI platforms would revise students' writing based on their proficiency and strengths as writers; that is, Chat GPT would overly correct a bilingual writer's essay and seemed to struggle with revising a more experienced writer's work by randomly and unnecessarily changing out vocabulary. However, by reading Bertoff, Downs, Annette Vee, Sidney I. Dobrin, Sandra Jamieson, Collin Brooke and Allison Carr, and other writing scholars—in conjunction with the evolution of students' own thinking about generative AI and writing—we prompt students to reflect on what substantial and sustained revision is.

The sustained revision students practice in this course is not limited to writing: students are also asked to revise their preconceptions of what "counts" as academic research by continually revisiting their research questions and findings through the assignment sequence (Purdy and Walker 28). The research students do is not a narrow, step-by-step, prefabricated process of marching through library databases. Rather, the questions students begin to explore in the early summary and response assignments are made more nuanced and complex as they query their own writing philosophies, analyze the collective data they and their classmates produce about student perceptions of generative AI writing tools, and locate relevant public arguments about generative AI. The research students do through this assignment progression is recursive and dynamic—focused on activities, not source types or locations (Purdy and Walker 30).

Writing about Writing and Critical AI Literacies

We thought a lot about the "writing-about-writing" pedagogical approach to FYC (Downs and Wardle, "Teaching about Writing"). The hallmarks of that approach—its focus on asking students to conduct primary research on their writing identities and processes, to read and work with writing studies scholarship, and to engage in critical reflection as they write—are clearly present in this course. This is a course about generative AI, of course, but at its center, it is a course about writing. We argue that the decisions writers make about whether to use generative AI in their process are, at their core, decisions not about platforms but about what writing is for and how writing happens. These decisions depend on a writer's ability to reflect on their writerly decisions. This deep, systematic reflection takes practice and needs to be taught (Taczak; Harris). We ask students to practice this reflection throughout the course, but most specifically in the Writing Philosophy (Assignment 3) and the Final Essay (Assignment 6). In these assignments, we guide students to notice what they do as writers, where they write, how they write, and why they write. We prompt them to consider what exactly changes when they use generative AI tools, and how each tool—and their decisions about how to use each tool—affects their writing processes and writing identities. We believe, as Kara Taczak argues, that "Reflection is a mode of inquiry: a deliberate way of systematically recalling writing experiences to reframe the current writing situation" (78). We deliberately weave reflection throughout the course design to help students "reframe" and consider how generative AI tools affect them as writers, learners, and students.

Our decision to emphasize the power and necessity of reflection in our course is supported by the MLA-CCCC Joint Taskforce on Writing and AI's October 2024 working paper, "Building a Culture for Generative AI Literacy in College Language, Literature, and Writing." The task force recommends using metacognitive reflective assignments and activities to help students understand how generative AI (which they refer to as "GAI") affects writing and writers. They propose new learning outcomes for college students, and two of these learning outcomes emphasize the kind of metacognitive reflection students practice in our course. First, students should be able to "explain the reasons for [their] informed choices about using or not using GAI for reading, writing, research, and learning processes" (7). Second, students should be able to "monitor how GAI affects their development as writers" (8). Students in our course are doing this work through the assignment sequence and the in-class explorations and reflections on various generative AI platforms. We hope that the assignments, readings, and activities help our students become more confident and knowledgeable about their choices to use or not use generative AI in certain situations. Our semester-long first-year writing inquiry is punctuated by frequent, deliberate reflection that, we hope, helps students develop the "critical generative AI literacy" called for by the MLA-CCCC Joint Task Force on Writing and AI.

Our course, like many in the writing-about-writing tradition, treats writing as an inquiry and a process and offers an iteration of what it might mean to use generative AI writing tools critically. We want students to articulate the limitations of generative AI writing technologies and also develop clear ethical boundaries for themselves as writers as they make decisions about whether and how to use generative AI. Indeed, one of the reasons we were excited to teach a generative AI-focused course as people only reasonably tech-savvy is that we are curious, and we know students are, too. We think this curiosity and lack of "right" answers make the inquiry authentic. While we agree with others that there are some things we do know—like AI is here to stay (Dobrin), we need to work with it ethically (Dobrin; Vee), and we should not use it as an excuse to police students (Jamieson)—we also are genuinely interested in the possibility of alternative perspectives and what students will come to believe through some guided inquiry and study. We believe that one of the ways this course fosters critical AI literacies is through its writing-about-writing foundation. We lean into writing studies scholarship, explicitly pairing essays about revision (Bertoff; Downs), authorship (Anson), writing pedagogy (Vee; Jamieson), and failure (Brooke and Carr) with reflections on writing and student experiments with AI to write.

Critical Reflection

While, of course, our different institutional contexts do matter, they mattered less than we expected. Both groups of students from Cornell University and SUNY Cortland loved engaging with a relevant topic, developing an explicit understanding of how to use generative AI ethically, and experimenting with generative AI tools in their writing in an approved setting. In Laura's two sections (an honors course with 12 students and a regular FYC course with 15 students) class discussion was rich and engaged; whereas in Kate's smaller basic writing course with 10 students, the full class discussions (as is often the case in this class) were more limited, with students working better in small groups. However, Laura's students struggled to enact deeper revisions, while with conferences in each unit, Kate's students were more successful with revision. Both groups of students loved the case study assignment and the opportunity to read and write about each other's writing philosophies. Both Laura's and Kate's students struggled with the Op-Ed (Assignment 5), and we think it is because four to five weeks is not enough time for first-year writing students to conduct independent research successfully.[3]

As is the case with any course taught for the first time, there are many changes we would make.

Changes to course readings:

- Read Chris M. Anson's article on AI and authorship much earlier in the Writing Philosophies unit.
- Use a shorter excerpt from Bertoff's article on revision and assign it later in the Writing Philosophies unit.
- Find more short pieces in the ever-expanding conversation about generative AI and add newer generative AI studies from education and other fields (e.g., Kizilcec; René F. et al. 2024; Alvero et al.).

Changes to assignments:

- Ask students to keep formal logs of the in-class generative AI experiments and give students credit for these logs (in our version, students simply kept their own notes).
- Shorten the length of the Writing Philosophy (Assignment 3) to one page, single-spaced, to make it easier to use in the Writing Philosophies Case Study (Assignment 4).
- Consider cutting the Op-Ed (Assignment 5) and turning the Final Essay (Assignment 6) into a more substantial final paper that, similar to the original Op-Ed assignment, asks students to cite class readings, class experiments, peers' writing, and perhaps one additional source students find through their own library or internet research.

One of the challenges of this course was the number of assignments. The assignment sequence includes six assignments, which is more than Laura or Kate had ever assigned previously, and would be a lot in any context! While the number of assignments looks a bit overwhelming for both students and teachers, most of the assignments are really quite short (2–3 pages), and three of them did not require revisions. Two of the classes (Kate's basic writing and Laura's honors section) had very low course caps, and thus, the workload was reasonable. For Laura's more traditional FYC section, which is capped at 22 students, the workload was much more challenging, and it was hard to respond to student work in a timely fashion. The Writing Philosophies Case Study (Assignment 4) might be particularly difficult with a larger class size because students are asked to read all their classmates' writing philosophies. This task could be amended easily enough, though, by having half the class read the other half's philosophies and vice versa. We also plan to change the initial Writing Philosophy (Assignment 3) so that students write just one page, making the reading load easier and encouraging a more succinct claim. Further, the first two assignments or the final assignment could be cut. We value the way the current design builds writing skills, but we understand that different contexts might demand fewer assignments.

Another issue with the course design is one familiar to many teachers: the difficulty of teaching sustained, reflective revision. Although we designed the sequence to emphasize revision across the assignments, this reflective recursivity did not happen automatically. Laura noticed this issue with her students; some resorted to simple editing or tweaking their writing or ideas, while others did not pick up on the connections that link each assignment, such as the move from the Writing Philosophies Case Study (Assignment 4) to their own Op-Ed argument (Assignment 5). Of course, we recognize that actually doing substantial, sustained revision across an entire semester is quite challenging, mature writing work. Our experience with our assignment sequence in this course confirms the findings of Lindenman et al.'s extensive 2018 study on student reflection in writing. These researchers, who studied the written work of first-year writing students at the University of Maryland, found that the reflections students wrote about their writing process and decisions "did not result in substantive or effective reimaginings of their work," even though this revision was one of the goals of the reflection assignments (584). This finding is important not just for our course design but also for the recommendations of the MLA-CCCC Joint Task Force on Writing and AI, which proposes using reflection as a way to teach students critical generative AI literacy. Asking students to reflect on their ideas and their writing is important and necessary, but reflection alone is not the answer. A reflective assignment will not magically prompt a student to engage in substantial, sustained revision because this kind of revision is hard work—"a sign and a function of skilled, mature, professional writing and craft" (Downs 67). Revision cannot be just a prompt; it must be discussed, scaffolded, and modeled.

Notably, generative AI writing tools helped us model what revision is (and what it is not) in the course. In one activity, we asked Gemini and ChatGPT to "revise" a paragraph from one of the course readings: Bertoff's essay, "Recognition, Representation, and Revision." The results were eye-opening and, in some cases, laughable. The "revisions" these two platforms did were mostly surface-level rearrangements, condensing, and editing of Bertoff's prose, and all the outputs lost Bertoff's signature incisive and witty style. The discussion that activity prompted led students towards a clearer delineation between "editing" and real "revision." Another interesting pattern Laura noticed in her courses was that revising seemed more difficult for her section of honors students. These students had a strong and immediate response to Brooke and Carr's essay on the necessity of failure in learning how to write. Many had succeeded (and even flourished!) so far as writers who do not revise, and the mere thought of failing was disturbing and distressing. Substantial revision requires honestly assessing what is working and what is not, and this reimagining requires risk—a step perhaps too far for some risk-adverse high-achieving students.

Finally, a perhaps surprising challenge we faced is that it is fairly easy to create an anti-generative AI spirit in the classroom. The majority of the readings we assigned raised considerable ethical and pedagogical issues with generative AI, from its environmental impact to its inescapable algorithmic biases. Many of our classroom experiments with different generative AI platforms ended up with students criticizing the limited or inaccurate writing produced by the chatbots. We found ourselves regularly trying to complicate this narrative by creating experiments and prompt engineering that resulted in stronger generative AI-created output, exploring lesser-known generative AI platforms that do a slightly better job referencing some sources used in creating outputs, and finding examples of how generative AI might be a tool for equity for certain learners and writers.

While only two out of ten students in Kate's small class argued against using AI (for their writing philosophies), all of the students developed a far more nuanced stance on AI—many noted that while AI can overtake a writer's learning process, there are ethical ways to use it that tend to require reflection, knowledge about writing, and just as much effort as writing something on your own. In Laura's classes, a few students remained vehemently against using generative AI as part of the writing process; two students advocated for its broad use (both in the classroom and in professional writing situations); and the remaining students took a similar balanced stance as Kate's students, with many echoing the MLA-CCCC Joint Task Force on Writing and AI's recommendation that students need to be taught how to use generative AI ethically and responsibly. Overall, we believe that by pairing discussions of and experiments with AI with composition scholarship on writing, students do gain a critical literacy around AI.

Notes

We do have IRB approval to study and use student writing from this class; unfortunately, we don't have the space to report those findings here.

We would be remiss in not honoring that the Writing Philosophies Case Study assignment has evolved from an assignment designed by Tracy Carrick, Kate's colleague at Cornell University. Carrick teaches a version of this assignment in which students develop an edited collection in which they analyze their peers' one-page snapshot stories of food experiences, interview peers for bios, and write a collection introduction that synthesizes trends in the selected stories. Tracy and Kate have also taught the assignment focused on students' experiences with language.

Specifically with the Op-Ed (Assignment 5), students tended to struggle with finding a focused set of sources and developing an argument with some depth.

Works Cited

Alvero, A.J., Jinsook Lee, Alejandra Regla-Vargas, René F. Kizilcec, Thorsten Joachims, and Anthony Lising Antonio. "Large Language Models, Social Demography, and Hegemony: Comparing Authorship in Human and Synthetic Text." *Journal of Big Data*, vol. 11, no. 138, 2024, pp. 1–28. doi.org/10.1186/s40537-024-00986-7.

Anson, Chris M. "AI-Based Text Generation and the Social Construction of 'Fraudulent Authorship': A Revisitation." *Composition Studies*, vol. 50, no. 1, 2022, pp. 37–46..

Bankhard, Jennifer, James Clements, James Condon, and P.T. McNiff. "An Abundance of Humanity: Teaching Writing in the Age of Generative AI." Conference for College Composition and Communication Annual Convention, 4 April 2024, Spokane Convention Center, Spokane, WA. Conference panel.

Bertoff, Ann E. "Recognition, Representation, and Revision." *Journal of Basic Writing*, vol. 3, no. 3, 1981, pp. 19–32. doi.org/10.37514/JBW-J.1981.3.3.03.

Brooke, Collin, and Allison Carr. "Failure Can Be an Important Part of Writing Development." *Naming What We Know: Threshold Concepts of Writing Studies*, edited by Linda Adler-Kassner and Elizabeth Wardle, Utah State UP / UP of Colorado, 2015, pp. 62–64.

Clements, James. "There Are Positive Uses of ChatGPT (But It Doesn't Matter.)" Conference for College Composition and Communication Annual Convention, 4 April 2024, Spokane Convention Center, Spokane, WA. Conference presentation.

Davis, Robert L., and Mark F. Shadle. "'Building a Mystery': Alternative Research Writing and the Academic Act of Seeking." *College Composition and Communication*, vol. 51, no. 3, 2000, pp. 417-46. Dobrin, Sidney I. "Generative AI Bots Will Change How We Write Forever — and That's a Good Thing." *The Hill*, 22 July 2023, thehill.com/opinion/technology/4107998-generative-ai-bots-will-change-how-we-write-forever-and-thats-a-good-thing/.

Downs, Doug. "Revision Is Central to Developing Writing." *Naming What We Know: Threshold Concepts of Writing Studies*, edited by Linda Adler-Kassner and Elizabeth Wardle, Utah State UP / UP of Colorado, 2015, pp. 66–67.

Downs, Doug and Elizabeth Wardle. "Teaching about Writing, Righting Misconceptions: (Re)Envisioning 'First-Year Composition' as 'Introduction to Writing Studies.'" *College Composition and Communication*, vol. 58, no. 4, 2007, pp. 552–84.

—. "What Can a Novice Contribute?: Undergraduate Researchers in First-Year Composition." *Undergraduate Research in English Studies*, edited by Laurie Grobman and Joyce Kinkead, NCTE, 2010, pp. 173–190.

Harris, Joseph. "Revision as a Critical Practice." *College English*, vol. 65, no. 6, 2003, pp. 577–592. doi.org/10.2307/3594271.

"General Education Requirements." *The State University of New York*, 2025, https://www.suny.edu/attend/academics/genedreq/.

Jamieson, Sandra. "The AI 'Crisis' and a (Re)turn to Pedagogy." *Composition Studies*, vol. 50, no. 3, 2022, pp. 153–57.

Kizilcec, René F., Elaine Huber, Elena C. Papanastasiou, Andrew Cram, Christos A. Makridis, Adele Smolansky, Sandris Zeivots, and Corina Raduescu. "Perceived Impact of Generative AI on Assessments: Comparing Educator and Student Perspectives in Australia, Cyprus, and the United States." *Computers and Education: Artificial Intelligence,* vol. 7, 2024, pp. 1–11. doi.org/10.1016/j.caeai.2024.100269.

Lindenman, Heather, Martin Camper, Jessica Enoch, and Lindsay Dunne Jacoby. "Revision and Reflection: A Study of (Dis)Connections between Writing Knowledge and Writing Practice." *College Composition and Communication,* vol. 69, no. 4, 2018, pp. 581-611.

"Working Paper 3: Building a Culture for Generative AI Literacy in College Language, Literature, and Writing." *MLA-CCCC Joint Task Force on Writing and AI,* Oct. 2024, aiandwriting.hcommons.org/working-paper-3/.

Purdy, James P., and Joyce R. Walker. "Liminal Spaces and Research Identity: The Construction of Introductory Composition Students as Researchers." *Pedagogy: Critical Approaches to Teaching Literature, Language, Composition, and Culture,* vol. 13, no. 1, 2012, pp. 9–41. doi.org/10.1215/15314200-1814260.

Rosenwasser, David, and Jill Stephen. *Writing Analytically.* 9th ed., Cengage, 2024.

Sura, Thomas. "Fostering Research Identities in Two-Course Writing Sequences: A Curricular Perspective." *Composition Forum,* vol. 32, 2015, compositionforum.com/issue/32/west-virginia.php.

Taczak, Kara. "Reflection is Critical for Writers' Development." *Naming What We Know: Threshold Concepts of Writing Studies,* edited by Linda Adler-Kassner and Elizabeth Wardle, Utah State UP / UP of Colorado, 2015, pp. 78–79.

Vee, Annette. "Large Language Models Write Answers." *Composition Studies,* vol. 51, no. 1, 2023, pp. 176–81.

"WPA Outcomes Statement for First-Year Composition (3.0)." *Council of Writing Program Administrators,* 17 July 2014, https://wpacouncil.org/aws/CWPA/pt/sd/news_article/243055/_PARENT/layout_details/false.

* The syllabus that accompanies this Course Design is available on the journal's website.

Laura J. Panning Davies is professor and chair of the English department at SUNY Cortland, where she teaches in the professional writing, first-year writing, and English education programs. She is co-author of *They Say / I Say with Readings* (W. W. Norton & Co.), and her research investigates writing pedagogy and writing program administration.

Kate Navickas is director of the Cornell Writing Centers and teaches in the Knight Institute for Writing in the Disciplines at Cornell University. She co-edited and contributed to *The Things We Carry: Strategies for Recognizing & Negotiating Emotional Labor in Writing Program Administration* (Utah State University Press, 2020). Her work is also published in *Pedagogy, Composition Forum,* and two recent collections.

Composing from Desire: Third Places in the First-Year Writing Curriculum

Charissa Che

Course Description

Writing for Intercultural Communicative Competence is a themed course I have designed and taught to undergraduates taking English 101: English Composition at Queensborough Community College (QCC), CUNY (The City University of New York).

This course nuances composition as a social practice that when motivated by desire, can bring about greater awareness, of both the self and others. The high-stakes assignments—the Autoethnography, Podcast, Third Place Paper, and Third Place Remediation—ask students to position themselves within the course concepts of third places and intercultural communicative competence. In investigating either a familiar or unfamiliar culture, students identify a conflict or tension within it, research its origins, and consider possible avenues to address or alleviate this conflict or tension.

Institutional Context

As of the 2020–2021 academic year, 8.9 million students were enrolled in community colleges, accounting for 41% of all undergraduates in the United States (Columbia University Community College Research Center). Part of the City University of New York, QCC hosts students from 109 different countries as of Fall 2023. Twenty-eight percent of incoming freshmen are "non-native" English speakers; Spanish, Chinese, Bengali, Creole, and Punjabi being the most prevalent non-English native languages spoken (OIRA 13).

These students' English writing competencies depend on a variety of factors: some speak a language other than English at home; others toggle between multiple languages; some speak English more fluently than their first language. Other considerations include international *and* domestic diaspora, dialects spoken *within* their first languages, age(s) of language(s) acquisition, cultural attitudes, generationality, educational background, and country of origin (Che 196).

Theoretical Rationale

Intercultural Communicative Competence, or ICC, describes an individual's ability to communicate and interact across cultural boundaries (Byram). To have ICC means being a *sojourner* in a new culture: someone who unlike the superficial motivations of the *tourist*, has an earnest desire to connect with others whose viewpoints may not necessarily coincide with their own, and in so doing, bridge ideological divides.

Reaching ICC entails moving through these steps: Possessing an *attitude* of openness and curiosity; gaining *knowledge* of the culture, its practices, and discourses; developing the ability to *interpret and relate* to the culture; *discovering and interacting* in real time with members of this culture; and finally, achieving *critical cultural awareness*—or, the ability to navigate different cultures with an openness to different points of view.

Relatedly, for Kramsch, third places are "actual, imagined, [or] virtual" contexts, driven by an individual's desire to self-identify ("Symbolic Dimensions" 366). She cites the 2000s as an "age of migration, diaspora and internet communication" that "opened up various possibilities of the self in the real or imagined encounters with others" ("Multilingual Subject" 102). With the increased rate at which cultural information is circulated, individuals are better disposed to escape "from a state of tedious conformity" that one might immediately find themselves in, to "a state of plenitude and enhanced power" ("Symbolic Dimensions" 354). Having emerged from this epoch, *third places* is a metaphor that attempts to capture a process of positioning the self both inside *and* outside the discourses of others.

To note, third places serve a similar purpose as, perhaps more familiarly, *contact zones* (Pratt) and *third spaces* (Bhabha), in that they also offer an outlet for individuals to straddle multiple cultures and take advantage of the hybrid identities that spring from them. However, *third places* offers a more flexible and agentive take on students' identity and language practices. Whether in pushing back against an oppressor, re-inventing one's own identity, forging solidarity among fellow marginalized peers, or exercising one's identit[ies] on one's own terms, *desire* is the core motivator (Kramsch, "The Multilingual Subject").

While the third place theoretical framework is over two decades old, it takes on a renewed importance given composition pedagogy's move toward including nontraditional literacies amid a rapidly evolving technological landscape. Nancy Bou Ayash writes that while "the study of language difference and its complex negotiation in academic literacy learning and development is certainly not new . . . it has gained a renewed scholarly visibility at local and transnational levels." She cites "globalized communication technologies, changes in migration patterns, and the linguistic heterogeneity of literate individuals and their resources" as factors that have made our language resources "more mobile and fluid" (555). Similarly, Bruce Horner writes that "recent changes in the pace and directions of global migration and in global communication technologies" have laid barer than ever the myth of linguistic homogeneity posited "as the norm for either post (or pre-post) secondary classrooms, faculty, and nations" (296). Indeed, the rapid proliferation of digital outlets means that we are not only adapting to and studying the affordances of non-standard Englishes, or the jargon of different academic disciplines, or the terminology specific to certain hobbies. We are also constantly adapting to new and often niche forms of web-speak that imbue old discourses with new, hybridized characteristics.

Another exigency for third place-informed pedagogies today emerges from our polarized sociopolitical climate. The "big picture" underlying third places is to help one find their place within "a horizon larger than the self" (Kramsch, "The Multilingual Subject" 102); what Xiaoye You might associate with a "dwelling place," or ethos born from "a perpetual calling for humans to assume ethical responsibility, through thought and action, for bringing a sense of order and meaning to our lives" (36). In this current moment, when intercultural contact is often associated with one group's political, economical, and ideological domination over another, third places can blur the dualities of Self/Other, and Us/Them and recast intercultural contact as an opportunity for symmetrical means of knowledge exchange, in which all parties' linguistic, cultural, and social spheres can be mutually influenced (Kramsch and Uryu 205–206). In disrupting linguistic homogeneity, we also reveal the effects of linguistic colonialism, whose ideologies have been correlated with a decline in heritage speakers (Do 68). With this understanding, heritage language speakers who may have felt pressured to cut ties from their primary discourse communities in favor of the dominant English-speaking one, may no longer view identity as a choice between binaries.

While the literature on third places has been discussed in relation to the "language learner" (Kramsch, "The Multilingual Subject" 97), this article widens the lens to consider the articulation and expression of self-identities, rather than English competency, as the goal. Achieving English proficiency is certainly a pragmatic objective of studying students' third places; however, understanding and applying them in our own writing pedagogies have far deeper implications on these students' sense of identity and belonging.

With an understanding of ICC and third places in mind, the course objectives invite students to do the following:

- think critically about their own and other cultures by evaluating and synthesizing differing cultural norms, values, practices, and tensions.
- develop a "Sojourner" mindset in exploring other cultures through primary and secondary research, immersing themselves within a culture and its practices, and engaging in cross-cultural identity negotiation.
- engage in various genres of composition, including multimodal work.

Throughout, students engage in an inquiry-based process in which they reflect on a third place they inhabit, or one they are curious to investigate, and chart their growth in intercultural awareness during their research process.

Students are introduced to third places by reading and viewing texts like Cathy Park Hong's "'Bad' English Is Part of My Korean American Heritage," an excerpt from her memoir, *Minor Feelings*, and Jamila Lyiscott's spoken word performance of "Three Ways to Speak English." They consider the personal significance of the various third places they inhabit. They then read James Paul Gee's "What is Literacy?" and Ann M. Johns' "Discourse Communities and Communities of Practice: Membership, Conflict, and Diversity," and consider the discourses of their own third places: the role that power plays in them, their norms and constraints, and the ideologies that govern them.

Then, they embark on the first formal assignment, the Artifact Autoethnography, in which they use a significant life event and related artifact as a vehicle to explore one of their third places. A form of narrative inquiry research, the autoethnography combines elements of autobiography/memoir and ethnographic research (Clandinin and Caine). As both the research subject and researcher for the assignment, students are positioned as experts on their third places and can speak on the desire underlying it within an academic framework.

Students are then introduced to the concepts of intersectionality and ICC by reading excerpts from Kimberlé Crenshaw's *On Intersectionality: Essential Writings* and Byram's *Teaching and Assessing Intercultural Communicative Competence: Revisited*. They examine intersections found in "How to Tame a Wild Tongue" by Gloria Anzaldua and "Voices of the Self" by Keith Gilyard. Students visually represent their various intersectional identities and their associated discourses with Discourse Community Mind Maps, then use them to converse with a peer whose discourse communities are seemingly disparate from their own. This interaction, subsequent research on their peer's third place, and lessons on interviewing for qualitative research projects culminate in the second formal assignment, the Podcast Interview.

In the final two high-stakes assignments, students choose to research a third place that is either their own, or is unfamiliar to them, and metacognitively reflect on their shifting positionalities in relation to its practices, literacies, ideologies, and discourses throughout the research and inquiry process. Their work results in a formal academic research paper, and a Third Place Remediation piece, in which they multimodally represent their third place and present it to the class, a lay audience. This component is contextualized with an excerpt from *Toward a Composition Made Whole* by Jody Shipka and examples of previous students' work. This act of "translating" an academic paper for a general audience allows them to exercise their rhetorical flexibility across genres.

Critical Reflection

Ann, a first-year writing student at QCC, learned Spanish as her first language but considers herself fluent in English.[1] While she believes that being bilingual positions her for more job opportunities, she struggles with college writing given a rift between what she wants to say, and her ability to say it. "I can't put the words in my head on paper in a way that it conveys what I'm really trying to say," she writes. "Sometimes I don't remember the word in the language I'm speaking so I switch to the other language." Being able to speak more than one language allows her to translate from one tongue to another to best articulate herself, but this is labor that also poses its own frustrations.

Ann began to play *Animal Crossing* during the COVID-19 pandemic, amid increased isolation and anxiety. Players of the online game build their own virtual villages in which they and anthropomorphic animals can go fishing, hunt for fossils, and socialize with other residents. This afforded her autonomy, alongside opportunities to foster relationships with fellow players. "*Animal Crossing* can be like a reset button, helping us to relax, socialize, forget about our problems, and freely express ourselves. . . You are the one who gets to choose how you will play the game, by the rules, or by using a little help," she writes. Additionally, aesthetic features such as "the soft yet catchy music, beautiful visuals, slow pace, and fun characters" have offered her peace. *Animal Crossing* fulfilled her "fundamental need" to relate to others during a time of solitude, and its effects remained post-lockdown: "Not only do video games lessen feelings of loneliness, but they can improve social skills that carry out to the real world!"

When it comes to college writing, the tug-of-war that Ann experiences in trying to "translate" her thoughts onto paper is a common experience of multilingual students. Eva Lam discusses Almon, a student who became too self-conscious about his "broken English" to speak up in class upon moving from China to the United States. Like Ann, he finds a third place in the virtual world, by founding a fansite for J-pop (Japanese-pop) singer Ryoko. Here, Almon is able to play the role of expert, friend, and even therapist to site members (Lam, "L2 Literacy"). As a result of engaging in a range of discourses (i.e., pop culture, religion, therapy, and netspeak) and genres (i.e., biographical, expressive, and narrative writing), Almon's confidence in his English writing abilities skyrocketed, as reflected in his improved writing in school.

Online environments possess unique affordances because they are immaterial, shared, and potentially ephemeral; yet, they permeate our experiences in the physical, "real world." Kramsch argues that the Internet has "diversified the modalities of meaning making" ("From communicative competence" 251), opening avenues for creative languaging among youths. "Many adolescents find in a foreign language a new mode of expression that enables them to escape from the confines of their own grammar and culture," she writes ("The Multilingual Subject" 101). The literacies of Almon's fansite and Ann's *Animal Crossing* can be viewed as "foreign languages" in which they find freedom in a new grammar and culture.

Manny, also a first-year writing student, learned Bengali as his first language, and is also proficient in English, Urdu, and Hindi. He feels his multilingualism allows him to get to know people of different backgrounds; yet, he adds, "I am not fluent [and] sometimes I face misunderstanding while talking with others." Like Ann, Manny faces frustration about not being able to adequately represent his ideas when communicating with others. His varying levels of language proficiency makes translating ideas challenging, and he often struggles to feel seen.

Unfailingly, he would attend class every day with a large pair of headphones around his neck, which he alludes to in his paper. "I believe music offers a very reliable pillar of support for people like me, people who feel alone. With society's integration of social media into everyday life, everyone wears a mask . . . I don't like that so instead of a mask I wear my headphones." Manny was in his late twenties at the time that he took my class, and this perhaps shaped his more ambivalent attitude towards social media, compared to his younger peers. His reflection recalls Kramsch's exigence for a third place framework: emergent digital technologies, while bridging communicative divides, are also causing us to rethink how we prefer to communicate if these new modalities *don't* suit our sensibilities.

Since the age of 10, hip-hop provided an oasis in which Manny could hear his experiences reflected in the lyrics of others. He writes, "I began developing a view of life through a very different lens, one that taught me the intricacies of what it means to be a minority in America." Although he has his own gripes about the genre's trajectory (he cites the progression of hip-hop, from the WuTang Clan and Biggie, to Jay-Z and Lil Wayne, to A$AP Rocky and Drake as something that left him "fiending" for "real hip-hop"), it was there for him through homelessness, mental illness, and drug addiction. "As hip-hop evolved it built a home for me in my broken house and this cold world," he writes. "I felt like I could always turn the volume up, tune out the outside world and tune into what peace feels like." For Manny, hip-hop was a lifesaving third place that helped him negotiate the challenges that came from being a racial minority while navigating the personal challenges that are "hidden" from the college classroom.

Through a sociocultural lens, hip-hop is also an opportune third place to invent and resist language, as seen from the global rap phenomenon in youth communities. Alastair Pennycook explores the discourse of the Japanese hip-hop group Rip Slyme, whose fans remixed Japlish (Japanese-English), AAVE, and self-referential "inside knowledge" into a new language, "raplish" (Pennycook 513). "Raplish" recalls Adam Banks' note on remixing as "an approach to activism and rhetorical performance" that synthesizes the "textual and technological" to "bridge old school and new school and print, oral, and digital literacies" (87). When viewed through this lens, remixing as a third place goes beyond metaphor and can inform multiple ways of composing to bridge linguistic and cultural differences. For Black students, welcoming third place discourses such as hip-hop, "raplish," and AAVE into the composition classroom recognizes diverse Englishes as artful. What's more, it can be seen as an Antiracist Black Language Pedagogy that fosters racial and linguistic justice: "consciousness-raising work" in which students can "make sense of, name, investigate, and dismantle anti-black linguistic racism and white linguistic hegemony" (Baker-Bell 6).

Willis is a student who recently moved from Hong Kong to the United States. Like Manny, Willis is dissatisfied with the societal and political norms in which he grew up and now finds himself among peers who do not necessarily relate with his experiences and views. Willis finds solace among the characters that he meets in *manga*, or Japanese comic books, finding a certain freedom in the "transnational discourse" of a culture that was outside of his own: "he was . . . associating himself with a third community of Japanese popular culture that does not necessitate any sociopolitical affiliations," observes Lam ("Border Discourses" 8). As Manny found kinship in the hip-hop lyrics, so did Willis feel that *manga* offered more relatable "everyman" characters through whom he could live vicariously.

Carmen, a white monolingual English speaker who grew up in the United States, is a gamer who plays *League of Legends*. For her paper, she explored the third place of *Dota II*, a similar online multiplayer game with a nonetheless "steep learning curve." As a female gamer in a male-dominated third place, she was accustomed to harassment when playing *League of Legends* and was curious to see if the same gender dynamics would unfold in this new third place. In conducting primary research, she watched others play *Dota II* on YouTube and was disheartened by what she found. "I noticed commentary that was very inflammatory and seemed exclusive of women," she wrote. "For example, one streamer said, 'She [a hero on the other team] had it coming wearing that (expletive) mini skirt.'" Her multimodal remediation was a video essay that depicted her experience with playing *Dota II* with a blend of photography, illustration, and graphic design, playing under her reading of a spoken word poem she had written. Amid visuals of the sexist dialogue she had seen used in her gameplay and drawings representing her feeling of isolation, she chanted,

"I want to be home." In immersing herself in this new third place, she had gained a renewed yearning for her old "dwelling place," *League of Legends*.

Evoking Kramsch, Carmen confesses her difficulty in reaching intercultural competence. "I cannot '[look] beyond words and actions and [embrace] multiple, changing and conflicting discourse worlds . . . '" ("Symbolic Dimensions" 356). "For me, interacting with . . . those who I don't understand or feel comfortable around is very difficult. That discomfort is one of the reasons why it took me so long to become part of the League community." While playing *Dota II* was "less toxic" than playing *League of Legends*, she ultimately decided to continue playing *League of Legends* because of the community she had worked hard to establish. Similar to Manny, she finds "peace" in being able to escape into her third place, even if she disagrees with some of its discourses.

Indeed, *communal* third places are not without their own constraints. Kramsch notes that achieving intercultural competence may be particularly difficult among Western cultures, citing the "American ideology of individualism" as something that "precludes any consideration that we might be 'culturally determined'" ("Symbolic Dimensions" 365). Yet we see this awareness in Carmen, who, while a monolingual English speaker who was born and raised in the United States, acknowledges the "culturally-determined" misogyny that often occurs within online gaming, as a female gamer.

On himself, Pennycook writes, "language is one of the things that *constitutes* my identity as a particular kind of subject" (514). If language is an ingredient of one's identity, writing pedagogies must consider how *multiple identities* work together in a student. In advocating for "the legitimacy of all language practices," we also advocate for the legitimacy of all *identity* practices (Flores and Lewis 97). Ayash elaborates on the potential of a pedagogy rooted in language multiplicity In demystifying language: "Interventions in language representations as themselves performative can take us forward by offering more nuanced ways of thinking about language use in academic literacies as embedded in rather than removed from the changing realities of our and our students' personal, professional, and civic lives" (574). There is power in using third places to inform writing pedagogies in that it disrupts the myth of a "truncated" student identity, such as that of an "English language learner," an "international student," or a student of a specific ethnic, class, or educational background. Third places consider students as full individuals.

Echoing Mary Bucholtz and Kira Hall's principle that identity is produced in linguistic interaction (585), Suhanthie Motha and Angel Lin describe language learning moments as "intersubjectively constituted, situated and co-constructed" (333). Writing assignments guided by a third place framework foster such moments to transcend prescribed "identity boxes," and can be instrumental in building solidarity, enabling creativity, and often, as a byproduct, improving academic writing.

At its core, the third place project asks students to reflect on their positionality with their chosen topic and metacognitively consider their experience throughout their research process. Reflecting on third places, whether our own or others', provides an insider's and outsider's perspective on what it means to be a member of a culture. With this self-reflexivity, students can gain a sense of greater rhetorical awareness, belonging, and empathy. Further, when enabled to "write themselves," students may be more inclined to see the merits of writing and revising as creative processes. Creativity, as Donald M. Murray writes, "requires a continuity of concern, an intense awareness of one's active inner life combined with sensitivity to the external world" (73). Third place-based writing, which encourages this insider/outsider awareness, is ideal for the cultivation of this creativity.

Research writing that incorporates personal writing also promotes pride in a student's heritage culture and identity in ways that conventional academic writing may not. Murray writes in "All Writing is Autobiography" that our goal as instructors should not be to "make sure our students write on many different subjects, but that they write and rewrite in pursuit of those few subjects which obsess them" (73). Soliday and Trainor argue for an "artisanal theory of composition" that puts spontaneous, "expressive instruction" rather than rules at the center of writing pedagogy, with the similar goal of helping students cultivate their self-identities in the classroom. By mobilizing technological resources, the authors write, instructors and students alike can feel less alienated by curricula and "abandon [their] institutional identities as users and clients to embrace more inventive, experimental, self-conscious identities" (144, 147). Similarly, Kramsch reminds us of the affective potential of third place writing among multilingual students in "capitalizing on the potential playfulness, heightened reflexivity and aesthetic sensibility of the increasing number of people around the world who, by choice or necessity, experience life in several languages" ("Multilingual Subject" 97). Shifting the academic discourse from efficiency and rubrics, towards the universality of play and invention may enable students to better navigate the tensions between constraint and creativity.

Drawing on Kramsch's initial exigency for third place pedagogies and considering the volume of digital third places found in the literature and my own students' projects, this course may incorporate more texts that explore emergent digital platforms as sites of identity invention moving forward. For instance, in *Writing About Writing*, first-year writing student Arielle Friedman discusses a Star Wars fan blog as a discourse community in "Galaxy-Wide Writing Strategies Used by Star Wars Bloggers." "Tunesmith Terror Techniques: Identifying Patterns in the Music of Horror Video Games" by Sean Kelliher looks at the discourses of Ludomusicology, the study of music in video games. "Cyberloafing: The line between rejuvenating and wasting time" by Chris Stokel-Walker examines the benefits and detriments of using the internet for non-work-related purposes while at work and can prompt thoughtful conversation among students regarding the function of third places *within* a first place. "How People *Actually* Use Their Smartphones" by Laura Haapio-Kirk and Georgiana Murariu is an approachable text that blends comics with essay writing to explore the conventions and uses of smartphones across cultures.

As we configure and reconfigure third place pedagogies in our classrooms for our present time, we should keep in mind that at their core is a resistance and critique of power structures. Third place and ICC pedagogies are inherently translingual in that they challenge English monolingualism, promote language difference, and encourage cultural exchange. As such, they cannot be divorced from conversations surrounding topics such as the role of race and racism in how language differences are practiced, negotiated, and recognized. Given current discourses of a "post-racial" society and "colorblind" racism, we should remember that to create a more linguistically just writing pedagogy is to create a more racially just one. To push back on English-only policies is to also challenge efforts in our educational and political institutions to codify and assimilate heritage language speakers to "White language supremacy" (WLS), which is based on a standardness that benefits White people while judging people of color as deficient (Inoue 357).

Therefore, translingual pedagogies are not without their risks. Ayash writes that attempts at "tapping into [diverse language] resources . . . get refracted through a monolingual structuring principle and regulated by the monolingualism of academic gatekeepers" (555). Despite the pushback third place-informed pedagogies may face from our institutions, our endeavor to decenter monolithic literacies and languages can only succeed if our students see their non-academic discourse communities as worth studying and possessing complex rhetorics, grammars, and conventions. As sites of invention, intercultural communication, resistance, healing, and community-building, third place-informed writing pedagogies offer a platform for linguistically and culturally diverse students to demonstrate their existing rhetorical dexterity within a culture that has systematically and ideologically privileged the rules of standardized English.

Note

1. All students have been given pseudonyms. Per my institution's HRPP (Human Research Protection Program) office, this study does not require IRB review as it does not meet the criteria of "human subject research," given that the data was not acquired via a "systematic investigation," but rather, a report of pre-existing coursework

findings. This work is considered a "Quality Assurance/Quality Improvement (QA/QI) activity," which according to section 5.5 of the CUNY HRPP Policy, are activities "whose purposes are limited to (a) implementing a practice that is expected, based on previous information, to improve a process, and (b) collecting and analyzing data regarding the implementation of the practice for clinical, practical, educational, or administrative purposes are not considered to meet the above criteria for research."

Works Cited

Anzaldúa, Gloria. "How to Tame a Wild Tongue." In *Borderlands: The New Mestiza – La Frontera*. Aunt Lute Book Company, 1987, pp. 53–64.

Ayash, Nancy Bou. "Conditions of (Im)possibility: Postmonolingual Language Representations in Academic Literacies." *College English*, vol. 78, no. 6, 2016, pp. 555–77.

Baker-Bell, April. "Dismantling Anti-Black Linguistic Racism in English Language Arts Classrooms: Toward an Anti-racist Black Language Pedagogy." *Theory Into Practice*, vol. 59, no. 1, 2020, pp. 1–14.

Banks, Adam Joel. *Digital Griots: African American Rhetoric in a Multimedia Age*. Southern Illinois U, 2010.

Bhabha, Homi K. *The Location of Culture*. Routledge, 2012.

Bucholtz, Mary, and Kira Hall. "Identity and interaction: A sociocultural linguistic approach." *Discourse Studies*, no. 7, no. 4–5, 2005, pp. 585–614.

Byram, Michael. *Teaching and Assessing Intercultural Communicative Competence: Revisited*. Multilingual Matters, 2020.

Che, Charissa. "Mind the (Linguistic) Gap: On 'Flagging' ESL Students at Queensborough Community College." *Writing Placement in Two-Year Colleges: The Pursuit of Equity in Postsecondary Education*, edited by Jessica Nastal, Mya Poe, and Christie Toth, The WAC Clearinghouse, 2022, pp. 191–222.

Clandinin, D. Jean, and Vera Caine. "Narrative inquiry." *Reviewing Qualitative Research in the Social Sciences*. Routledge, 2013, pp. 166–79.

Columbia University Community College Research Center. "Community College Enrollment and Completion." ccrc.tc.columbia.edu/community-college-faqs.html.

Crenshaw, Kimberlé. *On Intersectionality: Essential Writings*. Faculty Books, 2017.

Do, Tom, and Karen Rowan, editors. *Racing Translingualism in Composition: Toward a Race-conscious Translingualism*. UP Colorado, 2022.

Flores, Nelson, and Mark Lewis. "From Truncated to Sociopolitical Emergence: A Critique of Super-Diversity in Sociolinguistics." *International Journal of the Sociology of Language*, vol. 2016, no. 241, 2016, pp. 97–124.

Gee, James Paul. "What is Literacy?" *Journal of Education*, vol. 171, no. 1, 1989, pp. 18–25.

Gilyard, Keith. *Voices of the Self: A Study of Language Competence*. Wayne State UP, 1991.

Haapio-Kirk, Laura and Georgiana Murariu. "How People *Actually* Use Their Smartphones." *Sapiens*. 28 Oct. 2021, www.sapiens.org/culture/anthropology-smartphones.

Hong, Cathy Park. *Minor Feelings: An Asian American Reckoning*. One World, 2020.

Horner, Bruce. "Afterword: Postmonolingual Projections: Translating Translinguality." *Translingual Dispositions: Globalized Approaches to the Teaching of Writing*, edited by Alanna Frost, Julia Kiernan, and Suzanne Blum Malley, The WAC Clearinghouse, 2020, pp. 290–97.

Inoue, Asao. "How Do We Language So People Stop Killing Each Other, or What Do We Do about White Language Supremacy?" *College Composition and Communication*, vol. 71, no. 2, Dec 2019, pp. 352–69.

Johns, Ann M. "Discourse Communities I and Communities of Practice: Membership, Conflict, and Diversity." *Text, Role and Context: Developing Academic Literacies*. Cambridge UP, 1997, pp. 51–70.

Kelliher, Sean. "Tunesmith Terror Techniques: Identifying Patterns in the Music of Horror Video Games: Annotated Bibliography." Musicology and Ethnomusicology: Student Scholarship, 2021. digitalcommons.du.edu/musicology_student/103/.

Kramsch, Claire. "From Communicative Competence to Symbolic Competence." *MLA*, vol. 90, no. 2, 2006, pp. 249–52.

—. "The Multilingual Subject." *International Journal of Applied Linguistics*, vol. 16, no. 1, 2006, pp. 97–110.

—. "The Symbolic Dimensions of the Intercultural." *Language Teaching*, vol. 44, no. 3, 2011, pp. 354–67.

Kramsch, Claire, and Michiko Uryu. "Intercultural Contact, Hybridity, and Third Space." *The Routledge Handbook of Language and Intercultural Communication*, edited by Jane Jackson. Routledge, 2020, pp. 204–18.

Lam, Wan Shun Eva. "Border Discourses and Identities in Transnational Youth Culture." *What They Don't Learn in School: Literacy in the Lives of Urban Youth*, edited by Jabari Mahiri. Peter Lang, 2004, pp. 79–97.

—. "L2 Literacy and the Design of the Self: A Case Study of a Teenager Writing on the Internet." *Handbook of Research on New Literacies*, edited by Julie Coiro, Michele Knobel, Colin Lankshear, and Donald J. Leu. Routledge, 2014, pp. 1189–212.

Lyiscott, Jamila. "3 Ways to Speak English." TED video, filmed Feb. 2014, www.ted.com/talks/jamila_lyiscott_3_ways_to_speak_english.

Motha, Suhanthie, and Angel Lin. "'Non-Coercive Rearrangements': Theorizing Desire in TESOL." *TESOL Quarterly*, vol. 48, no. 2, 2014, pp. 331–59.

Murray, Donald M. "All Writing is Autobiography." *College Composition and Communication*, vol. 42, no. 1, 1991, pp. 66–74.

Office of Institutional Research and Assessment, Queensborough Community College. 2024. *Factbook 2023–2024*.

Pennycook, Alastair. "Global Englishes, Rip Slyme, and Performativity." *Journal of Sociolinguistics*, vol., 7, no. 4, 2003, pp. 513–33.

Pratt, Mary Louise. 1991. "Arts of the Contact Zone." *Negotiating Academic Literacies*. Routledge, 2012, pp. 171–85.

Shipka, Jody L. *Toward a Composition Made Whole*. U Pittsburgh P, 2011.

Soliday, Mary, and Jennifer Seibal Trainor. "Rethinking Regulation in the Age of the Literacy Machine." *College Composition and Communication*, vol. 68, no. 1, 2016, pp. 125–51.

Stokel-Walker, Chris. "Cyberloafing: The Line between Rejuvenating and Wasting Time." *BBC*, 7 Feb. 2020, www.bbc.com/worklife/article/20200206-cyberloafing-the-line-between-rejuvenating-and-wasting-time.

Wardle, Elizabeth, and Doug Downs, editors. *Writing About Writing: A College Reader*. 2nd ed., Bedford/St. Martin's, 2014.

You, Xiaoye. *Cosmopolitan English and Transliteracy*. Southern Illinois U, 2016.

* The syllabus that accompanies this Course Design is available on the journal's website.

Charissa Che is assistant professor of English at John Jay College of Criminal Justice, CUNY. She is associate editor of the *Journal of Basic Writing*, associate chair of the Two-Year College Association, and book review editor of *Teaching English at the Two-Year College*.

Where We Are: Teaching Writing in the Second Trump Administration

Composition in the Shadow of Campus Protests

Jonathan Alexander

The spring of 2024 saw numerous protest encampments emerge on university campuses throughout the nation and across the Western world. These encampments, comprised mostly of students and activists, protested US support for Israel's attack on Gaza and demanded that institutions of higher learning divest from any financial entanglements that might in any way be supportive of the Israeli government. Calls for boycotting Israeli academic institutions and engaging in other forms of sanction quickly came to be known as the BDS (boycott, divest, sanction) movement. Campus administrative responses to these encampments, which often took the form of occupying well-traversed walkways in an attempt to disrupt business-as-usual on the campuses, were varied, ranging from negotiations with the protesters leading to disbanding of the encampments to police actions, sometimes with startling force, to remove the encampments and squelch protest. Many students were suspended or arrested, facing serious interruptions to their degree progress; some faculty were also arrested and have faced disciplinary action on their campuses; and some administrators from prestigious universities were called before Congress to defend their campus's handling of the encampments and to face interrogations about allowing anti-Semitism to go unchecked at their universities. The crackdown on higher education since Trump's inauguration has only intensified, with the president withholding research funds and "fining" universities (as of this writing in the summer of 2025, UCLA was "fined" an outrageous $1,000,000,000) with demands to combat anti-Semitism by squelching all campus protests.

My understanding of composition today is inseparable from this political and historical context. If we understand composition as, at least in part, preparing students for literate and rhetorical participation in democratic structures, then such protests constitute a major and pressing opportunity to study, analyze, and understand the varieties and complexities of rhetorical engagement, debate, and embodied activity in the contemporary world. For sure, they are not the only ones available for study, but they are ones that are current and, often literally, right on our rhetorical doorstep—if not already in the house itself.

In "Rhetorical Education and Student Activism," Susan C. Jarratt and I argued in 2014 that protests, on our campus at least, were often co-present in educational contexts with the failure of university curricula to provide students with opportunities to study, understand, and experiment with varied forms of democratic engagement. In the absence of such curricula, students were frequently educating themselves on the rhetorics of such engagement, often inviting speakers and creating workshops to study forms of debate, activism, and protest. Our goal in writing the original article wasn't to advocate for a particular political position, but rather to point out that students were hungry for forms and platforms through which they could discuss, engage, and debate issues that were important to them. More importantly, part of my interest in these students' work was to begin to think through what a composition curriculum might look like if it took seriously students' desires for such political engagement. In my view, the recent appearance of encampments on many of our campuses only underscores precisely that same desire. And it is one that I think our field and our courses should be striving to fulfill, at least in part.

I do not have space in such a short piece to describe how such a desire might be met, but let me use what space I have to flesh out a bit more about why I have come to this conclusion.

Jacques Rancière has noted that politics often begins with a "groan," with an inarticulate but still voiced utterance that has yet to reach expressive content but nonetheless marks concern, pain, or problem. Many campus administrators across the country heard the groan of the encampments, often dismissing it or, if not wanting to dismiss it per se, then perhaps trying their best to avoid controversy, hoping the protests would simply go away. But I, with Rancière, might understand such encampments as the groans that are searching for a way to become articulate. They should not be dismissed just because the groan does not yet form a rational argument or cohere in ways that we, as members of an educational establishment, recognize. For me, this is where we in universities have failed to pay sufficient attention to and honor the groan; it is also where our discipline and courses might intervene and help our young people study and imagine forms of complex debate and engagement that turn those groans into generative claims, arguments, and actions.

Indeed, people often engage in protest when platforms for having difficult discussions have not been provided. Instead of actively providing those platforms, our campuses have typically instead enacted policies that, in some cases, have moved toward suspending students and then police action to remove protests, such as encampments. If these are our default policies, then they are failing to meet the needs of our students—and the needs and mission of our campuses as institutions of higher learning to make room for difficult discussions, for challenging dialogues. Composition courses seem precisely positioned in many of our curricular to underscore the value and even necessity of making room for difficult discussions, for engaging in challenging dialogues.

Why composition in particular? Let me begin to answer that question by considering the encampment on my own campus, which not only consisted of tents and spaces for meeting and conversation, but also had a library, a collection of books of interest in explaining both the focus of the occupation as well as the importance of the strategy of occupation. Books on a campus may not seem that odd, but the distribution of books—outside a library, bookstore, or classroom and instead directly on a major walkway from one part of campus to another and as part of an unauthorized encampment—is a call to rethink how we understand knowledge production, information dissemination, and debate. It constitutes a re-distribution of objects, namely the book, itself a metonym for knowledge production and dissemination, that signals a shift both in what knowledge is important and how that knowledge is shared. Indeed, part of the goal of many of the encamping protestors, on my campus and elsewhere, was to question what kinds of knowledge about the Palestinian genocide were being sanctioned and what kinds dismissed. Even the protestors' identification of the Israeli attack as "genocide" became a point of heated discussion and consideration—a consideration gesturing not only to a contested term but also to an academic apparatus of knowledge production that was frequently trying to control how the Israeli attack was being understood. Rancière himself notes that the occupation of universities often signals an attempt to "transform an instrument of reproduction of elites into its opposite—a forum open to everybody for discussion and for the invention of a non-hierarchical form of society" (101). While campus encampments might have not fully realized this kind of forum, despite good faith efforts of many in that direction, they still very often constituted attempts to intervene in discussions on campus about the attack on Gaza. Moreover, on my campus for instance, the encampment was one in which students, staff, faculty, and other protestors—including many Jewish-identified faculty—could find opportunities to share, exchange, and hear alternative thoughts and views.

At the very least, composition courses have the opportunity now to consider, study, and analyze why such forums emerged and how they engaged a variety of rhetorical practices to promote different ways of thinking. Doing so is not easy, or comfortable. In terms of the events from the spring of 2024, I myself was a bit taken aback by some of our own campus encampment's calls for intifada and the use of the phrase "from the river to the sea"—words and phrases that seemed to signal the need for violence. Others have talked to me since about how such words and phrases are actually calls for nonviolent agitation, but I understand how one might be confused. Indeed, that confusion is why we need discussion. Composition courses seem precisely positioned to consider the use of language and rhetoric in such circumstances. The goal of such discussions, to be sure, isn't to be partisan. But it is to take rhetorical action seriously and to value people's very deeply felt sense—and capacities—to shape their groans into positions, claims, and arguments. Honoring, studying, and equipping students to develop such capacities should be the point of our courses.

Of course, I offered a big "if" earlier—if we understand composition as, at least in part, preparing students for literate and rhetorical participation in democratic structures. I know not all readers understand composition in that way. Other colleagues are, not unjustly, deeply concerned with preparing students for a complex and ever-changing world of shifting (or vanishing) employment and career possibilities, not to mention preparing them for coursework in varied fields of study beyond the first-year comp requirement. But a failure to attend to the ways in which people—many of them quite young, many of them our students—are demanding opportunities to speak out, to foster debate, to provoke conversation, to experiment with rhetoric and to become powerful rhetors is to miss not just the opportunity of the historical moment; it is also to miss the opportunity to help prepare such students to create and fight for platforms and possibilities of free expression, meaningful exchange, and resistance to structures that would squelch such expression and exchange.

Ultimately, as I thought about the encampment on my campus, my feelings about it, students' varied responses to it, and our administration's ultimate clearing out of the protestors, I realized that the aim of the protest was not only to create unsettlement—an unsettlement necessary to call attention to the Palestinian genocide—but that, however committed our students are to the cause of the Palestinian people, this encampment was very likely also proxy for any number of other issues that we are not really talking about as a culture, or at least not substantively enough. And there are many issues we need to talk about, from climate catastrophe to the rise of fascism in our own country. But we aren't. We aren't talking about these issues on our campuses. And students are justly scared. They should be. Their world is on fire. Their protests in 2024, whatever their particular stated aims or goals, were a dramatic attempt to call attention to and demand debate about a variety of topics—not just to the immediate fires in Gaza (fires often literally caused by bombs that our tax dollars have paid for) but to the state of a world that is untenable, unsustainable, and even at times unimaginable. But we have to imagine it. We have to imagine it, and start seriously talking about it, with our students, our young people. To be sure, the composition course is not a course in which to adjudicate and solve historical, environmental, and political problems; I am not asking at all for courses in indoctrination of any kind. But I am making a case—and staking a claim—about a set of courses that absolutely should be committed to the study of rhetorical action in the world today. Our students need at the very least to be able to imagine that robust conversation and exchange about the topics that matter to them the most should be possible, even desirable. Anything less than such a pedagogical mandate for our field seems downright irresponsible, and our failure to address the addressability of contemporary issues with our students seems, frankly, unethical.

Works Cited

Alexander, Jonathan, and Susan C. Jarratt. "Rhetorical Education and Student Activism." *College English*, vol. 76, no. 6, 2014, pp. 525–44.
Rancière, Jacques. *Disagreement: Politics and Philosophy*. Translated by Julie Rose. U of Minnesota P, 1999.
—. *Uncertain Times*. Translated by Andrew Brown. Polity, 2024.

Jonathan Alexander is Chancellor's Professor and chair of the department of English at the University of California, Irvine. He is the author, co-author, or co-editor of over twenty books in the fields of rhetoric, writing studies, and sexuality studies.

"As Long as There's Fire," with Apologies to David Bowie

Ryan Skinnell

"I can't be a pessimist because I'm alive. To be a pessimist means that you have agreed that human life is an academic matter. So, I am forced to be an optimist."

~ James Baldwin, "A Conversation with James Baldwin"

As I write this in the beginning of the Fall 2025 semester, the University of California is grappling with Donald Trump's demand that they pay a $1 billion fine to settle an investigation into UCLA's alleged violations of Title VII of the Civil Rights Act (Kaleem). Brown and Columbia already bowed to the administration's settlement demands, and Harvard appears to be not far behind (Cantwell). The University of Pennsylvania agreed to ban trans athletes and vacated a trans student-athlete's records in several swimming events (Blinder). So-called DEI initiatives remain under withering attack everywhere (Student Basic Needs Coalition).

In addition to the Trump Administration's legal assaults on higher education, they've targeted higher education in other ways. Federal grant programs, including the National Endowment for the Humanities, have introduced American exceptionalism as an explicit requirement for funding and banned projects they see as promoting "gender ideology," "environmental justice initiatives or activities," or "discriminatory equity ideology" ("An Update"). The last I find particularly revealing—equity, in and of itself, is verboten in the federal imaginary. Trump also recently announced that grant application peer review would be overseen by political appointees and ordered that federal grants be made easier to cancel (Quinn). Of course, previously awarded projects in virtually every federal higher education grant program are already being cancelled ("U.S. Transportation").

As well, the Department of Education has been all but gutted. Smart money says it will be little more than a memory within the next year. The Secretary of Education, however, retains significant authority. Secretary Linda McMahon, formerly of World Wrestling Entertainment, recently issued a directive for the National Center for Education Statistics to collect information about race and/or ethnicity in university admissions. In a press release, she proclaimed, "We will not allow institutions to blight the dreams of students by presuming that their skin color matters more than their hard work and accomplishments. The Trump Administration will ensure that meritocracy and excellence once again characterize American higher education" (Office of Communications and Outreach). Her concern, which doesn't appear to have any grounding in the reality-based community, is that white applicants are being unfairly rejected because colleges and universities consider race and ethnicity in their admissions processes. She also recently announced $330 million in funding cuts for Minority Serving Institutions (MSIs) "that discriminate by conferring government benefits exclusively to institutions that meet racial or ethnic quotas" ("U.S. Department of Education").

And, of course, the Trump Administration has gleefully waded into one of the most contentious issues on college campuses to try and tilt the scales in his allies' favor. In April, Trump issued an executive order establishing an Artificial Intelligence Education Task Force and announcing a policy to "promote AI literacy and proficiency among Americans by promoting the appropriate integration of AI into education" (Trump). No doubt his interests are closely aligned with the economic interests of Big Tech CEOs who have been courting him since he was first elected in 2016. We might also speculate that he, like some of his allies, envisions a future with more machinic leverage over human and labor rights, though I'm not aware that he's explicitly said as much ("Why Are Big Tech"). In any case, needless to say, he's bullish on AI in the classroom and damn the torpedoes.

This is nowhere near a full accounting of the current onslaught against American education. The list of ways the second Trump administration has altered and continues to attempt to alter K-16 education could go on, and by the time this essay is published, this list may well evoke nostalgia for a better time. I hope I'm exaggerating, but whatever happens in the next few months and years, for better or worse, higher education will never again be what it was when I was a student, nor even when I was a young professor. The world has moved on.

This may seem an inopportune time, but I hope you'll permit me a brief tangent . . . as a reader and writer, I like litanies. The internet assures me that litanies are just long, tiresome, boring, repetitive, irritating, negative collections of grievances. Be that as it may, I like the way litanies accumulate heft by degree to demonstrate the magnitude of a thing. I'm reassured by Thomas B. Farrell's contention that "magnitude—in its myriad of manifestations—seems essential to the most important concerns of traditional rhetoric: namely, whether an audience may care about any topic sufficiently to attend to it, to engage it, and to act upon it" ("Weight" 472). Litanies, by way of magnitude, are part of our disciplinary inheritance. As writers and teachers of writing, we should pay them some attention.

As with litanies, so with lists. As Stephanie R. Larson points out in her affecting, award-winning book on rape culture, *What It Feels Like*, "listing doesn't seek to summarize or qualify the experience of violence but rather illustrates an enormity to a problem felt viscerally" (154). Lists and litanies structure information with the goal of making particular kinds of meaning. I like the way litanies and lists amplify the quantity of evidence in ways that Jenny Rice argues influence the quality of how readers experience information (68–70). Personally, I find the rhetorical implications intriguing.

I also like how lists and litanies clear space—at least potentially—for new ways of thinking in the face of inexorable accumulation. That is, litanies and lists both perform accumulation, but also provide a structure to information that can reveal critical patterns, aporias, or fissures. Larson contends, for instance, that #MeToo lists "inspired publics to understand vulnerability and fear from an embodied perspective," which in turn "reveals a kind of methodological hope in the sensations generated throughout the movement" (154). More specifically, the accumulation of Tweets about (mostly women's) personal experiences with rape and rape culture shook the common sense that sexual violence is primarily an isolated or individual problem. #MeToo lists literally reshaped how many people see the world. Similar effects can emerge from writing lists, not just reading them, too.

Now back to the matter at hand—the state of composition studies in a second Trump Administration. Things are, as the kids say, not good. But even as I articulate this most obvious observation, I'm called again to litany. Don't worry—this one is also really bad.

Just as a reminder, in the past half decade we've witnessed a global pandemic; an AI "revolution;" multiple wars and ongoing (and attempted) genocides; the widespread recrudescence of racist, classist, heteropatriarchal values in media and culture; the collapse of multiple global economies; an unrelenting, and rapidly intensifying, environmental polycrisis that Ira J. Allen pins to the whimsical acronym, CaCaCo (carbon, capitalism, and colonialism) (ix); and the global re-emergence of fascism, authoritarianism, and imperialism. Perhaps nearly as frightening, we cannot predict with any certainty where we will go from here, except to say, probably not back to "good" any time soon, if ever. Doomsaying of this sort is obviously scary and depressing, but I want to strike a hopeful note. It may also, I think, be a space of possibility, if we—by which I mean teachers of writing—can manage to discover what we have to contribute to current and future conditions.

A little more—briefly—on litanies and magnitude. Considerations of magnitude are not particularly abundant in rhetoric, less so in composition. The theoretical examinations that do exist are mostly relatively new—Larson's *What It Feels Like*, Christa J. Olson's *American Magnitude*, Rice's *Awful Archives*, Debra Hawhee's *Rhetoric in Tooth and Claw*—and they mostly trace back through Thomas Farrell's groundbreaking work on magnitude in the early 2000s ("Sizing" and "Weight") to Aristotle's work on *megethos* in *On Rhetoric* and *Poetics*.

In the latter, Aristotle says, "beauty requires magnitude, but magnitude that allows coherent perception" (*Poetics* 57). One effect of magnitude—of accumulation, of quantity, of heft—is that, taken past the point of "beauty," it arrests attention. Let me make this slightly less abstract. When something is too large to be perceived, humans find themselves overwhelmed and often frightened, maybe even paralyzed. In such circumstances, if they hope not to freeze or capitulate, they need to find ways of sensemaking in the face of overwhelming magnitude. They need to learn to refocus on what can be perceived—things that are smaller, closer, more manageable. Focus down, rather than shut down.

You'd be well within your rights to ask what any of this has to do with the question posed by the editors of this journal: Just where exactly are we? What exactly is the state and role of composition studies in the second Trump Administration? The answer, of course, is that we're overwhelmed and frightened. The magnitude of attacks on education, of seismic cultural shifts, of generative AI, of uncertain futures . . . it cannot be beautiful, certainly, for it is, in its entirety, un-perceivable. We literally cannot make it all cohere. That's the (really) bad news.

But there is, I think, (marginally) better news. In the face of overwhelming magnitude, as a rule, people do not stop perceiving. By choice or by force, we commonly re-focus on what can be perceived—things that are smaller, closer, more manageable. Lists, for example, or litanies, which you'll recall are a part of our disciplinary inheritance.

In 1512, Dutch humanist Desiderius Erasmus Roterodamus published his magnum opus, *De Copia*, subtitled *De duplici copia rerum ac verborum commentarii duo* ("Two commentaries on the twofold abundance of matter and words") (Erasmus). *De Copia* consisted of two books, both of which were concerned with the benefits and methods of abundance. Most famously, Erasmus described hundreds of possible variations of the phrase, "Your letter delighted me greatly," which has become more or less synonymous with "copia" more generally. At least, I'm going to treat it as such.

Copia is one of my favorite exercises to teach. I teach it in every class from first-year writing to graduate classes. It's delightful because students get to practice abundance, which they seem to enjoy, especially when they feel encouraged to use current slang: "Your DM rizzed me up, my dude." There's, like, laughter and stuff in the classroom, and no more so than when students witness my reactions to some of their variations. But I'm a teacher, so we can't just have fun for fun's sake. We have to think and talk about what we're doing and why.

By the end of ten or twenty minutes, we have an abundance of variations. It is too much for us to make cohere, so we gather to look for patterns, aporias, fissures. For Erasmus, the goal of abundance—of magnitude—is twofold. First, practicing abundance supports richness of style. Say things many ways to learn to say things many ways. Second, practicing abundance supports rhetorical invention. Say things many ways to discover how different choices open different options. In both cases, however, abundance begets focus and careful decision-making. Some might even say reflection, selection, and deflection. Erasmus did not describe copia as a method of learning to manage overwhelm and fright, but he did describe it as a method to avoid looking ridiculous, appearing tongue-tied, or boring audiences to death. We can extrapolate. I'm sure Erasmus wouldn't mind. Copia is a method for encountering overwhelming circumstances with lists and litanies. You invent as much as possible in order to discover possibilities from which you must narrow and select.

The point here is not that we can solve the world's problems with this one easy trick. It's that rhetoric and composition has theories and pedagogies for encountering magnitude. For instance, I learned important lessons about magnitude from my writing teachers. They taught me that readers need to be able to perceive coherently, which means that writers need to cultivate perception. I learned about signals and noise and how to draw and arrest attention. I learned about reading carefully to understand, not just to respond. I learned about restraint and about how refocusing on patterns, aporias, and fissures can help writers make things matter to readers (and themselves). This paragraph is a meta-copic exercise that I hope clears space for new ways of thinking about what we already know in the face of inexorable, catastrophic accumulation.

Lists and litanies offer but two ways of encountering magnitude, and they're not perfect. Listing the horrors, as I've done above, can actually be crippling. After I wrote the lists about education and the last decade of global catastrophes, I couldn't come back to this essay for several weeks. I genuinely didn't know how to make sense of what I'd listed. I'm still not sure I do, but the exercise did teach me some things.

The list of the Trump administration's attacks on education reveals to me that American education will never be the same again, which I suppose I knew, but not at the same visceral level before I started collecting them all together. But also, I remembered that the institutional structures most directly targeted are not synonymous with student learning, or even student access, necessarily. Additionally, while we can and should mourn the laying of waste, our colleagues have been telling us for decades, even centuries, that conventional education methods don't serve the vast majority of our students well. See, e.g., all the scholarship about antiracist and decolonial movements, all the scholarship about gender and feminism, all the scholarship about achievement gaps, all the scholarship about disparities in punishments for kindergarteners based on racial identity. You get the litany.

My earlier list of attacks on education, then, might reasonably invite us to new moments of invention that traverse realms of reconnaissance, rebuilding, subterfuge, sabotage, resistance, or retreat that already have roots in rhetoric and composition. I'm thinking, for example, of Vorris L. Nunley's "hush harbors," where enslaved Africans and African Americans gathered to practice banned religious and literacy traditions. I'm thinking of needlework that feminists used in the fight for suffrage (Goggin). I'm thinking of something as simple as changing a program's name so the crawling censorship bots get confused and misdirected. I don't know the answers, though I think some people are already inventing answers without us. Frankly, I don't think we're in any position to lead, much less commandeer, those efforts. But what I do know is that we are in a position, at least in modest ways, to help our students and ourselves refocus away from the whole magnitude—to apprehend it in smaller, closer, but meaningful ways. We have something to contribute that is not a solution, per se, but an offering. We might need to relearn what we know in this regard, but we are not defenseless or useless.

I'm compelled to make one final point about where I think we are: the magnitude of our current moment isn't (necessarily) partisan. *Everything* is too abundant at the moment—words, ideas, podcasts about crime, AI chatbots, peer-reviewed academic sources, obstreperous voices radiating from my electric teevee machine, TikTok dance variations, human rights abuses, thirty-minute recipes for boneless chicken thighs, Gen Z slang terms for having a crush, inescapable images of war and genocide on my social media feeds. We live in unprecedented abundance, and we need ways to make sense of it. The methods and pedagogies we have in the discipline may not—probably cannot—eliminate magnitude. But they are what we have that can genuinely help some people (ourselves included) encounter the world without freezing from fright and overwhelm. The modesty of our contributions must not be measured against the magnitude of the world's crises. Here's where we are: we need to figure out how to focus down to avoid shutting down.

In 2013, David Bowie released his first single in a decade. It was called, "Where Are We Now," eventually included on his penultimate album, *The Next Day*. "Where Are We Now" is a haunting, melancholic song covering themes including aging, loss, and regret. His refrain asks the question, "Where are we now, where are we now?" He answers cryptically: "The moment you know, you know, you know." Listeners could be forgiven for supposing that it's all too much for him to take in—too much to make sense of.

But resignation and paralysis don't appear to be in his plan. Bowie ends the song with a litany: "As long as there's sun, as long as there's rain, as long as there's fire, as long as there's me, as long as there's you." Listeners are left to interpret his meaning. In my interpretation, the magnitude of loss and regret can only really be understood, or even approached, by refocusing on what he can apprehend—that which he has learned to make matter. As long as there's fire, there is possibility. And at least for now and the foreseeable future in composition studies, there's still no shortage of sun, rain, fire, me, and you, even if the world has indeed moved on.

Works Cited

Allen, Ira J. *Panic Now? Tools for Humanizing*. U of Tennessee P, 2024.

Aristotle. *Poetics*. Translated by Stephen Halliwell, Loeb Classical Library, Harvard UP, 1995.

Aristotle. *On Rhetoric: A Theory of Civic Discourse*, 2 ed. Translated by George Kennedy, Oxford UP, 2007.

Baldwin, James. "A Conversation with James Baldwin." American Archive of Public Broadcasting (GBH and the Library of Congress), 24 Jun. 1963, americanarchive.org/catalog/cpb-aacip-15-0v89g5gf5r.

Blinder, Alan. "Penn Agrees to Limit Participation of Transgender Athletes." *New York Times*, 1 Jul. 2025, www.nytimes.com/2025/07/01/us/penn-title-ix-transgender-swimmer-trump.html.

Bowie, David. "Where Are We Now?" *The Next Day*, Columbia, 2013.

Cantwell, Brendan. "Exactly What Is in the Ivy League Deals with the Trump Administration—and How They Compare." *The Conversation*, 14 Aug. 2025, theconversation.com/exactly-what-is-in-the-ivy-league-deals-with-the-trump-administration-and-how-they-compare-262912.

Erasmus, Desiderius. *Copia: Foundations of the Abundant Style / De duplici copia verborum ac rerum commentarii duo*. Translated by Betty I. Knott, in *Collected Works of Erasmus*, vol. 24, edited by Craig R. Thompson, U of Toronto P, 1978, pp. 279–660.

Farrell, Thomas B. "Sizing Things Up: Colloquial Reflection as Practical Wisdom." *Argumentation*, vol. 12, 1998, pp. 1–14.

—. "The Weight of Rhetoric: Studies in Cultural Delirium." *Philosophy & Rhetoric*, vol. 41, no. 4, 2008, pp. 467–87.

Goggin, Maureen Daly. "Fabricating Identity: Janie Terrero's 1912 Embroidered English Suffrage Signature Handkerchief." *Women and Things, 1750–1950: Gendered Material Strategies*, edited by Maureen Daly Goggin and Beth Fowkes Tobin, Routledge, 2009, pp. 17–42.

Hawhee, Debra. *Rhetoric in Tooth and Claw: Animals, Language, Sensation*. U of Chicago P, 2017.

Kaleem, Jaweed. "'Uncharted Territory': Newsom and UC Go to Battle Against Trump's UCLA Sanctions." *Los Angeles Times*, 11 Aug. 2025, www.latimes.com/california/story/2025-08-11/newsom-trump-ucla-grant-freezes-antisemitism.

Larson, Stephanie R. *What It Feels Like: Visceral Rhetoric and the Politics of Rape Culture*. Penn State UP, 2021.

Nunley, Vorris L. *Keepin' It Hushed: The Barbershop and African American Hush Harbor Rhetoric*. Wayne State UP, 2011.

Office of Communications and Outreach. "U.S. Secretary of Education Linda McMahon Directs National Center for Education Statistics to Collect Universities' Data on Race Discrimination in Admissions." *U.S. Department of Education*, 7 Aug. 2025, www.ed.gov/about/news/press-release/us-secretary-of-education-linda-mcmahon-directs-national-center-education-statistics-collect-universities-data-race-discrimination-admissions.

Olson, Christa J. *American Magnitude: Hemispheric Vision and Public Feeling in the United States.* Ohio State UP, 2021.

Quinn, Ryan. "Trump Order on Grants Puts Politics Above Peer Review, Researchers Say." *Inside Higher Ed*, 13 Aug. 2025, www.insidehighered.com/news/government/science-research-policy/2025/08/13/trump-order-puts-politics-above-peer-review.

Rice, Jenny. *Awful Archives: Conspiracy Theory, Rhetoric, and Acts of Evidence.* Ohio State UP, 2020.

Student Basic Needs Coalition. "Attacks on DEI Programs Are Making Students Rethink Their College Choices." *Teen Vogue*, 16 Apr. 2025, www.teenvogue.com/story/attacks-dei-programs-students-college-choices.

Trump, Donald J. "Advancing Artificial Intelligence Education for American Youth." *The White House*, 23 Apr. 2025, www.whitehouse.gov/presidential-actions/2025/04/advancing-artificial-intelligence-education-for-american-youth.

"An Update on NEH Funding Priorities and the Agency's Recent Implementation of Trump Administration Executive Orders." *National Endowment for the Humanities*, 24 Apr. 2025, www.neh.gov/news/update-neh-funding-priorities-and-agencys-recent-implementation-trump-administration-executive.

"U.S. Department of Education Ends Funding to Racially Discriminatory Discretionary Grant Programs at Minority-Serving Institutions." *U.S. Department of Education*, 10 Sept. 2025, www.ed.gov/about/news/press-release/us-department-of-education-ends-funding-racially-discriminatory-discretionary-grant-programs-minority-serving-institutions.

"U.S. Transportation Secretary Sean P. Duffy Defunds Woke University Grants." *U.S. Department of Transportation*, 2 May 2025, www.transportation.gov/briefing-room/us-transportation-secretary-sean-p-duffy-defunds-woke-university-grants.

"Why Are Big Tech Companies a Threat to Human Rights?" *Amnesty International*, 29 Aug. 2025, www.amnesty.org/en/latest/news/2025/08/why-are-big-tech-companies-a-threat-to-human-rights.

Ryan Skinnell is professor of rhetoric & writing and director of first-year writing at San José State University. He has published six books, including *Faking the News: What Rhetoric Can Teach Us About Donald J. Trump* (2018) and *Rhetoric and Guns* (2022). He has also published more than one hundred articles, essays, and reviews for academic and non-academic audiences on topics ranging from demagoguery, fascist rhetoric, and contemporary political discourse to American education, bureaucracy, and faculty development. He is currently finishing a book on Adolf Hitler's rhetoric.

Composition Among the Ruins

Lydia Wilkes

It is the end of the world.

> —Richard E. Miller, *Writing at the End of the World*

Twenty years ago, the world seemed to be ending to Richard Miller. The future of the humanities required reckoning with violent events like 9/11 that jeopardized education as the best means for securing a brighter future. While schools endlessly counted the ways the world is ending, absent from school, he claimed, was training in how to build new worlds in which meaning-making practices like reading and writing continue to matter (x).

Miller certainly imagined a world in which those practices continue to matter. But I wonder if he could have imagined how much they'd be challenged and transformed in just twenty years. That voters would re-elect a charlatan who, as a wannabe dictator, promised to destroy public education as part of a Christian nationalist agenda. That synthetic text, image, sound, and video would threaten not only public education and writing as human endeavors, but also, through synthetic truth and AlphaPersuade, any semblance of a shared reality controlled by humans, and, through synthetic intimacy amid an epidemic of loneliness, the very human relationships that comprise a society (Center; "People").

To speak to the former, an academic friend asked me this summer whether I thought the university would still exist in fifteen years. Yes and no, I responded, as I considered the effects of enrollments at different types of institutions, their endowment sizes, rescinded federal research funding, dwindling public faith in the value of higher education, and culture war accelerants poured by high-ranking government officials on existing anti-intellectual, anti-science, and anti-higher education fires that have long burned in the US. I recalled that colleges were closing at a rate of one per week in 2024, often due to financial mismanagement (Marcus). I struggle to imagine the large public state universities at which my friend and I work, Ivy League universities, or large community college systems disappearing in fifteen years. But some regional comprehensives, smaller private colleges, HBCUs, tribal colleges, and HSIs? The outlook seems bleak.

Campuses that don't close may be transformed from bastions of free and critical thought and expression to citadels of far-right ideological training, as has happened at New College of Florida, the first instance of a state governor capturing a progressive public liberal arts college for far-right takeover (Dailey).

Prior to the takeover, New College was a place where a famous white nationalist could be exposed to other perspectives that led him to question and eventually renounce white nationalism (Saslow). Attacks on student protestors' freedom of speech and assembly from many campuses' upper administrations, followed by an array of punishments for those daring to dissent from US-sponsored genocide, remind us that many upper administrators do not share our commitment to free and critical thought and expression. Attacks on academic freedom do the same, with Texas A&M University firing a children's literature professor at the behest of the state's governor, removing the dean and department head from their administrative duties, and announcing a full audit of all courses across the A&M System after a student confronted the professor about teaching gender identity beyond the gender binary (Priest). Colleges and universities across the country fired employees for their speech on social media following the lethal shooting of the far-right Christian nationalist activist Charlie Kirk, rapidly eroding First Amendment protections and chilling speech in classrooms and online (Binkley). As several states implement anti-DEI legislation, the Utah state legislature has gone further by replacing first-year writing at Utah State University with a classical education model rooted in Western civilization that emphasizes the rise of Christianity, intended as a test case for the rest of the state and, should it succeed, as a national model for the far-right Christian nationalist takeover of curricula (Cabrera; Kurtz et al.).

Less than a month after that conversation, Congress passed a budget reconciliation bill that, among other things, limits student loan amounts to "use debt as a tool of social control," a clear attempt to deny all but the wealthy access to higher education and thereby resegregate US society (Taylor and Schirmer). Astute observers claimed the bill "may portend an extinction event for higher education as we know it" (Taylor and Schirmer).

Though he was keenly aware of education's many ails at the turn of the millennium, I doubt Miller could have imagined an extinction event for higher education. I doubt he, or most anyone else, could have imagined that large language models and GPT technology would pose an existential threat to humanity, as "50% of AI researchers believe there's a 10% or greater chance that humans will go extinct from our inability to control AI" (Center).

I wonder, what am I failing to imagine?

Even amid ruthless attacks on the post-World War II educational order, I struggle to imagine that my three-year-old niece won't have a college or university to attend in fifteen years. I struggle to imagine the university that employs me, or the colleges and universities that employ my friends and colleagues, crumbling wholesale in that time. I struggle to imagine an end to this world's business as usual.

It's tempting to anticipate a backlash against the current administration's attempts to return the US to the Gilded Age when literacy rates were lower and most people did not graduate from high school. As the administration hastens the ongoing transfer of wealth from poor to rich, part of a trend toward neofeudalism according to some political theorists (e.g., Dean), the pendulum swing from right to left may seem inevitable, particularly if we take twentieth century history as a guide: if the administration succeeds, "the counter-revolution they set in place could well be the defining trope of the 2030s and beyond" (Zeitz).

Perhaps that would be the case, and certainly it would seem to bode well for mass literacy, composition, and higher education in their present configurations . . . *if* we could count on a stable climate to keep providing reliable ecosystem services, among other things, like clean water and pollination. But we're already experiencing years with 1.5C of warming over pre-industrial levels as this world's business as usual continues to imperil us, our more-than-human kin, and the planet (Poynting et al.). Humanity has two to three more years of burning carbon at the current rate before we will lock the planet into 1.5C of warming, eventually causing "'catastrophic inland migration'" as millions of people abandon the coasts due to sea level rise (qtd. in Carrington; Poynting).

Overshadowing a possible extinction event for US higher education in 2025 is the sixth mass extinction of our more-than-human kin (Kolbert, *Sixth*). Overshadowing the possible collapse of US higher education is collapse itself.

It's the End of the World as We Know It . . .

Our present way of life in the Global North—the world as we know it— is simply not sustainable with the resources on this planet. While techno-optimists extol new technologies as solutions to planetary problems, such technologies do nothing to address the resource overconsumption driving resource scarcity and resulting crises like increasing inequality, democratic backsliding, war, famine, and much more. In response to resource overconsumption, these techno-optimists point to gains in efficiency as a way to mitigate that overconsumption, but when new technologies increase efficiency, increased demand results, a phenomenon known as the Jevons paradox. This happens because greater efficiencies lower prices and when goods and services are cheaper, people use more of them, further fueling resource overconsumption (Rosalsky). Infinite economic growth, our business-as-usual model, is not possible on a finite planet (Meadows et al.).

How much time do we have left with the world as we know it? A 1972 prediction by an MIT team, recently tested with contemporary evidence, holds up: collapse will happen around 2040 (Herrington). Just fifteen years away.

But this is misleading. It's not as though things will be normal in 2039 and in ruins in 2040. Rather, we're living now through a period of staggered collapse propelled by polycrisis or multiple intersecting crises that intensify and amplify each other (Allen ix). Staggered collapse is as much political, economic, and social as it is environmental: all these systemic aspects of our lives are crumbling unevenly, affecting people differently based on factors like wealth and location.

It's bad enough that staggered collapse is harming people now. Worse yet, far-right ideologues holding political power are accelerating it, simultaneously preparing for collapse and hastening its arrival so the chosen few can abandon this collapsing world for the supposed safety of a luxury bunker, floating corporate city, or terraformed colony on Mars (Klein and Taylor). The "end-times fascism" of ultra rich tech bros, MAGA isolationists, and Christian nationalists, all committed to apartheid and genocide to determine who deserves to survive collapse, seeks salvation through Armageddon (Klein and Taylor). This end game sheds new light on the trends that now comprise our reality: cruelty, exclusion, and necropolitics directed at surplus humanity (that's us) secure a future for the wealthy few.

So, is that it? So long to the university? So long to composition? So long to this world?

. . . And I Feel . . . ?

> Worlds end.
> And worlds begin.
>
> —Richard E. Miller, *Writing at the End of the World*

Pause for a moment. Take a deep breath. Look out the window. Better yet, go touch grass. Who's out there right now in the more-than-human world? Bees and butterflies and birds, though diminished in health and numbers, are still here. Plants and trees still nourish us with food, protect us with shade. The sky is still blue and not white, as geoengineering may one day color it (Kolbert, *Under*). The good, green Earth still cares for us (Kimmerer).

Maybe you're feeling despair right now—or hope, two common emotional responses to the magnitude of losing this world (Barnett, *Ecological*). Maybe you can't believe all of this will end so soon. Maybe you're grieving this loss before it happens, coming to care yet more for this achingly beautiful world, to act yet more to protect it (Barnett, *Mourning*). Maybe you're panicking.

Panic, according to rhetorician Ira J. Allen, is a "rational response to an unbearable reality" of polycrisis and collapse (28). Panicking now, while relative resource abundance and social stability still exist for many in the Global

North, is "a first emotional step in developing tools for humanizing" (29) as this world ends and billions of regular, panicked people invent new worlds. Laying the groundwork for such new worlds can (and should) happen now, but there's no guarantee those worlds will be better than this one. End-times fascists are, after all, hastily building new worlds on exclusion and dehumanization.

Allen's bet on panicking now, and doing so wisely, is for us to "invent ways of being human together" that give us "a chance at doing better than the worst" (29). Indeed, our species' survival "will take nothing less than the transformation of our collective ways of being in the world" (145). How we choose to act politically together now amid an abyss of uncertainty and risk affects who we will be in the decades to come, what sorts of worlds we might create.

All of this sounds daunting and exhausting to me. While I welcome the possibility of humanizing in the ruins of this world, I have felt stuck in what Allen calls the carbon-capitalism-colonialism assemblage ensnaring us all.

Yet, like Allen, I know humans have been remaking worlds for the entirety of our existence by trying on ways of acting together, discarding some, embracing others (Graeber and Wengrow). To take only one example, Native peoples of the Mississippi River Valley rejected a violent, coercive social order in favor of more egalitarian social relations that, hundreds of years before contact, they arranged their societies to protect (Graeber and Wengrow). While a habitable planet exists, we'll continue to reinvent ourselves, our universities, our meaning-making practices, and our worlds—for better or worse.

Composition Among the Ruins

All of this may seem completely removed from your next class meeting. But if staggered collapse hasn't reached you or your students yet, it will.

When collapse does arrive, it's tempting to think that we'll somehow escape capitalism's clutches, but the harsh reality is that "[w]e're stuck in the worst-case scenario where the world ends but we still have to go to work" (Wildfire). That work may look different, but assuming something like higher education still exists in fifteen years—a safe assumption, I think—what might composition among the ruins of this world do?

If a far-right order prevails, we can engage in malicious compliance with it while carving out refuges for free thought, feeling, and being together, for imagining and building otherwise worlds (e.g., King et al.). Within such refuges, composition among the ruins can and should be devoted to the building of next worlds. By promoting social justice and refusing dehumanization, composition in its current form is guided by principles and practices that can build better next worlds, but as the liberalism on which composition is based crumbles under sustained fascist attack, composition itself likely needs change as well—to be reinvented by academics and non-academics alike acting in coalition. What this reinvention might look like is unclear to me, but it's abundantly clear that this work can't wait for collapse, as, per Allen, we're far more able to do it now than we will be in five, ten, or fifteen years as collapse staggers toward us through natural disasters, shredded social safety nets, civil conflict, pandemics, etc.

How might we go about building next worlds? One way is to create spaces for imagining alternative worlds that are better than the worst and, within those spaces, cultivating tools for humanizing. Allen offers solidarities, sustaining disruptions, novelties, and archaisms as four of these tools.

Let's stay with solidarities. Transgressing the boundaries fascism thrives upon, people form solidarities across significant differences, without erasing them, based on shared humanity, struggle, responsibility, and reciprocity, thereby refusing fascism's social divisions (Allen; Hunt-Hendrix and Taylor). Suffused with risk and possibility alike, solidarity is "a disposition *toward making new worlds possible* [...that] we can practice" (Allen 99, emphasis in original). It's certainly one we can study and teach in our courses amid staggered collapse. Composition and rhetoric teacher-scholars are well-positioned to cultivate this tool for humanizing—and others—because we habitually center the humanity of our students and coach their development toward humanistic goals like the free and clear expression of well-developed ideas that account for alternative perspectives and increased knowledge of both an academic subject and the self (through reflective writing, for instance).

What tools for humanizing will you imagine? As fascists constrict free thought and speech, what tools for humanizing will you emphasize? How might you collaborate with others to create refuges where you might have a chance to invent next worlds that could be better than the worst? How might you invite students to collaborate on this invention, if you can take such a risk? What next worlds might we imagine together and, with today's and tomorrow's practices for making meaning, set about composing?

Acknowledgments

The author wishes to thank Joshua Trey Barnett for his timely question and Patricia Roberts-Miller and Amy Robillard for their feedback.

Works Cited

Allen, Ira J. *Panic Now? Tools for Humanizing*. U of Tennessee P, 2024.
Barnett, Joshua Trey. "Introduction." *Ecological Feelings: A Rhetorical Compendium*, edited by Joshua Trey Barnett. Michigan State UP, 2025.
—. *Mourning in the Anthropocene: Ecological Grief and Earthly Coexistence*. Michigan State UP, 2022.

Binkley, Collin. "Colleges Face High Stakes in Responses to Republican Outcry over Staff Comments on Charlie Kirk." *Associated Press*, 19 Sept. 2025, apnews.com/article/kirk-college-free-speech-clemson-trump-2b7aacd948f2e9f7bd1e95283fe-ec8d3

Cabrera, Alixel. "USU Professors Brace for Change as Legislature Imposes Western Civilization Courses." *Utah News Dispatch*, 24 Mar. 2025, utahnewsdispatch.com/2025/03/24/usu-professors-resistance-as-legislature-imposes-western-civilization-courses/

Carrington, Damian. "Only Two Years Left of World's Carbon Budget to Meet 1.5C Target, Scientists Warn." *The Guardian*, 18 Jun. 2025, www.theguardian.com/environment/2025/jun/18/only-two-years-left-of-world-carbon-budget-to-meet-15c-target-scientists-warn-climate-crisis

The Center for Humane Technology. "The A.I. Dilemma." *YouTube*, 9 Mar. 2023, www.youtube.com/watch?v=xoVJKj8lcNQ

Dailey, Ryan. "DeSantis Seeks to 'Recapture Higher Education,' Mold Sarasota's New College with Conservative Takeover." *Orlando Weekly*, 9 Jan. 2023, www.orlandoweekly.com/news/desantis-seeks-to-recapture-higher-education-mold-sarasotas-new-college-with-conservative-takeover-33299099

Dean, Jodi. "Communism or Neo-Feudalism?" *New Political Science*, vol. 42, no. 1, 2020, pp. 1–17. doi.org/10.1080/07393148.2020.1718974

Graeber, David, and David Wengrow. *The Dawn of Everything: A New History of Humanity*. Farrar, Straus, and Giroux, 2021.

Herrington, Gaya. "Update to Limits to Growth: Comparing the World3 Model with Empirical Data." *Journal of Industrial Ecology*, vol. 25, no. 3, 2021, pp. 614–26. doi.org/10.1111/jiec.13084

Hunt-Hendrix, Leah, and Astra Taylor. *Solidarity: The Past, Present, and Future of a World-Changing Idea*. Pantheon, 2024.

Kimmerer, Robin Wall. *Braiding Sweetgrass: Indigenous Wisdom, Scientific Knowledge, and the Teachings of Plants*. Milkweed Editions, 2013.

King, Tiffany Lethabo, Jenell Navarro, and Andrea Smith, editors. *Otherwise Worlds: Against Settler Colonialism and Anti-Blackness*. Duke UP, 2020.

Klein, Naomi, and Astra Taylor. "The Rise of End Times Fascism." *The Guardian*, 13 Apr. 2025, www.theguardian.com/us-news/ng-interactive/2025/apr/13/end-times-fascism-far-right-trump-musk

Kolbert, Elizabeth. *The Sixth Extinction: An Unnatural History*. Macmillan, 2015.

—. *Under a White Sky: The Nature of the Future*. Penguin Random House, 2022.

Kurtz, Stanley, Jenna Robinson, and David Randall. "General Education Act: Model Legislation." *Ethics and Public Policy Center*, 12 Nov. 2023, eppc.org/publication/general-education-act-model-legislation/

Marcus, Jon. "Colleges are Now Closing at a Pace of One a Week. What Happens to the Students?" *The Hechinger Report*, 26 Apr. 2024, hechingerreport.org/colleges-are-now-closing-at-a-pace-of-one-a-week-what-happens-to-the-students/

Meadows, Donella H., Dennis L. Meadows, Jørgen Randers, and William W. Behrens III. *The Limits to Growth: A Report for the Club of Rome's Project on the Predicament of Mankind*. Potomac Associates, 1972.

Moody, Josh. "Texas A&M President Steps Down under Pressure." *Inside HigherEd*, 18 Sept. 2025, www.insidehighered.com/news/governance/executive-leadership/2025/09/18/texas-am-president-steps-down-under-pressure

"People Are Lonelier than Ever. Enter AI." *Your Undivided Attention*, 30 May 2025, www.humanetech.com/podcast/people-are-lonelier-than-ever-enter-ai

Poynting, Mark. "Three Years Left to Limit Warming to 1.5C, Leading Scientists Warn." *BBC*, 18 Jun. 2025, www.bbc.com/news/articles/cn4l927dj5zo

Poynting, Mark, Erwan Rivault, and Becky Dale. "2024 First Year to Pass 1.5C Global Warming Limit." *BBC*, 9 Jan. 2025, www.bbc.com/news/articles/cd7575x8yq5o

Priest, Jessica. "Video of Clash over Gender-Identity Content in Texas A&M Children's Lit Class Leads to Firing, Removals." *The Texas Tribune*, 8 Sept. 2025, www.texastribune.org/2025/09/08/texas-am-video-professor-student-gender-identity-content/

Rosalsky, Greg. "Why the AI World is Suddenly Obsessed with a 160-Year-Old Economics Paradox." *NPR*, 4 Feb. 2025, www.npr.org/sections/planet-money/2025/02/04/g-s1-46018/ai-deepseek-economics-jevons-paradox

Saslow, Eli. "The White Flight of Derek Black." *The Washington Post*, 15 Oct. 2016, www.washingtonpost.com/national/the-white-flight-of-derek-black/2016/10/15/ed5f906a-8f3b-11e6-a6a3-d50061aa9fae_story.html

Taylor, Astra, and Eleni Schirmer. "The Republican Plot to Un-Educate America." *The New Republic*, 23 Jun. 2025, newrepublic.com/article/197017/budget-bill-kill-higher-education

Wildfire, Jessica. "Bird Flu Capable of Airborne Transmission." *The Sentinel-Intelligence*, 6 Jun. 2025. www.the-sentinel-intelligence.net/bird-flu-capable-of-airborne-transmission/

Zeitz, Joshua. "The Gilded Age Is Back—And That Should Worry Conservatives." *Politico*, 2 Mar. 2025, www.politico.com/news/magazine/2025/03/02/trump-musk-bezos-gilded-age-corporations-economy-00205454

Lydia Wilkes is assistant professor of English and writing program administrator at Auburn University. Her scholarship has appeared in *College Composition and Communication* and several edited collections. She co-edited *Rhetoric and Guns* (Utah State University Press, 2022) and *Toward More Sustainable Metaphors of Writing Program Administration* (Utah State University Press, 2023).

Until I Hit Ocean

Patti Poblete

This isn't so much an article as a trio of confessions.

I'm Not an American Citizen

To be clear, while I was born in Canada, I am considered a permanent resident of the United States. I've lived in this country since I was ten years old.

We won't talk about the time I didn't realize my green card had expired for six months and I lived in sheepish fear until I could drive six hours to the closest federal office where they would give me a temporary stamp in my passport until my official piece of plastic arrived by certified mail.

We won't talk about the time I spent a year teaching abroad, and when I returned, the customs agent asked how I could be considered a "permanent" resident of the country if I wasn't actually residing there, and left me standing, terrified, at that airport kiosk for several minutes while he went to consult with others about, I don't know, whether I would have to live in LAX for the rest of my natural life?

My parents are from the Philippines, but they moved to Canada in the 70s. Most of the family moved to North America during that time; nobody talks about why. After we moved to Southern California, my parents and younger sister opted for dual citizenship. My brother and I did not. When people ask why we opted to become permanent residents instead of citizens, my brother and I typically shrug and mumble something about not wanting to do jury duty.

I can't speak for my brother, but it's a bit more complicated for me.

I Have No Metric for "Normal"

I grew up in a fundamentalist community. Like, it wasn't a bad one—if you've only ever read about the Seventh-Day Adventist church, it was probably an aside in a book mostly concerned with somebody who was later significant in the Civil Rights movement. (I honestly couldn't tell you why, but that's the only literature in which I've ever run across the denominational name.) Oh, and stuff about health food. We're very up on health food.

Things we are down on: Gambling. Alcohol. Spiritual intermediaries. Dancing and subsequent shenanigans. Non-conformity. The Catholic church circa Martin Luther. Vulgar language. Bacon.

Anyway.

It was 2004. Ronald Reagan had just died. I was in the third pew from the front in church, sitting with my fellow English grad students. We were receiving our master's degrees that weekend, and the second day of ceremonies was a dedication in church. As part of the program, whoever was up at the pulpit asked us to observe a moment of silence in Reagan's honor. Then they asked us to stand for it. "What?" I muttered to the friend next to me. "I'm not doing that," she murmured back.

In my master's program, my nickname, which I'd like to think was affectionate, was the Feminist.

It was 2004. I woke up and discovered George W. Bush had been re-elected for a second term. I cried. Like, literally, I broke into tears and went onto my Livejournal and told my online friends that America didn't want me. Didn't want me—immigrant, progressive, brown, queer, creative, intellectual—personally.

This past summer, while I was rooting through my parents' garage shelves in search of old DVDs, I found a framed photograph of W and his wife. I assume my parents received this after making some sort of monetary donation to a campaign. They never hung it up or anything; we're not total weirdos.

I'd never seen it before that moment.

One of the jokes I often tell folks, after I did PhD school in the Midwest and taught in the South for several years, is that when I went on my last job search, I fled West until I hit ocean. (Technically, I hit the Puget Sound estuary, but "ocean" is much more dramatically satisfying.) This is a misrepresentation, however: My goal was to go west, but more to get into the same time zone as my family. That I also seemed to be fleeing a surge of legislative attempts to censor educators was a happy (?) coincidence.

That's My Secret, Cap: I'm Always Angry

::insert Mark Ruffalo GIF here::

It was 2000. Our history class read Karen Armstrong's *A History of God*. As part of class discussion, our professor asked us why we shouldn't define Christianity by what Christians have done, rather than what they purport to believe. As a result, multiple students complained the professor was promoting atheism, and the campus chaplain decried him for being anti-Christian.

It was 2011. At Purdue University, international students accounted for a bit over 11% of the undergraduate student body ("Fall 2010 International Student"). Amongst the English teaching assistants, a few of the graduate students complained they weren't able to teach "normal" classes anymore because of the high percentage of English language learners. At the Writing Lab, multiple international students signed up for tutoring the first week of classes; we discovered they were told to do so prior to completing any coursework. This was a phenomenon that occurred every quarter without fail.

It was 2017. Iowa State University hosted its annual Iowa State Conference on Race and Ethnicity. A student interrupted President Steven Leath's opening address, citing his lack of advocacy for minoritized and multiply marginalized students. After a number of students departed in a coordinated walk-out, Leath grumbled about the lack of civility and, astonishingly, invoked his close working relationship with a Black colleague as proof of his anti-racism.

It was 2021. In Arkansas, legislation banned teaching "divisive concepts" about race and gender. The law didn't extend to higher education, but at a public university, we still felt the subsequent chilling effect.

It was 2023. At my new community college in Washington state, I assigned readings from Cheryl E. Ball and Drew M. Loewe's *Bad Ideas About Writing* to my first-year composition classes, including essays that support bilingual education and inclusive learning. I had them watch the short film "Immersion," which depicts the struggle of an English language learner when in an English-only educational environment. In my student evaluations, students suggested I was pushing a liberal agenda that was inappropriate for the class. Thankfully, when I met with my dean and tenure committee, they voiced their support for my curricular choices. (Still, just about every quarter, at least one student would complain.)

It's 2025. The last time I visited home, my parents told me to make sure I didn't post anything controversial on social media. Just in case, though of what, they didn't specify.

Does this count?

Works Cited

Armstrong, Karen. *A History of God: The 4000-Year Quest of Judaism, Christianity, and Islam*. Alfred A. Knopf, 1993.
Ball, Cheryl E. and Drew M. Loewe, editors. *Bad Ideas about Writing*. Open Access Textbooks, 2017. textbooks.lib.wvu.edu/badideas/badideasaboutwriting-book.pdf.
"Fall 2010 International Student and Scholar Enrollment & Statistical Report." *International Students and Scholars*. Purdue University, 2010. www.purdue.edu/gpp/iss/_documents/EnrollmentReport/iss_statisticalreportfall10.pdf.
"Immersion." *Media That Matters*. YouTube, 2009. www.youtube.com/watch?v=I6Y0HAjLKYI.

Patti Poblete [poh-BLEH-teh] is English faculty at South Puget Sound Community College and part of the editorial team for *WPA: Writing Program Administration*. Previously, she acted as WPA at Henderson State University. Her research includes public and digital rhetorics, writing pedagogy, and cultural criticism. Ask her about dragons.

Book Reviews

Navigating AI's Writing Revolution: A Review Essay and Call for Deliberation

Augmentation Technologies and Artificial Intelligence in Technical Communication: Designing Ethical Futures, by Ann Hill Duin and Isabel Pedersen. Routledge, 2023.

AI and Writing, by Sidney I. Dobrin. Broadview Press, 2023.

Teaching and Generative AI: Pedagogical Possibilities and Productive Tensions, edited by Beth Buyserie and Travis N. Thurston. Utah State University, 2024. uen.pressbooks.pub/teachingandgenerativeai/

Reviewed by Jason Tham, Texas Tech University

The emergence of generative artificial intelligence has triggered what might be characterized as one of the most significant pedagogical disruptions in composition studies since the advent of digital writing technologies. Within months of ChatGPT's public release in November 2022, writing instructors found themselves grappling with fundamental questions about authenticity, authorship, and assessment. These questions were made more urgent when AI demonstrated its capacity to accelerate writing processes to unprecedented speeds. However, amid the push for rapid adaptation and integration, a crucial question emerges: in our haste to keep pace with technological acceleration, might we be overlooking the pedagogical value of deliberate deceleration—slowing down to allow room for human reflection and meaning making? The three books under review here represent early scholarly responses to this disruption, each offering distinct perspectives on how the field might navigate what Sidney Dobrin aptly terms the "many unsettled questions" surrounding AI's role in writing education. Collectively, they reveal both the urgency with which our field has responded to generative AI and the evolution of that response over time. From Ann Hill Duin and Isabel Pedersen's prescient framework for ethical technological integration, published before the widespread adoption of generative AI, to Sidney I. Dobrin's foundational approach to teaching writing with AI, to Beth Buyserie and Travis N. Thurston's collection of pedagogical examples and critiques emerging from classroom experience, these works trace a trajectory from anticipatory theoretical frameworks to practical implementation strategies. Yet notably absent from this progression is sustained consideration of whether acceleration itself—i.e., the drive to quickly integrate, adapt, and optimize— might be antithetical to the deeper learning objectives that composition studies has long championed.

Articulating Pedagogical Maturation

The Buyserie and Thurston collection *Teaching and Generative AI: Pedagogical Possibilities and Productive Tensions*, published in 2024, represents the field's most mature response to AI integration challenges. Emerging after more than a year of classroom experimentation with AI tools, the collection benefits from accumulated pedagogical experience and nuanced understanding of AI's capabilities and limitations. The collection's subtitle, emphasizing both "possibilities" and "tensions," reflects a sophisticated understanding that emerged as initial panic gave way to sustained engagement. Unlike earlier responses that often focused on managing AI as a potential threat, this collection approaches AI as a complex pedagogical reality requiring thoughtful integration rather than prohibition or uncritical adoption.

The collection's distinctive strength lies in its grounding in sustained classroom experience. Where earlier texts necessarily relied on theoretical frameworks or limited pilot studies, Buyserie and Thurston's contributors draw on extensive pedagogical experimentation to offer nuanced analysis of what works, what doesn't, and why. The book's interdisciplinary scope reveals how different fields, from composition studies to engineering to digital humanities, have developed distinct approaches to similar challenges around academic integrity, creativity, and authorship. This comparative perspective, unavailable to earlier publications, allows readers to understand AI integration as part of broader pedagogical innovation rather than a crisis unique to writing instruction.

However, the collection's pedagogical orientation also constrains its critical scope. The focus on managing AI within existing educational structures, while valuable for immediate implementation, limits consideration of how AI might fundamentally transform educational goals and methods. The interdisciplinary approach that constitutes the book's strength paradoxically highlights the challenge of developing coherent cross-disciplinary frameworks for AI integration, as different fields' solutions often prove incompatible or contradictory.

Most significantly, even this mature collection reveals the field's continued emphasis on adaptation and integration rather than resistance or deliberate deceleration. The "productive tensions" that the editors highlight—between efficiency and pedagogy, between innovation and tradition, between student agency and technological capability—may themselves reflect a missed opportunity to advocate for pedagogical practices that intentionally preserve space for reflection, contemplation, and genuinely human forms of meaning-making. Rather than resolving fundamental questions about AI's role in education, the collection's emphasis on managing these tensions suggests the field remains committed to accommodation rather than principled resistance to acceleration culture.

Presenting a More Momentary Response

Dobrin's *AI and Writing*, published in August 2023 as one of the first textbooks specifically addressing generative AI in writing instruction, occupies a crucial historical position in the field's response to AI. Released approximately nine months after ChatGPT's public launch, the book represents an early attempt to move beyond initial panic toward systematic pedagogical integration.

Dobrin's timing allowed him to address the immediate concerns that dominated early 2023 discussions while developing more comprehensive approaches to AI integration. His dual focus on conceptual understanding and applied guidance reflects the field's recognition that effective AI integration required both theoretical frameworks and practical strategies. The book's emphasis on "transferable skills that can assist student writers in many contexts and on many platforms" (quote from book jacket) positioned it as essential reading for instructors scrambling to understand how AI might fit into their established curricula. The book's historical contextualization proves particularly valuable for its moment, as Dobrin situates AI developments within longer trajectories of technological disruption to writing practices. By comparing AI to innovations like the printing press and word processors, he provides crucial perspective for a field experiencing what many perceived as an unprecedented crisis.

However, the book's timing also reveals certain limitations. Written during the early months of public AI engagement, when ChatGPT dominated discourse and other AI platforms remained less developed, Dobrin's analysis necessarily focuses on a narrower range of AI capabilities than would be possible today. The book's structure, with ethics and bias addressed primarily in concluding chapters rather than integrated throughout, suggests that the pressure to provide immediate practical guidance may have constrained deeper critical engagement with AI's systemic implications. More problematically, the emphasis on efficiency and practical application may inadvertently reinforce what could be called "acceleration culture"—the assumption that faster writing processes are inherently better ones.

Grounding in Anticipatory Frameworks and Ethical Design

Duin and Pedersen's *Augmentation Technologies and Artificial Intelligence in Technical Communication*, published in 2023 but completed before widespread public engagement with generative AI, takes the most expansive and theoretically sophisticated approach among these three texts. Their timing proves particularly significant: writing before the ChatGPT moment, they were able to develop frameworks unconstrained by immediate crisis response, positioning AI within a broader ecosystem of augmentation technologies that enhance human capability or productivity.

The book's prescient focus on ethical design proves especially valuable given how quickly concerns about AI's environmental impact, labor displacement, and perpetuation of social biases became central to public discourse. Where later texts would necessarily respond to immediate pedagogical pressures with calls for rapid adaptation, Duin and Pedersen's framework encourages "slow thinking" about technological integration—deliberate, reflective consideration of long-term implications rather than reactive implementation. Their examination of "augmentation technologies" beyond generative AI, including "cognitive, physical, sensory, and emotional enhancements to the body or environment" (10), now reads as remarkably forward-thinking given the rapid development of multimodal AI systems and the growing integration of AI into various aspects of human-computer interaction. The book's focus on "interrogating" rather than simply implementing these technologies established a critical foundation that would prove essential as the field grappled with AI's rapid mainstream adoption.

Nevertheless, the book's pre-ChatGPT timing still means it lacks engagement with the specific challenges that emerged once generative AI became widely accessible to students and instructors. While the ethical frameworks remain relevant, the text provides limited guidance for the immediate classroom dilemmas that would soon dominate professional discourse. More significantly, it cannot address what may be the most crucial pedagogical challenge: how to maintain space for deliberate, reflective learning processes when AI tools promise instant results.

Confronting Current Conditions

Since these books' publication, the AI landscape has continued its rapid evolution, revealing both the prescience and limitations of their early analyses. The competition between major AI platforms (e.g., Google Cloud AI,

Microsoft Azure AI, OpenAI, IBM watsonx, Amazon SageMaker, etc.) has intensified, with each developing distinct strengths in areas like creative writing, coding, data processing, and multimodal capabilities. This diversification suggests that the field's initial focus on ChatGPT, while understandable, may have been too narrow.

More significantly, institutional responses have evolved from initial prohibition to more nuanced policies, with writing programs in higher education developing policies to address the use of AI and how it is connected to writing (Davis et al.). This institutional shift reflects the field's growing recognition that AI integration requires sophisticated policy development rather than blanket restrictions. The emergence of AI-specific pedagogical strategies also suggests that the field has moved beyond treating AI as simply another writing tool. Instructors are now developing assignments that explicitly incorporate AI collaboration, with students learning to use ChatGPT and other AI applications, including AI image generators, to develop and enhance their skills rather than avoiding these technologies.

However, significant challenges remain. Questions about academic integrity continue to evolve as detection technologies prove unreliable and institutional policies struggle to keep pace with technological development. Environmental concerns about AI's computational requirements have become more prominent, though they receive limited attention in these early texts. Most significantly, the rapid pace of technological change means that specific technical guidance quickly becomes outdated, while broader conceptual frameworks retain their relevance.

It's Altogether Temporal--Changes, Themes, and Tensions

The chronological progression of these three texts reveals significant evolution in the field's approach to AI integration. Duin and Pedersen's pre-ChatGPT framework emphasizes long-term ethical considerations and systematic approaches to technological adoption. Dobrin's response to the ChatGPT moment focuses on immediate pedagogical needs while establishing conceptual foundations. Buyserie and Thurston's collection reflects pedagogical maturation, with contributors drawing on sustained classroom experience to offer more nuanced analysis of integration challenges.

This temporal progression illuminates how external pressures have shaped scholarly priorities. Duin and Pedersen had the conceptual space to develop comprehensive ethical frameworks, while later authors necessarily responded to immediate crisis conditions in educational settings. The evolution from anticipatory theory through foundational response to experienced reflection suggests the field's growing sophistication in approaching technological integration.

Despite their different historical moments and audiences, these three texts reveal several convergent themes that suggest emerging consensus within the field. All three emphasize the importance of critical engagement over wholesale adoption or rejection of AI technologies. They share a commitment to ethical integration that considers implications beyond immediate productivity gains. And they recognize that effective AI integration requires new literacies and pedagogical approaches rather than simple adaptation of existing practices.

Together, these texts' temporal positioning also reveals ongoing tensions within the field's evolving response to AI. The practical orientation of *Teaching and Generative AI* and much of Dobrin's *AI and Writing* reflects the immediate pressures facing instructors and students. In contrast, Duin and Pedersen's focus on ethical design futures suggests the need for longer-term strategic thinking that extends beyond immediate pedagogical concerns. This tension between immediate practical needs and longer-term strategic considerations reflects broader questions about the field's role in technological adoption. Should composition studies focus primarily on helping students and instructors adapt to existing AI technologies, or should it take a more active role in shaping how these technologies develop and are deployed? The books under review suggest different answers to this question, with practical guides emphasizing adaptation and critical frameworks emphasizing active intervention in technological design.

Making a Case for Slow Pedagogy

What emerges most clearly from examining these three texts together is not their individual contributions but their collective avoidance on AI refusal (Sano-Franchini et al.): none seriously considers whether the pedagogical imperative should be adaptation to AI's acceleration rather than resistance to it. While all three books advocate for "critical" or "ethical" engagement with AI technologies, they largely accept the premise that educational practices must evolve to accommodate technological capabilities rather than asking whether those capabilities align with educational goals.

This acceptance of acceleration culture may represent a fundamental misunderstanding of composition studies' core mission. If writing pedagogy has traditionally emphasized process over product, reflection over efficiency, and critical thinking over rapid response, then AI integration that prioritizes speed and convenience may be pedagogically counterproductive regardless of its technical sophistication. The question becomes not how to integrate AI effectively, but whether integration itself serves student learning or merely institutional pressures for efficiency and innovation.

Consider the implications of what some scholars and I have called "slow pedagogy" in the context of AI integration (Tham, "Whose Time Is It"). Rather than teaching students to prompt AI systems effectively, slow pedagogy might emphasize extended periods of prewriting, multiple revision cycles, and sustained engagement with difficult ideas. Instead of using AI to accelerate research processes, it might insist on the pedagogical value of confusion, struggle, and gradual understanding. Rather than optimizing writing workflows, it might preserve space for what appears inefficient but proves educationally essential: the *time* required for genuine intellectual development.

Such an approach would be controversial in contemporary educational contexts increasingly dominated by efficiency metrics and technological optimization. Yet it might represent composition studies' most important contribution to broader conversations about AI and education, that is, the argument that not all human activities should be optimized, and that learning processes require forms of temporal engagement that resist acceleration.

This is not an argument for Luddite rejection of AI technologies, but for pedagogical intentionality about when and how they are integrated. It suggests that composition and professional communication instructors might serve students better by modeling slow thinking and deliberate decision-making (Tham, "Rhetoric and Socially Responsive Design") than by demonstrating AI optimization techniques. It proposes that maintaining human agency in an era of automation might require deliberate practices of deceleration rather than adaptive acceleration. While these three texts represent important early contributions to AI scholarship in composition studies, they collectively reveal some limitations in the field's current approach. Beyond their overwhelming focus on how generative AI replaces or supplements conventional writing processes, namely thinking, ideating, drafting, composing, editing, and publishing, they share an acceptance of acceleration as inherently desirable. Even Buyserie and Thurston's collection, despite its inclusion of disciplinary approaches beyond writing, remains primarily concerned with AI as a tool for optimizing productivity rather than questioning whether optimization itself serves educational goals. These texts have yet to seriously consider whether the temporal dimensions of learning—or the time required for reflection and deliberation—might be incompatible with AI's accelerated processes.

Furthermore, the focus on mere content generation may inadequately prepare students for the broader reality of AI integration in contemporary life. Students encounter AI not only when writing essays but when applying for jobs, preparing for interviews, managing personal budgets, creating talking points for presentations, planning travel, seeking purchase advice, or comparing products. More fundamentally, they encounter AI as part of the broader societal expectation that all processes should be optimized for speed and efficiency. They engage with AI-generated content across multiple modalities—audio, visual, video, and felt senses—not just text. The field's emphasis on AI as a writing tool, while understandable given our disciplinary focus, may miss both the broader critical literacy demands of automated content production and the more fundamental question of whether acceleration itself serves human flourishing.

The implications of this limitation extend beyond pedagogical completeness to questions of equity and preparedness. Students who understand AI only as a writing assistant may be unprepared for workplace environments where AI shapes decision-making processes, client communications, and strategic planning. They may lack critical frameworks for evaluating AI-generated content in contexts where traditional notions of authorship and authority become complex or irrelevant. Our own obsession with text-based AI applications may leave students vulnerable to more sophisticated forms of AI-mediated persuasion and manipulation. As AI systems become more integrated into social media algorithms, news curation, and commercial recommendation systems, critical literacy demands understanding how automated systems shape information environments across all means of expression.

To be fair, when considering the professional and civic implications of AI literacy, these three texts effectively address academic integrity and classroom applications; they provide guidance for navigating AI's role in job markets that are increasingly shaped by algorithmic screening, workplace communication increasingly mediated by AI tools, or civic participation increasingly influenced by AI-generated content and automated information systems. Together, these books reveal significant areas needing further scholarly attention. Most notably, a lot of our research studies focus primarily on English-language, North American educational contexts, with limited consideration of how AI technologies might affect global writing practices or multilingual writers. This limitation becomes more significant as AI technologies increasingly shape international communication and as questions about linguistic diversity in AI training data become more prominent. These books also demonstrate the challenge of writing about rapidly evolving technologies. Since our scholarly and pedagogical methods are often inferior to emergent technological features, we should not just adopt and adapt. These experimental books show us that future scholarship might benefit from emphasizing critical theoretical approaches over specific technological implementations.

Additionally, scholars of writing and rhetoric should engage with the broader political economy of AI development. Questions about corporate control of AI technologies, labor implications of automation, and the environmental costs of computational intensity receive limited attention. Future scholarship might benefit from more sustained engagement with these systemic issues. Again, as leading-edge publications, these books reveal the field's ongoing struggle to balance technological integration with traditional pedagogical values. While the authors advocate for thoughtful engagement with AI rather than wholesale rejection, they provide only some guidance for navigating situations where AI use might conflict with established educational goals or assessment practices. Future scholarship on AI may benefit from additional time for reflection on the complexities that continue to emerge surrounding the use of AI in writing and other facets of our lives—time that these scholars did not have, particularly those who responded in the immediate aftermath of the emergence of ChatGPT and other early generative technologies.

Toward Slow Thinking

Through the summaries of these books and syntheses of their constraints, I aim to suggest that sustainable AI integration will require approaches that extend well beyond writing instruction and, more controversially, beyond the assumption that technological capabilities should determine pedagogical practices. If our goal is to develop genuine critical literacy for an era of automated content production, composition studies may need to expand its conception of literacy to include not only AI content evaluation and algorithmic awareness across professional and personal contexts but also deliberate practices of deceleration that preserve space for uniquely human forms of cognition and decision-making.

This approach would necessarily be interdisciplinary, involving collaboration with fields like human cognition and psychology, media/mass communication, digital humanities, design studies, and information science to develop more comprehensive curricula. But it would also be counter-cultural, explicitly advocating for slow pedagogy as resistance to acceleration culture. Such an approach might involve assignments that intentionally require extended time periods, reflection processes that cannot be accelerated, and explicit instruction in "slow thinking," including forms of deliberation that resist optimization.

The case for slow thinking (and by extension, slow pedagogy) rests on several premises that these texts do not adequately address. First, learning processes require temporal engagement that cannot be compressed without fundamental alteration. Second, critical thinking depends on forms of confusion, struggle, and gradual understanding that AI systems are designed to eliminate. Third, democratic citizenship requires deliberative capacities that are weakened rather than strengthened by optimization technologies. And fourth, human agency in an automated world may depend more on our capacity for intentional deceleration than on our ability to keep pace with accelerating systems.

Most importantly, this approach suggests that the field's response to AI cannot remain primarily adaptive but must actively engage with fundamental questions about what forms of human activity should be preserved from optimization. The three texts under review provide valuable foundations for this broader project. Their collective insights point toward the need for more philosophically grounded approaches to AI literacy that prioritize human flourishing over technological integration.

As we continue to navigate AI's implications for writing pedagogy and practice, these early texts provide valuable foundations for ongoing dialogue. Their emphasis on critical engagement, ethical consideration, and pedagogical innovation offers a constructive framework for approaching future developments. Their articulations of technological evolution and shifting expectations indicate a broader challenge of preserving human agency in an automated world.

The conversation these books begin—about the relationship between human creativity and machine capability, about the ethics of technological integration, and about the future of writing instruction—will undoubtedly continue to grow and change. But I must close here by reiterating that our conversation needs to expand beyond questions of integration to fundamental questions about deceleration and deliberation. The contribution of these books lies not in providing absolute solutions but in establishing frameworks for inquiry that future scholarship can build upon, challenge, and ultimately transcend in service of genuinely humane approaches to technological change. Such a project demands our collective and sustained attention.

Works Cited

Davis, Katlynne, Jason Tham, D. Mollie Stambler, Jialei Jiang, Jessica Campbell, Gustav Verhulsdonck, and Daniel Hocutt. "What Do We Talk About When We Talk About AI Literacy? Tensions in Current Institutional Guidelines and Recommendations for a Slow, Reflective Future." *Programmatic Perspectives*, forthcoming.

Sano-Franchini, Jennifer, Megan McIntyre, and Maggie Fernandes. *Refusing GenAI in Writing Studies: A Quickstart Guide*. refusinggenai.wordpress.com/

Tham, Jason. "Rhetoric and Socially Responsive Design: Critical Perspectives for Writing, Technology, and Social Change." *Writing & Rhetoric Across Borders Speaker Series*, 9 May 2025, Department of Writing, Rhetoric, and Discourse, DePaul University, Chicago. Invited Lecture.

—. "Whose Time Is It, Anyway? Writing, Labor, and the Illusion of Efficiency." *Composition Forum*, forthcoming.

Jason Tham is associate professor of technical communication and rhetoric at Texas Tech University. He is editor of *Computers and Composition*. He is author of several books on design thinking approaches in writing and communication practices.

Feminist Technical Communication: Apparent Feminisms, Slow Crisis, and the Deepwater Horizon Disaster, by Erin Clark, Utah State University Press, 2023, 179 pp.

Reviewed by Brigida R. Blasi, University of Wyoming

When reading *Feminist Technical Communication*, I found Erin Clark's challenge to traditional understandings of efficiency in technical communication most impactful. Through a case study of her own examination and consumption of the technical communication surrounding the Deepwater Horizon Disaster (DHD), Clark makes a case for applying what she terms "apparent feminisms" to reframe technical communication in crisis situations to prioritize human health, environmental justice, and communal well-being. Clark states that the book is meant to be both an introduction to feminist technical communication and an argument for "intersectional feminist approaches as vital for the future of technical communication as a field" (3). At its core, the book's call to expand what counts as meaningful and ethical efficiency seems poised to inspire critical conversations among scholars and practitioners alike. As part of a larger movement within technical communication that seeks to prioritize justice, inclusivity, and accessibility, her arguments against efficiency for efficiency's sake make it an important resource for anyone looking to reimagine technical communication beyond its accepted and traditional boundaries.

Clark begins with a preface focusing on her positionality to and within the multitude of intersectional approaches she weaves into her own methodology of apparent feminism while acknowledging that "no one can create a one-size-fits-all feminism" (xiv). It is admirable that she begins her study by examining her own privilege and positionality in depth. As she points out frequently, technical communication practitioners (as well as people in general, I would argue) would do well to emulate this honest effort towards self-reflection, particularly when adopting, critiquing, or adapting the methodologies of people coming from different backgrounds, experiences, and ways of knowing.

In chapter one, "Feminist Technical Communication," Clark delves into her overarching argument. She advocates for an intersectional feminist approach to technical communication for two reasons: First, it is essential for current graduate students to learn this methodology as the field evolves and becomes more focused on social justice; Second, technical communication's traditional understanding of efficiency (making information fast and easy to access) forces or influences a loss of critical information, particularly in cases of environmental or health-related crises. This second point stands as the book's most compelling argument, which anchors her broader call for more ethical and socially responsible practice. Her case studies show how lost information in overly efficient systems benefits the powerful while harming those most affected. She traces feminist technical communication to the 1990s, highlighting figures like Mary M. Lay and Katherine T. Durack, then aligns with scholars like Angela Haas to emphasize intersectionality and the need to amplify marginalized voices.

In chapter two, "Apparent Feminisms," Clark discusses her own experiences during her PhD work and as an instructor, which influenced her move toward a methodology she has termed "apparent feminisms" throughout her academic career, beginning with her dissertation (Frost, 2013). After repeatedly finding ingrained misogyny and bias blindness in her students, she developed "apparent feminisms" as a flexible, adaptable, and transient framework for introducing feminist perspectives into varied and unexpected fields of technical communication. Building on the work of other scholars, Clark pushes back against the myth of neutrality in technical communication. Apparent feminisms, as a methodology, aims to make feminist perspectives conspicuous and inspire coalition-building to address social and political issues, with the intention of inspiring a more socially conscious approach to technical communication that balances efficiency and ethical responsibility.

Clark introduces the eponymous concept in chapter three, "Slow Crisis," using this and a reconsidered definition of "disaster" as frameworks for rethinking efficiency and risk. She describes slow crisis as something that develops gradually over time, often going unnoticed until becoming critical, such as the long-term health effects on local communities in the aftermath of an environmental disaster. This builds on the work of other scholars, such as Rob Nixon's concept of "slow violence," which applies to situations like domestic abuse (p. 75). Using both health and environmental case studies, Clark argues that non-feminist, strict interpretations of legal rhetorics often disadvantage the victims of slow crisis. Overall, she argues that traditional views of efficiency fail to address these drawn-out crises, advocating for feminist methodologies that prioritize long-term social and cultural factors in risk communication.

In chapters four, "Disaster," and five, "An Approach Feminist Analysis of the Deepwater Horizon Disaster," Clark applies apparent feminisms to her examination of the 2010 DHD, critiquing how corporate definitions of efficiency prioritize economic recovery over long-term human health, noting that reports on the DHD rarely addressed the health risks, such as central nervous system damage and cancer. She contrasts the local focus on health and ecological risks with the broader economic focus seen in national reporting. She further explores local, unofficial transcultural communication like guerilla media and blogs as immediate, digital tools used by people with marginalized voices to challenge those dominant, efficient narratives. By making the case that local communities needed to employ guerilla media in order to disseminate truly useful information, Clark makes a strong argument for a more intersectional efficiency model. Her analysis emphasizes the ethical responsibility of technical communicators to integrate these diverse perspectives, ideally reshaping technical communication to be more socially just and inclusive.

In the final chapter, "Looking Forward, Looking Back," Clark reexamines the DHD through multiple historical lenses, illustrating how different notions of efficiency shaped the narratives constructed around it. She emphasizes not just the overlooked long-term human health impacts, but also the equally marginalized role of women in environmental justice movements. She again tries to enforce her argument for the concept of apparency in feminist theory, stressing the importance of making marginalized bodies and perspectives visible in technical communication. Beyond reiterating her argument for a redefinition of efficiency, she calls for apparent feminists to actively engage in revising origin stories and making feminist perspectives more visible, advocating for community and interdisciplinary collaboration as essential to achieving social justice.

Stating more than once that her methodology is meant to be flexible and adaptable, Clark acknowledges the transient nature of apparent feminisms. However, she also admits that she questioned whether the broader turn toward social justice in technical communication has rendered her methodology redundant before writing this book. Her grappling with these questions highlights the interdependence of apparent feminisms with other frameworks in health, ecology, and environmental rhetoric. While her methodology offers significant insights, its strength lies in its ability to intersect with and amplify broader social justice movements rather than standing as a singular approach.

The book presents some challenges for readers. She calls the book "messy" because she, simply put, tries to do too much in fewer than 200 pages (33). Frequent shifts between personal narrative and academic analysis can feel disjointed, and the book's ambitious scope—covering feminist historiography, personal narrative, and applied theory—can make it hard to follow. While these issues don't diminish the book's significance, they can make it difficult to absorb, especially given the lack of concrete, practical examples. Whose responsibility is it to employ these more empathetic, community-based approaches to technical communication? What are practical ways this can be implemented? What would that look like in comparison to what was produced during the DHD? In the end, Clark is not offering concrete solutions, likely on purpose. Instead, she is asking her readers to consider their own privilege and positionality, just as she does in her preface, to more carefully deliberate on how information is used, manipulated, and absorbed.

Overall, Clark has created for her readers a series of examples and questions to consider not just in practice, but in life. Her call for a redefinition of efficiency to include long-term human health and ecological sustainability is compelling, offering valuable insights for both scholars and practitioners. Overall, *Feminist Technical Communication* is an important contribution to the field, providing a powerful argument for the integration of feminist and, more broadly, social justice perspectives into technical communication. It could be the impetus for some interesting classroom conversations, particularly for students interested in communication in government, health and human services, or environmental sciences. The book offers a perspective that challenges traditional economic-centric views in technical communication. In essence, this book is Clark's call to action for technical communicators to challenge oppressive systems through collaborative, accessible, and community-focused efforts in their work.

Works Cited

Durack, Katherine T. "Gender, Technology, and the History of Technical Communication." *Technical Communication Quarterly*, vol. 6, no. 3, 1997, pp. 249–60, https://doi.org/10.1207/s15427625tcq0603_2.

Frost, Erin A. 2013. "Theorizing an Apparent Feminism in Technical Communication." Order No. 3574642, Illinois State University.

Haas, Angela M., and Michelle F. Eble, editors. *Key Theoretical Frameworks: Teaching Technical Communication in the 21st Century*. Utah State UP, 2018.

Lay, Mary M. "Interpersonal Conflict in Collaborative Writing: What We Can Learn from Gender Studies." *Journal of Business and Technical Communication*, vol. 3, no. 2, 1989, pp. 5–28, https://doi.org/10.1177/105065198900300202.

Nixon, Rob. *Slow Violence and the Environmentalism of the Poor*. 1st ed., Harvard UP, 2011, https://doi.org/10.4159/harvard.9780674061194.

Brigida R. Blasi is the head of education and outreach at the American Heritage Center at the University of Wyoming. She is also a member of the inaugural cohort of UW's new PhD program in public humanities.

Masking Inequality with Good Intentions: Systemic Bias, Counterspaces, and Discourse Acquisition in STEM Education by Heather M. Falconer, The WAC Clearinghouse, 2022, 162 pp.

Reviewed by Shuvro Das, Virginia Tech

Heather M. Falconer's *Masking Inequality with Good Intentions: Systemic Bias, Counterspaces, and Discourse Acquisition in STEM Education* interrogates the tension between liberal commitments to diversity and the reality of persistent systemic biases. Grounded in ethnographic research and a critical rhetorical framework, Falconer investigates how White Institutional Presence (WIP), race- and gender-evasive ideologies, and disciplinary discourse norms shape the trajectories of BIPOC (Black, Indigenous, People of Color) students within an undergraduate research program. For compositionists concerned with writing across the curriculum, linguistic justice, and identity negotiation, this book offers a vital lens into how discourse acquisition functions as both a mechanism of institutional inclusion and a site of epistemic gatekeeping.

Falconer's study follows six BIPOC students in PRISM (Program for Research Initiatives in Science and Math), a research mentoring initiative at a Hispanic-Serving Institution. Through interviews, program artifacts, and observations over multiple years, she analyzes how participants experience STEM writing, mentorship, and identity formation. Drawing on critical race theory, decolonial thought, and discourse theory, Falconer builds a compelling case that STEM education is not a neutral space but one that is "structured by exclusionary white cultural logics that systemically marginalize women, racial minorities, and other underrepresented groups" (2). These structures, she argues, are often masked by well-meaning diversity rhetoric that fails to interrogate the epistemological assumptions underlying scientific communication and pedagogy.

The book opens with a deeply reflective introduction in which Falconer situates her positionality as a white, first-generation, working-class woman in STEM. She recounts the microaggressions and barriers she encountered, positioning her narrative as both context and catalyst for the study. This autobiographical framing enables Falconer to model the kind of vulnerability and critical reflexivity she later encourages in faculty. Importantly, she argues that underrepresentation in STEM is not simply a pipeline issue, but a cultural one: "Too often, equity efforts take these biased disciplinary norms as neutral baselines rather than interrogating their marginalization of pluralistic identities and ways of knowing" (5). This framing helps readers understand that Falconer's goal is not simply critique, but the reimagining of STEM teaching through more inclusive, identity-affirming pedagogies.

Chapter one, "The Intersection of Language, Culture, and Power," introduces the concept of the "discoursal self" and explores how students are positioned—and position themselves—within STEM's rhetorical landscapes. Falconer lays out five premises for understanding student identity in disciplinary contexts, from learning as a social activity to the role of institutional feedback in shaping belonging. To underscore how these premises operate in lived experience, Falconer draws on critical race theory and intersectionality, arguing that discoursal identities are shaped by overlapping oppression and inseparable from structural inequality in STEM. As she writes, "race and racism intersect with other forms of oppression to the degree that it is nearly impossible to parse the negative impacts of one oppression from another" (28). This chapter illustrates why simply teaching scientific genres is insufficient without attending to the cultural values they embed and reinforce. By linking student identity development to discourse acquisition, Falconer sets up the book's larger argument that equity requires disrupting the institutional narratives that privilege white, middle-class norms.

In chapter two, "Lifting the Curtain," Falconer sharpens her critique by presenting White Institutional Presence (WIP) as the ideological foundation of STEM culture. She defines WIP as the pervasive privileging of white norms, values, and discourse in higher education, which remain largely invisible to those they benefit. She emphasizes how these standards are normalized, writing, "The belief that one's knowledge, values, and norms are universally and exclusively correct is central to White ascendancy" (53). She examines how WIP operates in practice by noting that while PRISM was created to diversify STEM participation, its mentors often reinforced dominant standards around scientific writing and performance. This chapter's significance lies in showing how equity efforts can replicate exclusion if they fail to interrogate disciplinary assumptions. For compositionists, the critique of WIP offers a lens for examining similar dynamics in our own classrooms and programs.

Chapter three, "The Psychological Costs of Race- and Gender-Evasive Ideologies," continues to build the case that dominant STEM discourse environments marginalize underrepresented students by neglecting the structural realities tied to identity. Falconer contrasts the experiences of Anne, a Black woman, and Madalyn, a white woman, who shared a research lab but experienced it in vastly different ways. While Madalyn received mentoring and affirmation, Anne was excluded from authorship and denied meaningful rhetorical support. "Race- and gender-evasive ideologies become a means of reinforcing a system that is inherently racialized and gendered under the guise of fairness or meritocracy" (88), Falconer writes. By tracing how feedback, writing instruction, and mentorship are distributed inequitably, this chapter underscores how access to discourse and legitimacy in STEM is mediated by whiteness and gender norms. This makes a strong case for identity-aware mentoring and writing instruction, advancing Falconer's larger goal of redefining what equitable participation looks like in STEM fields.

Chapter four, "Performing Race and Gender in Science," extends the book's central theme by analyzing how students' racial and gendered identities are not just background characteristics but are actively performed and interpreted within scientific communities. Drawing on speech act and positioning theory, Falconer asserts that "institutional spaces are not only built through discourse but also maintained through repetitive performances that align with dominant ideologies" (112). The stories of Anne, Ruben, and Amrita demonstrate how student identities are read by faculty and peers through culturally dominant scripts, affecting their access to meaningful work and recognition. Ruben's experience of demotivation due to repeated microaggressionsand Amrita's success under a mentor who affirmed her background show how mentoring either reinforces or disrupts normative expectations. This chapter reveals how scientific legitimacy is contingent not just on rhetorical fluency, but also on being read as fitting within dominant cultural expectations—again reinforcing the need to build counterspaces, educational environments that challenge the exclusionary logics of traditional STEM discourse and value diverse identities as epistemic resources.

Chapter five, "Structuring Communities of Understanding and Support," turns the book's theoretical critiques into tangible pedagogical possibilities by exploring how PRISM operated as a counterspace. Falconer identifies three mechanisms that made PRISM effective in creating this supportive environment: narrative identity work, reframing scientific discourse as cultural, and strong mentor-mentee alignment. Particularly compelling is her discussion of "mentored writing," where faculty scaffolded students' rhetorical learning without demanding assimilation into dominant norms. As one participant observed, "Explicitly talking about these realities also helped to counteract the imposter syndrome" (145), highlighting how naming structural inequities can empower and support students. This chapter is key to the book's overall contribution, demonstrating how STEM programs can cultivate spaces of belonging that resist dominant cultural logics through intentional discourse practices.

The final chapter, "Building Equity with Counterspaces," synthesizes the book's findings and foregrounds its practical implications. Drawing on multiple scholars, Falconer defines counterspaces as educational environments that actively resist dominant norms and affirm the identities, experiences, and epistemologies of marginalized students. Falconer argues that equity in STEM requires more than demographic representation; it necessitates rethinking the values, norms, and ideologies embedded in scientific institutions. She cautions, "good intentions alone do not prevent harmful practices" (154). Her recommendations—including mentoring transparency, collective faculty reflection, and positionality sharing—offer strategies for challenging exclusionary practices and reshaping institutional culture. This chapter reaffirms the book's central thesis by offering a blueprint for building counterspaces that are rhetorically and relationally constructed.

The book offers valuable insights into how race and gender shape discourse acquisition in STEM through narratives from Falconer and her students. While class is addressed implicitly in some of these narratives, it could benefit from more consistent theorization. The analysis might also be further strengthened by more sustained attention to other vectors of marginalization—such as disability, sexuality, or linguistic difference. Another limitation is that while the book advocates for space for student resistance to oppressive norms, it provides few concrete examples beyond code-switching between languages. More discussion of how educators can productively negotiate student resistance would be valuable. Additionally, though Falconer's work analyzes student experiences and surfaces powerful insights, programmatic implementation details remain somewhat vague. More specifics on successfully operationalizing these concepts across institutional contexts could strengthen the recommendations.

Masking Inequality with Good Intentions makes a vital contribution to composition studies by illuminating how discourse, power, and identity intersect in STEM education. For writing instructors, program administrators, and researchers invested in anti-racist and justice-oriented pedagogy, Falconer's work offers a powerful framework for building more inclusive and reflective writing spaces. Her articulation of counterspaces as identity-sustaining environments is especially relevant at a moment when higher education must not only increase the representation of diverse individuals but also reckon with and transform the institutional and programmatic norms and structures that continue to marginalize them. Building equitable STEM programs requires shifting from asking students to write their way into acceptance to reshaping the values that define scientific legitimacy. For anyone committed to fostering more just, pluralistic visions of STEM teaching and learning, this book offers a clarion call to move beyond box-checking representation.

Building on these insights, what makes this book especially valuable for composition studies is its practical and conceptual relevance across contexts. Writing instructors and WAC/WID practitioners can draw on Falconer's concept of mentored writing to reframe instruction around identity-affirming rhetorical practice. Program administrators will find her analysis of White Institutional Presence a useful tool for developing more equitable assessment criteria and faculty training initiatives. Researchers in rhetoric and technical communication can build on her methodology to examine how discourse and identity interact in other institutional or professional spaces.

Shuvro Das is a PhD student in the rhetoric and writing program and a graduate teaching assistant of technical and professional writing in the department of English at Virginia Tech. His research interests include queer rhetoric, technical and professional communication administration, cultural rhetoric, transnational rhetoric, and writing across the curriculum.

Cultivating Critical Language Awareness in the Writing Classroom, by Shawna Shapiro, Routledge, 2022, 360 pp.

Reviewed by Ananta Khanal, University of Louisville

Focusing on critical examinations of language, identity, privilege, and power, *Cultivating Critical Language Awareness in the Writing Classroom* by Shawna Shapiro offers a nuanced exploration of how these elements shape the pedagogical approaches to writing classrooms. After critically examining the history of writing instruction—pragmatism and progressivism—Shapiro introduces a Critical Language Awareness (CLA) pedagogy that foregrounds the sociopolitical dimensions of language and advocates for inclusive and justice-oriented practices in writing instruction. The book's primary objective is to highlight the significance of CLA in diverse educational contexts and to introduce pedagogical pathways that foster both academic rigor and linguistic diversity. This book is organized into three parts, each comprising several chapters. Part one, "Foundations of CLA Pedagogy" (chapters 1–3), introduces its historical roots, key concepts, and guiding principles. Part two, "Four Pathways for CLA Pedagogy" (chapters 4–7), presents four instructional strategies in detail. Part three, "Charting Your Own Journey with CLA Pedagogy" (chapters 8–10), offers guidance for designing CLA-informed curricula suitable for diverse institutional and classroom contexts.

In chapter one, "Why Do We Need CLA Pedagogy?" Shapiro explores the relevance of CLA pedagogy in classrooms, building on integrated literacy approaches by extending what Alastair Pennycook (1997), as cited by Shapiro, calls "critical pragmatism" (14). This stance challenges the status quo while addressing students' real-world needs. Shapiro argues that CLA pedagogy invites students to examine how language both reflects and resists systems of power, cultivating three core outcomes: "self-reflection, social justice, and rhetorical agency" (18). Therefore, Shapiro highlights the importance of this pedagogy in an era that often treats linguistic diversity as a deficit rather than a lived reality.

After establishing the significance of this pedagogy, Shapiro builds on its conceptual foundations by tracing the intellectual roots of CLA in chapter two, "What is CLA? History and Concepts." Shapiro traces the pedagogical and theoretical evolution of CLA to the UK's "Knowledge about Language" movement (29) and the 1989 "Language in the National Curriculum" (LINC) initiative (35), both of which sought to connect language instruction to real-world communication. While these reforms integrated sociolinguistic awareness into public education, Shapiro argues that US writing instruction has remained resistant—partly because of curricular decentralization, the literary dominance in English departments, and sociopolitical reaction against progressive reforms. She goes on to critique critical linguistics for its abstraction and Freirean critical literacy for its limited focus on language, proposing CLA as a more balanced and pedagogically grounded alternative.

In chapter three, "How and Why Does CLA Pedagogy Work? Principles and Best Practices" Shapiro defines the CLA approach and elaborates its six principles. In the first section, Shapiro articulates CLA not as a static method but as a dynamic, reflexive, student-centered, and justice-driven orientation to teaching language. She contrasts CLA with traditional grammar instruction in the US, which often treats language as fixed and error-based. Instead, Shapiro advocates a rhetorical approach to grammar, one that invites students to examine their own linguistic attitudes and biases. In the second section, she presents six principles of CLA pedagogy—valuing all linguistic identities; linking language to social justice; engaging minds, hearts, and bodies; connecting awareness to action; navigating tensions around linguistic norms and standards; and building on best instructional practices—to form a coherent and adaptable framework. These principles not only clarify the aims of CLA but also prepare the ground for its practical application, as explored in part two.

Part two, "Four Pathways for CLA Pedagogy", is the heart of the book, where Shapiro translates theory into curriculum. Each of the four "pathways" offers a unique entry point into CLA pedagogy, with unit structures, essential questions, transferable skills, suggested readings, and assignment ideas outlined across chapters four through seven. The first, the "Sociolinguistics Pathway" (chapter four), positions language as a lens for examining identity and injustice. Drawing on sociolinguistics, the study of language variation in society, Shapiro investigates how language both shapes and reflects social identities. The pathway centers around ten essential questions aligned with CLA goals, guiding students in analyzing linguistic variation, attitudes and prejudices, and institutional profiling. To help students engage with these questions in meaningful ways, Shapiro includes assignments like "Media 'Show-and-Tell'" (94) and role-playing exercises, inviting students to interrogate the social meanings of language in their everyday lives. Shapiro claims this pathway is particularly effective in linking CLA with anti-racist pedagogies and critical inquiry.

Furthermore, the "Critical Academic Literacies [CAL] Pathway" (chapter five) challenges the dominant norms of academic discourse by disrupting deficit-based models like English for Academic Purposes (EAP) and Writing in the Disciplines (WID). Rather than training students to master disciplinary genres, CAL invites them to question the ideological underpinnings of academic language. Students examine disciplines as linguistic communities, interrogate grammar concepts and controversies, and advocate for linguistic pluralism. Assignments such as "Linguistic Sleuthing" (142) and "Writing Beyond the Classroom" (165) empower students to reimagine the discourses of academia. Therefore, this pathway reinforces the book's central claim that cultivating academic literacy through CLA pedagogy simultaneously fosters critical awareness of how language practices are shaped by and reproduce systemic inequalities.

The third pathway, the "Media/Discourse Analysis Pathway" (chapter six), expands CLA into digital and public spheres to explore how media shapes both personal experience and collective understanding. Here, Shapiro argues that students must be both critical consumers and ethical producers of discourse. This pathway is grounded in ten essential questions and three interlinked areas: examining language and identity in digital spaces, cultivating critical news literacy, and critiquing dominant narratives. Assignments like "News Media Autobiography" (197) and "What's Trending?" (202) ask students to analyze online language use, recognize rhetorical framing, and engage publicly through genres such as news and editorials. This pathway is potent in its capacity to make abstract concepts like discourse and ideology tangible and relevant to students' lived experiences.

The fourth and final pathway, the "Communicating-Across-Difference Pathway" (chapter seven), emphasizes the role of language in shaping everyday relationships and fostering community. Drawing on insights from psychology, intercultural communication, and conflict resolution, this chapter examines how language can both disrupt and nurture human connections. Shapiro explores key issues through three connected aspects: interpersonal communication, navigating difficult classroom conversations, and "Writing-as-(Re)Design" (237), which uses design thinking to encourage empathetic and intentional writing. Assignments such as the "Power of Language Essay" (229) and "Fishbowl Conversation and Report" (235) encourage students to listen actively, reflect thoughtfully, and respond with empathy. This pathway is especially valuable for instructors aiming to cultivate inclusive and dialogic classroom environments.

After outlining the four pathways, Shapiro turns in part three, "Charting Your Own Journey with CLA Pedagogy," to the challenge of adapting CLA to specific teaching contexts and student needs. Chapter eight, "Tailoring CLA Pedagogy to Your Teaching Context," offers instructors a concrete framework for curricular design grounded in "needs—and assets—analysis" (261). Drawing on examples from her courses at Middlebury College—such as "Language and Social Justice" and "Narratives in the News Media"—Shapiro illustrates how instructors can align CLA pedagogy with diverse institutional realities. She further emphasizes the importance of accessibility and inclusivity, advocating the use of Universal Design for Learning (UDL) principles to ensure engagement for all types of learners.

Chapter nine, "Infusing CLA into Classroom Instruction," shifts from broader frameworks to daily teaching, addressing how instructors can implement CLA principles in routine classroom practices. Shapiro provides strategies for embedding CLA into speaking assignments, reading discussions, peer review, and feedback practices. Her sample feedback guidelines offer actionable tools for responding to student writing. Rather than emphasizing "correctness," she urges instructors to focus on rhetorical clarity, intentionality, and impact. This chapter guides educators beyond surface-level grammar instruction and toward deeper linguistic engagement that fosters critical awareness of how language shapes and reflects power and identity.

The book concludes with chapter ten, "Going Further with CLA," a visionary call to extend CLA beyond the classroom and into faculty development, co-curricular programming, and broader institutional contexts. Shapiro's concept of "CLA for Life!" reframes critical language awareness as not merely an academic practice, but a civic and ethical orientation and lifelong pursuit. From mental health counseling to workplace communication, she illustrates how CLA principles can improve everyday interactions and foster more thoughtful and inclusive environments.

Cultivating Critical Language Awareness in the Writing Classroom is not merely a teaching guide; it can serve as a transformative pedagogical strategy. One of the book's strengths lies in how it makes equity, agency, and justice feel actionable in real classrooms. Though its scope is broad, Shapiro's clear structure and adaptable pathways keep it accessible. She also thoughtfully acknowledges the challenges CLA pedagogy faces in individualistic social contexts like the US, yet offers multiple strategies that empower educators to respond with purpose and pedagogical intentionality. This book is especially well-suited for first-year composition instructors aiming to foster inclusive and reflective writing practices. These include assignments such as autoethnographic reflections on identity and language, genre analysis, and social issue investigations. Her "Guidelines for providing feedback on language" (305) is particularly valuable, offering a thoughtful and practical approach rooted in respect, clarity, and critical engagement. This book also provides program directors with tools for conducting needs-and-assets analyses, designing learning outcomes that emphasize linguistic justice, and integrating CLA principles into program-wide curricula at both undergraduate and graduate levels. For scholars, researchers, and educators in rhetoric and composition, it provides adaptable classroom activities, sample assignments, and assessment frameworks that can be used to foster critical discussions on language, power, and identity.

Overall, Shapiro proposes more than a pedagogy; she offers a call to action. By inviting instructors to reimagine writing classrooms as spaces of critical inquiry, ethical engagement, and linguistic affirmation, she positions educators not merely as instructors of writing but as facilitators of justice. I consider this book to be an essential read for anyone committed to transforming language education through the lenses of identity, privilege, and power toward a more equitable and inclusive future.

Ananta Khanal is a PhD student in rhetoric and composition and a graduate teaching assistant in English at the University of Louisville.

"K for the Way:" DJ Rhetoric & Literacy for 21st Century Writing Studies, by Todd Craig, Utah State University Press, 2023, 228 pp.

Reviewed by Megan Palmer, Northeastern University

As I write this, I click play on the album that brought me into the Hip Hop scene: *Enter the Wu-Tang (36 Chambers)*. Cliché, maybe, but how many book reviews start with the sonic landscape they are written in? What happens when our aural interests inform our scholarship? Our pedagogy? Dr. and DJ Todd Craig answers these questions and more in *"K for the Way:" DJ Rhetoric & Literacy for 21st Century Writing Studies*, where he puts the sonic at the forefront, bringing writing studies into conversation with the perspective of the DJ. He defines DJ Rhetoric as the methods, modes, and discursive practices DJs use in their communication and creation. Craig defines DJ Literacy as the "sonic and auditory practices of reading, writing, critically thinking, speaking, and communicating through and with the rhetoric of Hip Hop DJ culture" (24). These definitions set a foundation for Craig's inquiry, namely: "What implications might a Hip Hop DJ Rhetoric, Literacy, and Pedagogy have on English Studies for (re)-imagining and (re)-envisioning contemporary Writing Studies?" (31). Across seven chapters, Craig answers this question by introducing readers to the world and rhetorics of Hip Hop DJs and what these can offer to writing classroom pedagogy.

Craig opens chapter one, "Planted Seeds Grow Trees: The Impetus for the Urgency of "K for the Way": DJ Rhetoric and Literacy for Twenty-First-Century Writing Studies," with a familiar form of classroom writing: a literacy narrative. But instead of discussing how he learned to read and write, his literacy narrative paints a vivid portrait of how he learned the culture, technologies, and values of the DJ, positioning himself as both a writing scholar and an expert in Hip Hop culture. He traces the scholastic study of Hip Hop in fields like new media and design studies, communication studies, Black studies, and Hip Hop studies—while noting that it seems "less prominent, or even relevant, for Composition/Rhetoric as a field" (8). Craig's motivation lies in filling this gap, as he personally knows the Hip Hop DJ to be a digital griot whose linguistic and discursive practice can expand our ideas about what writing can do. Chapter one also introduces readers to his methodology of hiphopography, as coined by James G. Spady. Hiphopography takes a non-hierarchical approach to research, blending ethnography, oral/social history, and biography, intentionally minimizing the lines between researchers and the community they are researching. The conversations Craig includes throughout the book are personal and connected, with many DJ interviewees vouching for Craig as they connected him to other DJs (a form of sponsorship explored in chapter two). Scholars conducting community-engaged research may find his discussions about methodology especially thought-provoking, as they offer a model that ensures the values and practices of the partnering community are a non-negotiable part of the methodology.

In chapter two, "'Itchin' for a Scratch': Pushin' Toward a DJ Rhetoric on the 1s and 2s," Craig explains the importance of the DJ practice of "sponsorship"—a form of networking, vouching, and apprenticeship that connects DJs as they're coming up in the community. As such, instead of having a list of DJs to reach out to directly for interviewing, Craig began with a much shorter list of DJs in his immediate circle, who would then connect him with the DJs in their circles, establishing his credibility as a researcher and DJ. This approach embodies the norms of the DJs he was studying and allows Craig to overcome some of the insider/outsider challenges that accompany conducting research in a community one belongs to. In this chapter, Craig also traces Hip Hop's musical and community roots—emphasizing that this text and the DJ literacies he's elevating are undeniably and unapologetically Black. This naming feels especially important as it articulates the stakes of this work both in and out of the classroom and reminds us that literacy can take many forms.

Scholars seeking classroom application will particularly appreciate chapters three and four. In chapter three, "Jackin' for Beats V2.0: The Intertextuality (Re)Mix," Craig argues that DJ discursive practices can support classroom goals of remix and citation. He suggests that DJ understandings of bitin' (lifting someone's loop wholesale and disregarding its context or even passing it off as your own), jackin' (lifting someone's loop directly, but giving credit to where it came from and respecting its original context), and transformin' (sampling someone's work while both acknowledging the original roots and making something completely new) can be a more useful framework to discuss citation than black and white arguments about plagiarism. Situating this work in writing studies, Craig cites Alistair Pennycook, juxtaposing bitin', jackin', and transformin' alongside Pennycook's ideas about transgressive and non-transgressive intertextuality. This framework challenges Western academic assumptions about textual ownership and originality, with Hip Hop's intertextual legacy being another way to decolonize our ideas about student plagiarism. By embracing these community-based, oral traditions that prioritize creative transformation and a more interpersonal kind of integrity, we can move beyond purely punitive approaches to student writing, instead encouraging them to recognize collaborative knowledge-making traditions. To demonstrate these discursive practices to students, Craig brings in concrete, real world examples, like Vanilla Ice using the backbeat of "Under Pressure" in "Ice Ice Baby" as a clear demonstration of bitin' characterized by a lack of honesty.

In chapter four, "'A Whole Lotta Somethin' from Nufin': Racism, Revision, and Rotating Records: The Hip Hop DJ in Composition Praxis," Craig digs into what DJ literacies have to offer the revision process. Craig's description of the assignment itself is short, but citing Nancy Sommers' "Revision Strategies of Student Writers and Experienced Adult Writers," he makes it clear to composition scholars the connections to the radical/global revision his assignment draws on:

> Toward the end of the semester, I ask students to choose any of the major essays they have written for our class . . . identifying three to five sentences that serve as the core of the premise . . . I ask them to keep those three to five sentences, delete the rest, and use the chosen sentences as the focal point of their new writing. (106)

To situate this practice in students' existing cultural capital, Craig brings in a musical example: A Tribe Called Quest's revision of their first album, notably the song, "Bonita Applebum." Treating both the lyrics and other sonic elements as text, he asks students to analyze the two versions of the same song, identifying instances of radical revision, and the strategies of adding on (addition), cutting away (deletion), flipping (substitution), and swapping (reordering) that DJs (and Sommers) utilize respectively. Here, I yearned for a more multimodal version of this text, one that could leverage the affordances of linked videos or a playlist. The songs are cited like any other 'academic' text, and they are a critical element of immersing oneself in the scholastic and cultural space of the book. Readers, particularly those who may not be as familiar with Hip Hop, would be remiss not to explore this sonic intertextuality during their reading experience.

Where the book till this point foregrounds academic scholarship and supplements it with DJ interviews, chapters five (co-written with Carmen Kynard) and 6 flip this script and put the DJs' voices front and center—hiphopography at work. Chapter five, "'Sista Girl Rock': Women of Color and Hip Hop Deejaying as Raced/Gendered Knowledge and Language," examines the experiences of six women DJs, noting the gendered affordances and limitations of Hip Hop culture. Drawing on Hip Hop feminism, Craig and Kynard bring these DJs into the conversation, not just as DJs, but as public pedagogues sharing their DJ rhetoric in public K-12 schools and community education projects. Chapter six, "The Get Down Parts Keeps Gittin' Down: The DJ in the Center of the Comp 'Contact Zone,'" similarly digs into the stories of five more DJs, who speak on their own expertise, instead of as supplemental to academic theory. As Craig has been saying all along, they are worth studying.

At times *K for the Way* can feel like a scathing indictment of the field of rhetoric and composition, and fairly so. His critique extends to CCCC's "Students' Right to Their Own Language," which, he argues, fails to reflect the same commitment to teachers and researchers bringing their own languages into publication and conferences. But despite the lack of Hip Hop in writing studies—and the resistance of many scholars who insist it isn't worth their study—Craig is not disheartened. He is energized. He is committed to incorporating Hip Hop into his classroom and his scholarship. This energy is what fuels the closing chapter seven, "'Learn Levels to This Whole Thang . . . Trying to Make a Slow Change': Spinnin' the Words for Comp3.0," which is written in the style of a musical outro. Here, Craig imagines a Comp 3.0 where writing and rhetoric is pushed to expand the rhetorical strategies we bring into the classroom—as Craig says, "with or without the field's permission and acknowledgement" (171).

More than anything, *K for the Way* is an invitation. Whether you're new to the Hip Hop scene, have been a b-boy or b-girl since the 90s, or have your own DJ literacy narrative to share, this text is for you. At a concrete level, Craig provides pedagogical tools throughout the text, including assignments that instructors can use to bring more sonically oriented remix, revision, and citation strategies into the classroom. At a more theoretical level, Craig challenges readers to fundamentally reimagine how writing gets made, shared, and evaluated. Craig asks readers to think differently about the examples we bring into writing classrooms and whose voices we consider worth listening to. *K for the Way* is an invitation to do better by, for, and with students—particularly our Black students—by centering the cultural capital they bring to the classroom. DJ Todd Craig won't hold your hand, and he won't pull any punches. But his bold vision for Comp 3.0 is an invitation to think about writing more inclusively and sonically. If a song has ever moved you, you know that music is text, is meaning, is knowledge, and Craig argues that DJs are the ones making it.

Megan (Meg) Palmer is a PhD student in the English department at Northeastern University. Her research interests include digital humanities, the first-year writing experience, and community engaged learning. Meg is an avid reader and can often be found singing in her barbershop quartet, Past Curfew.

Multimodal Composing and Writing Transfer, edited by Kara Poe Alexander, Matthew Davis, Lilian W. Mina, and Ryan P. Shepherd, Utah State University Press, 2024, 288 pp.

Reviewed by *Abigail Robinson, Virginia Tech*

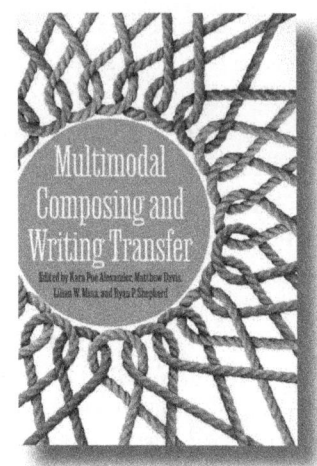

Multimodal Composing and Writing Transfer is the nexus between two ongoing areas of scholarly interest and research in rhetoric and composition studies. The authors in this collection consider how multimodal composing practices and pedagogies complicate the field's understanding of student writing transfer. They answer the call brought forth by Chris Anson in the foreword to clear "a path for continued and much-needed research on the nature of transfer in a digital world" (xvi), by engaging with the intersections of multimodality and transfer studies in a variety of places (e.g., first-year composition, writing curriculums, and writing centers), through a plethora of methods (e.g., interviews, surveys, and case studies), and with an abundance of genres and media (e.g., video editing software, ink drawings, social media, and websites). *Multimodal Composing and Writing Transfer* emphasizes how critical pedagogies, curricular revisions, and research support student multimodal transfer inside and outside of the classroom.

In the introduction, Alexander, Davis, Mina, and Shepherd provide a succinct literature review on multimodality and transfer in the field of rhetoric and composition. They trace the concept of multimodality to the New London Group's "A Pedagogy of Multiliteracies: Designing Social Futures" and discuss its contemporary application in composition studies. Transfer, particularly in multimodal context, is similarly linked to the New London Group's foundational work as well as to initiatives such as Douglas Downs and Elizabeth Wardle's Writing about Writing curriculum. Taken together, they describe multimodal transfer as a process that "involves adapting knowledge of communicative modes to understand, develop, and enhance communication across other modes and contexts" (14). Following the introduction, the ten chapters are divided into three parts, "Multimodality and Transfer in the First-Year Writing Curriculum," "Multimodality and Transfer in the Vertical Curriculum," and "Multimodality and Transfer across the Writerly Life." This expanding purview allows for a thorough exploration of transferable composing practices and the influences of context and media across writing development.

The three chapters in part one explore multimodal transfer in first-year writing. Chapter one, "Seeing It, Hearing It, Feeling It: Digital Methods for the Study of Transfer across Media" by Crystal VanKooten, presents a case for using editing software to investigate student transfer. She combines her students' audio-visual presentations with their reflections from interviews to illustrate how digital tools can help to analyze the complex process of transfer across media. In chapter two, "Making Transfer Matter across Digital Media Platforms: First-Year Writers' Design of Multimodal Campaigns for Social Advocacy," Jialei Jiang draws upon students' survey and interview responses to show how digital platforms such as Wix, Canva, and Vyond support or obstruct transfer. In chapter three, "On the Labor of Writing Transfer: Bodies and Borderlands Discourses in Translation," Joseph Anthony Wilson and Josie Rose Portz employ a case study approach to investigate how Zhannat, a student in East Kazakhstan, uses translation as a method of knowledge transfer in her multilingual course project. The authors in part one employ various established and new research approaches to investigate multimodal transfer in first-year writing. The multimodal projects discussed also provide excellent assignment examples such as audio-visual projects, websites, and multilingual presentations that encourage student transfer. More so, the authors identify key connections between multimodality and transfer such as rhetorical awareness and critical engagement which are expanded on throughout the collection.

The authors in part two explore how students engage in multimodal writing transfer across curricula. In chapter four, "Equipping Tutors to Transfer Multimodal Writing Knowledge to Writing Center Contexts," Kara Poe Alexander, Becca Cassady, and Michael-John DePalma use survey and interview data to investigate how writing center tutors use their multimodal knowledge when working with peers. They argue for more critical education about multimodal misconceptions and reflective "literacy linking," as well as "more opportunities for tutoring of multimodal texts" (100; 101). In chapter five, "'It's Not Like I Can Put a Picture of a Paper on Instagram, You Know?': Genre and Multimodality in Writing Knowledge Transfer across Contexts," Anna V. Knutson examines how one student applies knowledge from academic genres to her personal blog, arguing that students should be encouraged to draw upon their unique literacies and skills when composing in writing courses. Her findings highlight how elements such as text length and genre conventions can foster the development of transferable writing knowledge. In the sixth chapter, "The Other Curriculum: Social Media and Its Connection to University Writing," Ryan P. Shepherd explores how students engage in writing beyond the classroom that is often overlooked in formal instruction. Reexamining interviews with six undergraduates, he finds that students' awareness of multimodal transfer declines over time as they move further from early writing courses. Together, the three chapters in part two provide useful accounts of composing practices across curricula. The authors note the struggles of transfer, specifically between academic and nonacademic genres and media. By recognizing these challenges, the authors identify important connections between transfer and concepts such as genre, text length, and rhetorical flexibility that point to the need for integration into classes and curricula.

The four chapters in part three expand on the calls in part two to investigate how transfer occurs across time and contexts. In chapter seven, "Drawing Worlds Together: Tracing Semiotic Practices along Histories of Literate Activity," Kevin Roozen presents a longitudinal study of Laura as she reflects on the impact of drawing on her personal, academic, and professional life, arguing that multimodal transfer spans a lifetime. In chapter eight, "Rhetoric in its Fullness: Metalanguage and Multimodal Transfer," Logan Bearden draws on data from prior research to argue that explicit rhetorical metalanguage is needed in course and program outcomes to provide students with the language to recognize and utilize their transferable multimodal skills. In a similar vein, in chapter nine, "A Curriculum Delivered, a Curriculum Remembered: Multimodal Transfer in Writing and Rhetoric Major Alumni," Travis Maynard examines multimodal transfer among alumni, focusing on how six graduates utilize their rhetorical knowledge gleaned from major coursework in Florida State University's editing, writing, and media concentration to their professions and everyday lives after graduation. In the tenth chapter, "If You Build It, They Will Use It: Composing Infrastructures, Communities of Practice, and Instructor Dispositions," Jeff Naftzinger compares two literature and two rhetoric and composition graduate instructors, finding that communities of practice play a significant role in both how multimodal composing is viewed and integrated into teaching pedagogy. The findings in part three align with those of previous chapters, though emphasis here is placed on how instructors and administrators might revise their programs and curricula to support multimodal transfer. The longitudinal research methods presented in these chapters provide a complex, holistic understanding of how multimodal transfer is dependent upon time and locations, both inside and outside of the classroom.

This book ends with an afterword by Kathleen Blake Yancey, who draws upon both personal anecdotes and the work presented in this collection to further the calls to "map the universe of multimodality, transfer, and most especially, the intersections between them" (228). Yancey encourages the field of rhetoric and composition to ground its work in a shared vocabulary, conceptualize writing across a lifetime, incorporate writers' identities and communities, and engage in dialogue with students about multimodal transfer.

Multimodal Composing and Writing Transfer is an excellent resource for researchers, instructors, and administrators, whether one is familiar with multimodal transfer or is encountering the concept for the first time. The collection offers a wide range of adaptable research methods for studying transfer, including longitudinal studies, interview and survey-based research, and inventive approaches such as video editing. These methods allow researchers to explore transfer not only in academic settings, but across personal composing practices and across life, further investigating the influences of time, place, and even memory on multimodal transfer. Additionally, instructors will find concrete assignment ideas that pair multimodal projects with reflective practices, as well as strategies for helping students draw on their existing literacies, languages, and other strengths as rhetorical resources. This collection also provides administrators with practical strategies for supporting multimodal transfer at the curricular level, such as revising program outcomes to incorporate rhetorical metalanguage and expanding writing center services to support multimodal transfer. Across these perspectives, the collection offers both theoretical insight and practical guidance for fostering multimodal transfer in meaningful, sustainable ways. All in all, this edited collection is a worthwhile read for those interested in student writing transfer across a variety of modalities, contexts, or stages of writing development. With its unique insights from the authors, this collection paves the way for more disciplinary research and discussion about the notable intersections between multimodal composing and writing transfer.

Abigail Leigh Robinson is a PhD student in rhetoric and writing and a graduate teaching assistant at Virginia Polytechnic Institute and State University. Her research and scholarly interests include visual and material rhetorics, writing pedagogies, and multimodal composing practices.

PARLOR PRESS
EQUIPMENT FOR LIVING

Now with Parlor Press!

Studies in Rhetorics and Feminism
   New Series Editors: Jessica Enoch and Sharon Yam

Emerging Conversations in the Global Humanities
   Series Editor: Victor E. Taylor

New Releases

Plato's Nightmare by Steven B. Katz

The SoTL Guide: (Re)Orienting the Scholarship of Teaching and Learning by Nancy L. Chick, Peter Felten, and Katarina Mårtensson

Storied Objects: A Graphic Narrative Reflection on Material Metaphors and Digital Writing by Erin Kathleen Bahl

Xeno >> Glossia: An Illuminated Study of Christine de Pizan by Marci Vogel

Rhetorical Reception: One Hundred and Fifty Years of Arguing with Sex in Education by Carolyn Skinner

City Housekeeping: Women's Labor Rhetorics and Spaces for Solidarity, 1886–1911 by Liane Malinowski

Kenneth Burke's Rhetoric of Identification by Tilly Warnock

Forthcoming in 2026

Shaping Rhetorical Studies: The Research of RSA Fellows, with Commentary edited by Cheryl Glenn and Richard Leo Enos

Teaching and Learning with Rhetorical Listening: Alternatives to Self-Censorship and Silence in High School and College Classrooms edited by Krista Ratcliffe and Jessica Rivera-Mueller

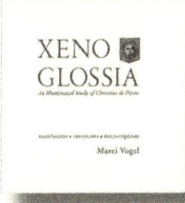

Check Out Our Website!

Discounts, blog, open access titles, instant downloads, and more.

parlorpress.com

Composition Studies **Discount:** Use CS20 at checkout to receive a 20% discount on all titles not on sale through January 1, 2026.

www.ingramcontent.com/pod-product-compliance
Lightning Source LLC
Chambersburg PA
CBHW031437160426
43195CB00010BB/766